Digital Matters

W9-ABS-529

Digital Matters analyses the complex interaction between the material and immaterial aspects of new digital technologies. It draws upon a mix of theoretical approaches including sociology, media theory and history, cultural studies and the philosophy of technology, to suggest that the Matrix of science fiction and Hollywood is but an extreme example of the way in which contemporary technological society enframes and conditions its citizens.

Digital Matters provides a novel perspective upon on-going digital developments by using, in addition to current thinkers, the work of past theorists not normally associated with digital issues. This provides a fresh insight into the roots and causes of the social matrix that lies behind the digital Matrix of the popular imagination. In so doing, the authors highlight the way we should be concerned by the power of the digital to undermine physical reality but also to explore the potential the digital has for alternative, empowering social uses. The book's central aim is to impress upon the reader that, for reasons they may not have suspected, the digital does indeed matter.

Jan Ll. Harris holds degrees from the universities of Oxford, Nottingham and Salford. His research focuses upon the intersection of continental philosophy and the philosophy of technology, and the cultural impact of digital technology.

Paul A. Taylor is a senior lecturer in Communications Theory at the Institute of Communication Studies, University of Leeds. His research interests focus upon digital culture and critical theories of the mass media. He is the author of *Hackers: Crime in the Digital Sublime* (Routledge, 1999) and co-author of *Hacktivists: Rebels with a Cause?* (Routledge, 2004).

Digital Matters

Theory and culture of the matrix

Jan Ll. Harris and Paul A. Taylor

Routledge
Taylor & Francis Group

LONDON AND NEW YORK

First published 2005 by Routledge
2 Park Square, Milton Park, Abingdon, Oxon OX14 4RN

Simultaneously published in the USA and Canada
by Routledge
270 Madison Ave, New York, NY 10016

Routledge is an imprint of the Taylor & Francis Group

© 2005 Jan Ll. Harris and Paul A. Taylor

Typeset in Bembo by Prepress Projects Ltd
Printed and bound in Great Britain by TJ International Ltd, Padstow,
Cornwall

British Library Cataloguing in Publication Data
A catalogue record for this book is available from the British Library

Library of Congress Cataloging in Publication Data
A catalog record for this book has been requested

ISBN 0–415–25184–2 (hbk)
ISBN 0–415–25185–0 (pbk)

For John and Sylvia (J.Ll.H.)

Paul would like to thank all those university personnel of a bureaucratic mindset without whom this book would have been finished a lot sooner

Contents

Preface

> Today, after more than a century of electric technology, we have extended our central nervous system itself in a global embrace, abolishing both space and time as far as our planet is concerned. Rapidly, we approach the final phase of the extensions of man – the technological simulation of consciousness . . . Any extension, whether of skin, hand, or foot, affects the whole psychic and social complex.
>
> (McLuhan 1995 [1964]: 3–4)

> The technological plane is an abstraction: in ordinary life we are practically unconscious of the technological reality of objects. Yet this abstraction is profoundly real: it is what governs all radical transformations of our environment.
>
> (Baudrillard 1997: 5)

The term 'matrix' has, since the release of the first instalment of the Wachowksi brothers' films, become inseparably associated with Keanu Reeves, black leather trench coats and bullet-stopping kung fu. In the following pages we will attempt to restore to this term some of its earlier associations; indeed, a quick review of the other uses to which this term has been put will serve to prefigure some of the conceptions and causes of what we shall here call the *matrix* (the use of the lower case serving to distinguish it from the cinematic and cyberpunk resonances of the *Matrix*).

The word 'matrix' has been variously deployed to describe, among others:

- the substance, situation or environment in which something has its origin, is embedded or takes its form from;
- the intercellular substance of cartilage, bone and connective tissue;
- the master mould from which a given gramophone record is pressed;
- the major metal in a given alloy;
- a rectangular arrangement of circuit elements used to generate one set of signals from another;
- the womb [from *mater* (mother) also providing the source of *matter*].

Thus, the term 'matrix' has associations with the environment that shapes; the supporting structure of organic form; the reproduction of media; signal transposition; the creation of hybrid or alloyed materials; the womb and biological reproduction; and, finally, with matter itself. In the following chapters we will touch upon many of these associations, and in this manner demonstrate that the matrix as a trope for our relation to technology is a far more flexible and polyvalent term than the vision of technology in the eponymous film. Exploiting these resonances, as well as the more popular notion of *The Matrix*, we hope to address the concept of *digital matters* (recalling that matrix and matter have a common origin in the term *mater*) understood in terms of the womb of reproducibility out of which our culture and society is fashioned. Moreover, we will argue that this digital matrix is the latest term in a succession of techno-informatic environments that have historically determined our individual and collective expression.

The title, *Digital Matters*, is deliberately chosen for its ambivalent meaning. On the one hand, it is intended to signify the perhaps most obvious meaning of 'issues relating to the subject of digital technology' whilst, on the other hand, we also want to draw attention to a central tension of digital technology: its materiality. As McLuhan and Baudrillard point out (see above), technology is often assumed to involve a process of abstraction, an escape from the matter/matrix within which the human has been fashioned and reproduced. But the effects of this immaterial form are frequently felt within society at a material level, either by individuals using digital technologies or, more subtly, by the alterations it produces on the whole cultural environment – McLuhan's psychic and social complex. The paradox of this *im/materiality* (a term we adopt to express this double articulation) manifests itself in numerous ways. For instance, we might note that much of contemporary capitalism is simultaneously abstract in appearance yet powerful in its material effects for those on its receiving end. The evanescent figures on plasma screens in Wall Street have very direct effects for those working in the *maquiladora* factories of Latin America. In this context, the matrix describes both the physical technological infrastructure of advanced capitalism and the abstract forces that, although difficult to pin down, constitute the very real vectors of influence within digital matters.

In developing our analysis of digital matters, and in order to move beyond the emerging doxa in the field of self-styled cyberstudies, we employ a disparate range of theorists, some of whom may seem, at first glance at least, rather tangential to digital concerns. This is deliberate, and serves to place the problematic of digital matters in a broader socio-historical and theoretical context than is customary. A ready outline of our method and its rationale can be gained through considering the following, from Michel de Certeau:

> We witness the advent of number. It comes with democracy, the large city, administrations, cybernetics. It is a flexible and continuous mass, woven tight like a fabric with neither rips nor darned patches, a multitude of quantified heroes who lose names and faces as they become the ciphered river of

the streets, a mobile language of computations and rationalities that belong
to no one.

(de Certeau 1988: v)

Here, de Certeau adumbrates the complex admixture of factors involved in
digital matters. His stress is on a generalized numericity, most fully realized in
the calculation and processing of the digital but with its origins in a range of
numerizations, in the installation of the rule of numbers. It is urban, democratic
(the count as the index of democracy), and facilitates the administration of the
polis. It abstracts and so produces an existential anonymity ('just a number'):
the noble subjects of history become the 'ciphered river of the streets'. Most
important, however, is the inextricable relation between number as abstraction,
enframement and circumspection and the fluidity it induces. This mixture
of mobility and abstract codification is one we will encounter repeatedly, not
least in Deleuze's notion of a society of control (i.e. our own) – one whose
despotism is all the greater for its flexibility, its attention not to the norm but to
the exception. All of this constitutes the context, the matrix no less, in which
digital matters emerge and operate.

The above quotation also describes how with modernity comes a certain
deadening of life's particularity. This is a theme that we shall explore and which
has a respectable theoretical lineage, for instance in the Frankfurt School's
notion of *instrumental reason,* understood as the privileging of the general or the
abstract over the particular and reaching its apotheosis in the form of the *totally
administered society.*[1] We analyse in the following chapters the various aspects of
this obtundence of particularity as it is developed in the context of digital matters.

---

1 Adorno's *oeuvre* consistently addresses capitalism's tendency to privilege the general over the
   particular with the concept of identity thinking – e.g. in *Negative Dialectics* (Adorno 1973) –
   whilst in *One Dimensional Man* (Marcuse 1968) describes the totally administered society and
   his account of its operational thinking provides an invaluable introduction to the way in which
   social values become subordinate to the requirements of society's technological infrastructures.

Introduction
The im/materiality of digital matters

> Communication is envisaged less as an exchange of meanings, of ideas . . . and more as performance propelled into movement by variously materialized signifiers. It is enframed into hardwares, guided by rules and styles and 'crowned' by signified effects that, once sufficiently routinized, can appear as realms of their own. To hold, as Derrida did in *Grammatology*, that signifier and signified cannot be isolated against each other would constitute the minimal claim of the program. The deconstructionist project uncovered implications of the minimal claim, pursuing the infinite play of meanings as traces without ultimate origin and control. The present enterprise takes another direction. It is concerned with potentials and pressures of stylization residing in techniques, technologies, materials, procedures, and 'media'.
>
> (Gumbrecht and Pfeiffer 1994: 6)

Gumbrecht and Pfeiffer's above argument for the increased need to attend to the materiality of communication usefully highlights the basic approach of this book. Like Gumbrecht and Pfeiffer, we have centred our project upon tracing the origins of agendas of control and demonstrating how techniques and procedures come together in digital matters. Indeed, their statement could almost be taken as a manifesto for various theorists who seek to compensate for the relative overconcentration in recent times upon the signified to the exclusion of the signifier. As already touched upon, we cannot create an opposition between a neutral and incorporeal conception of information and communication and the material channels that transmit this information. Instead, communication and information must be understood as an im/material performance in which none of the factors involved can be privileged over the other; medium and message must be approached as a single im/material complex. We consistently emphasize throughout this book that digital modes of communication are not neutral and, although premised upon the rapid flow of information in the seemingly immaterial and neutral form of binary 1s and 0s, this mode of propulsion has historical antecedents in both earlier forms of media and the substance of city environments. We examine in detail the notion of *enframement* and how, whilst the virtual realities of digital matters may appear as radical new realms of their own, they nonetheless have their precedence in a history of technological enframing, and more specifically in the evolution of media technologies as a part of this history.

A growing interest in the work of Friedrich Kittler, as well as volumes such as Gumbrecht and Pfeiffer's *Materialities of Communication* (1994), suggest that there exists a small but stubborn body of theorists who '. . . are looking for underlying constraints whose technological, material, procedural, and performative potentials have been all too easily swallowed up by interpretational habits' (Grumbrecht and Pfeiffer 1994: 12). This position would involve a break with notions of creative reception on the behalf of users/viewers/readers in favour of a concern with the tools they employ. Thus, the work of the so-called 'hardware faction' can be seen as the media equivalent of technological determinism. The often highly speculative theory of Baudrillard, as it is commonly understood, would tend to place it against these concerns, in that one definition of the condition of hyperreality is that of 'the exaltation of signs based on the denial of the reality of things' (Baudrillard 1990a: 63). However, as we shall see, the exaltation of signs that Baudrillard believes characteristic of our epoch is not an escape from materiality or hardware but the product of a certain configuration of the latter.

These theoretical innovations hold out the possibility of understanding the increasing prevalence of the trope of immateriality in cyberdiscourse without subscribing to its simple-minded ontology. From Adam Smith's invisible hand to the more recent expressions of e-commerce literature – for example, *Living on Thin Air* (Leadbetter 2000), *The Weightless World* (Coyle 1998), *Being Digital* (Negroponte 1995) and *The Empty Raincoat* (Handy 1995) – weightlessness and abstraction are taken seriously as aspects of the social and economic order. These works refer exclusively to new information technologies but, as this book shows, the im/material tension of digital matters has its roots much earlier in the history of technology. Whatever is presently understood by the phrase 'the matrix', it is safe to assume that for most people it has connotations relating to digital phenomena. We will see in the subsequent chapters how, to match its simultaneously abstract and material nature, the matrix can be conceived of in both much more philosophical and grounded ways than attention to mere digitality on its own affords.

Digital matters – beyond the material?

By their very nature, the technologies of information and communication – 'media' in the broad sense of that term – are technocultural hybrids. On the one hand, they are crafted things, material mechanisms that are conceived, constructed and exploited for gain. But media technologies are also animated by something that has nothing to do with matter or technique. More than any other invention, information technology transcends its status as a thing, simply because it allows for the incorporeal encoding and transmission of mind and meaning.

(Davis 1998: 4)

The above quotation incorporates several of this book's key themes stemming from the notion of digital matters and the technological matrix they are premised upon. It addresses basic questions about the relationships between:

1 technology and culture;
2 matter and technique; and
3 a crafted object and transcendent informational encodings.

However, despite using Davis to identify a number of our key concerns, there exists a major divergence between the language of the above summary and our perspective, namely that, following the particular inflection given to Derrida's thought in Kittler's project and in keeping with our own notion of im/materiality, we challenge the opposition between the notions of an ideal in terms of mind and meaning and of a technology that is diacritically distinguished by its relation to matter – in other words an opposition between the incorporeal and the secondary of the materialities of communication. This classical logocentric binarism is precisely the mode of thought that we seek to undermine with our focus upon *im/materiality*. As we shall see in our exploration of Kittler's work, sense and significance and the subject that produces them are inseparable from the media network in which they are expressed. We shall return to this theme later; for now, let us explore the themes that we have extracted from Davis.

Technology and culture

The extent to which technology can be perceived as an autonomous entity independent of human agency is a perennial issue of debate. One of the most powerful challenges to an intellectual tradition that emphasized the impuissance of the human in the face of the technics has been that offered by Bruno Latour in his *We Have Never Been Modern* (1993). Here, Latour argues that our culture is marked by a strong tendency to set the social and cultural against the material and technological (previous quotation). This tendency, or what he terms 'the modern constitution', has political, epistemological and philosophical ramifications. Within the context of our focus it serves to preclude the creation of an adequate framework within which technology and its consequences can be addressed, resulting instead in misplaced and sterile binaries. In the place of this cleavage of technics and culture, Latour argues for techno-cultural hybrids. These hybrids are irreducible; they cannot be divided into the composite components, but instead consist of multiple transactions between 'culture' and 'matter' or 'technique' (these terms must all be put in suspension since any term that might be attributed to one or the other is simply another instance of hybridity).

This position (prosaically reduced to the doxa of 'social constructivism') has been responsible for consigning a tradition of critical technical determinism to terminal unfashionability. Whilst we acknowledge the insight and originality of Latour's thesis and the richness of the empirical material uncovered by social constructivism (see, for example, MacKenzie and Wajcman 1985), we argue, nevertheless, that the earlier notions of technical determinism and their vision of a systemic, culminative dimension to the technological retain their validity, although we accept that it is necessary to modify the determinist thesis in the light of the kind of reading put forward by Latour. As a result, in contrast to Latour, we argue that the culture and affective life of those living within digital networks is qualitatively different to earlier techno-cultural assemblages, and thus that the concept of modernity and the temporal vector that underpins it remains valid.

Matter and technique

Our argument that contemporary life is characterized by what we have dubbed the im/material as an irreducible admixture of abstract or incorporeal information and matter and technique is not new. When, in *Manifesto of the Communist Party*, Marx and Engels (1977 [1848]): 46) declared that 'all that is solid melts into air', they succinctly summarized capitalism's simultaneous ability to expand physical production whilst undermining that very physicality. The implications of this statement have become all the more apparent in recent decades and have continued to receive theoretical attention, particularly in the efforts of thinkers such as Negri, Virno, Lazzarato, and Deleuze and Guattari to formulate a neo-Marxism. Works such as Kern's *The Culture of Time and Space 1880–1918* (1983) and Berman's *All That is Solid Melts into Air: the experience of modernity* (1983) trace the cultural emergence and registration of crucial transitions in the im/materiality of capitalism. These authors tend, however, to concentrate upon the fragmentary and ephemeral experience of modernity. Berman, for example, describes how modernity 'pours us all into a maelstrom of perpetual disintegration and renewal, of struggle and contradiction, of ambiguity and anguish' (ibid.: 15). Our focus, whilst recognizing and discussing this experience of disorientation (especially in Part II), is directed much more to how, beneath such apparent flux, certain underlying networks operate – matrices of control that are at once abstract and material.

The various aspects of digital matters and the matrix explored in the following pages make a succinct summary of their theme difficult but, by way of a preliminary definition, we might say that the matrix represents for us

> *the underlying and frequently invisible (but nevertheless powerful) socio-technical framework that circumscribes and dampens human agency in the contemporary world.*

We aim, however, to avoid the criticism of Kern proffered by Harvey, namely that Kern's account of changing conceptualizations of time and space, lacking 'any theory of technological innovation, of capitalist dynamics across space, or of cultural production, . . . offers only "generalizations about the essential cultural developments of the period."' (Harvey 1990: 266). To better tackle the essentially paradoxical nature of contemporary capitalism's im/materiality, we attempt to follow Harvey's injunction to explore the interrelation between capital, culture and technology. Thus, we seek a fuller understanding of the im/materiality of contemporary communication's matrix through a synergistic analysis of theories of technological and media development; new theories of the dynamics of advanced capitalism's abstract spatialization; and cultural theory/fiction. The cross-fertilization of resources in this tripartite analysis aims at establishing a deeper understanding of the nature of the digital zeitgeist than that offered by the meretricious 'dot.com' industries, whose 'deranged optimism' Thomas Frank describes as the 'corporate salivating' of 'business pornography' (Frank 2001).

A crafted object and transcendent informational encodings

In keeping with this book's consistent emphasis upon the im/material, we emphasize the particularity of interaction with physical objects and explore the experience of 'flows' first encountered in the urban environment and now, according to certain commentators, a generalized condition of digital culture understood as 'the space of flows/the flow of spaces' (Castells 2000). Above, Davis talks in terms of transcendence when contrasting the world of objects and their incorporeal transformation into data, and we have indicated our unease with respect to this vision of transcendence. Instead, we offer something like a genealogy of the object, drawing in part on Martin Heidegger's account of the conversion of the products of artisanal production into the object understood as merely a unit in an overarching standing reserve – or as *enframed*. While this is not the place for a discussion of the philosophical subtleties of Heidegger, we note that this transformation is a process both of *withdrawal* and of unconcealment and, as such, allows us to understand something of the process that we have been collectively subject to in the last few centuries. Thus, rather than stressing information's transcendence, following Lash (2002), we stress its *immanence*, its colligation with a range of material processes and its strict inseparability from them. Thus, the status of the object is not that of increasing redundancy in the face of incorporeal data but, rather, the subject of transformations or deformations: operations that articulate the deeper logic of the matrix.

The vexed question of pessimism

> . . . the power of the image to beget image, and of technology to reproduce itself via human intervention, is utterly in excess of our power to control the psychic and social consequences . . . It is the medium that is the message because the medium creates an environment that is as indelible as it is lethal.
>
> (McLuhan cited in Moos 1997: 90)

Whilst in this book we consistently highlight the strict inseparability of developments in media with the evolution of capitalism, we are also perhaps more sympathetic to those theorists who do not allow a well-intentioned humanism to distort the harsher conclusions of their analyses. Readers can make up their own mind, but we at least want to provide them with an accurate account of the theorists we highlight, all of whom partake, to some degree, of the fatalism Baudrillard has enshrined in his notion of *Fatal Strategies* (1990b). The optimism or pessimism of a theorist ultimately rests upon his or her interpretation of the nature of the society–technology dialectic, if indeed he or she recognizes such a dialectic (we think here of Kittler). Raymond Williams states that technology's determinative influence is 'necessarily in complex and variable connection with other social relations and institutions' (Williams cited in Freedman 2003: 177):

> Determination is a real social process, but never (as in some theological and Marxist versions) a wholly controlling, wholly predicting set of causes. On the contrary, the reality of determination is the setting of limits and the exertion of pressures, within which variable social practices are profoundly affected but never necessarily controlled. We have to think of determination not as a single force, or a single abstraction of forces, but as a process in which real determining factors – the distribution of power or capital, social and physical inheritance, relations of scale and size between groups – set limits and exert pressures, but neither wholly control nor wholly predict the outcome of complex activity within or at these limits, and under or against these pressures.
>
> (Williams cited in Freedman 2003: 133)

Of particular interest for our purposes and the analysis of Part II is Williams's use of the phase *mobile privatization* to describe the particular form this complex relationship takes with modern media. We see how the capitalist social environment is supported by media technologies the consumption of which reinforces the wider consumption patterns of a commodity-dominated culture.

Mumford also subscribed to a dialectical interpretation of the relationship between material culture and its immaterial, symbolic representations. His particular version of this dialectic, however, raises the possibility that it will end in the triumph of single term (a subject we explore in detail with Chapter 1's account of Jacques Ellul's interpretation of the absolute dialectic), and so he voices the fear that humankind's situation may be changing 'from creators of machinery to that of creatures of the machine system' (Mumford cited in May 2003: 112). This observation is reminiscent of McLuhan's allusion to Butler's 1872 novel *Erewhon,* which argues for humanity as the vehicle of transmission for technological reproduction, such that: 'Man becomes, as it were, the sex organs of the machine world, as the bee of the plant world, enabling it to fecundate and to evolve ever new forms.' (McLuhan 1995 [1964]: 46) For Mumford, *technics* (a term he uses to indicate not only material technology but also its attendant forms of knowledge) contained the potential for both positive and negative social consequences, which he claimed 'have recurrently existed side by side: one authoritarian, the other democratic, the first system-centred, immensely powerful, but inherently unstable, the other man-centred, relatively weak, but resourceful and durable' (Mumford cited in May 2003: 116).

Mumford's appeal to a democratic technics that can be opposed to the powerful, totalizing effects of technological systems makes him part of a group of writers with similar hopes. Raymond Williams (1967) similarly calls for *democratic communications*, Feenberg (1999) (as we will see in the next chapter) speaks of a need for *democratic rationalization,* whilst Thompson refers to a *reconstruction of the public sphere* (1994) leading to *a reinvention of publicness* (1995). The common failing of these approaches is that they all appeal to a neutral or extra-technological social field that can constructively direct the use and nature of media technologies. In arguing for regulation and control, however, they refuse the perspective of thinkers such as Kittler, who argue that our very notions of what constitutes appropriate regulation are themselves products of the media networks in which we are constituted. From this perspective, Williams's charge that McLuhan's determinism is by default ideologically compromised constitutes a *tu quoque* – in other words, the myth of neutrality itself conceals a latent ideology:

> . . . what is happening in America is not the design of an articulated ideology. No *Mein Kampf* or *Communist Manifesto* announced its coming. It comes as the unintended consequence of a dramatic change in our modes of public conversation. But it is an ideology nonetheless, for it imposes a way of life, a set of relations among people and ideas, about which there has been no consensus, no discussion and no opposition. Only compliance. Public consciousness has not yet assimilated the point that technology is ideology.
>
> (Postman 1987: 162)

However, it should be emphasized that McLuhan's ultimate position on technology is difficult to establish. In the popular mind he is regarded as an optimistic advocate of electronic technologies, a view perpetuated by his frequent appearances in televised debates in the 1960s, and compounded by his revival in the 1990s as the godfather of the *Wired* generation. But McLuhan's global village was predicated upon explicitly acknowledged cultural disruption and destruction: 'The American stake in literacy as a technology or uniformity applied to every level of education, government, industry, and social life is totally threatened by the electric technology' (McLuhan 1995 [1964]: 18). Ostrow notes that the Californian techno-evangelists who have brought McLuhan out 'from behind a potted palm again' (Moos 1997: xvi) gloss over their exhumed guru's warnings: 'No place in the reverie of interactive computer-generated virtual reality do we find a warning that "the pressure of the mass media leads to irrationality" nor the fact that it is "urgent to modify their usage"' (1997: xvi).

In contrast to his purported technophilia, McLuhan's own repeated argument was an urgent and growing need to engage critically with electronic media rather than to judge them sententiously:

> In the electric age we are discovering new modes of rationality. I am not saying this is a 'good' thing. I'm simply trying to understand what is happening

> and how it's done . . . I don't approve of the global village. I say we live in it
> . . . We have to discover *new patterns of action, new strategies of survival.*
>
> (McLuhan 1995 [1964]: 50, 58, 67 [our emphasis])

Perhaps in keeping with critical engagement is McLuhan's equivocation with respect to electronic technology. Thus, he declares both that 'my own observation of our almost overwhelming cultural gradient toward the primitive – or involvement of all the senses – is attended by complete personal distaste and dissatisfaction. I have no liking for it' (1995 [1964]: 65) and that 'We are now compelled to develop new techniques of perception and judgement, new ways of reading the languages of our environment with its multiplicity of cultures and disciplines. And these needs are not just desperate remedies but roads to unimagined cultural enrichment' (1995 [1964]: 137). This ambivalence is played out repeatedly in McLuhan's writing – for example, he states that 'Most media . . . are pure poison – TV, for example, has all the effects of LSD. I don't think we should allow this to happen' (McLuhan cited in Moos 1997: 72), while at the same time maintaining that 'the computer is the LSD of the business world, transforming its outlooks and objectives' (McLuhan 1995 [1964]: 83).

What is certain amidst such ambivalence is that McLuhan believed that technologies had profound and wide-reaching effects on the milieus into which they were introduced. It is relatively easy to demonstrate the dramatic effects and unforeseen consequences of physical technologies upon our physical environment. McLuhan used the example of the car and the roads it brings in its wake: 'The motorcar's environment creates roads and surfaces. It doesn't simply occupy a space. It creates its own space . . . When you look at the car in terms of what it does to people, it becomes a horrifying story . . . People were unable to see the road system that came with the car' (McLuhan 1995 [1964]: 76) It is less easy, however, to demonstrate some of the implications for the more immaterial but still important social environment, and for their effects upon the self-identity of those who participate in these environments. McLuhan believed that media technologies, like psychedelic drugs, had the ability to alter the sensory ratios of those who engaged with them and, like the beloved compounds of his first generation of readers, that their effects were both profound and intangible – and that they, like all forms of personal and collective transformation, were the objects of fear and fascination in equal measure.

Part I – theorizing the im/material matrix: technics triumphant

> . . . technical systems, once built and operating, do not respond positively to human guidance. The goals, purposes, needs, and decisions that are supposed to determine what technologies do are in important instances no longer the true source of their direction. Technical systems become severed from the ends originally set for them and, in effect, reprogram themselves

and their environments to suit the special conditions of their own operation.

(Winner 1977: 227)

... private space has been invaded and whittled down by technological
reality. Mass production and mass distribution claim the *entire* individual,
and industrial psychology has long since ceased to be confined to the factory. The manifold processes of introjection seem to be ossified in almost
mechanical reactions. The result is not adjustment but *mimesis*: an immediate identification of the individual with *his* society, and through it, with the
society as a whole.

(Marcuse 1968: 10 [emphasis in original])

Winner (1977: 229) defines *reverse adaptation* as 'the adjustment of human
ends to match the character of the available means'. Reverse adaptation thus
describes the subsumption of ends by means: that which intercedes or facilitates,
escapes its role and instead of being purely instrumental comes to determine
the process that it was simply meant to enable. Once this translation of ends
through means into merely means is under way, technical efficiency becomes
the dominant frame of reference to the exclusion of all other considerations.
Technology no longer merely fulfils our desires; it translates them into new
ones that increasingly can be fulfilled only by recourse to buying technologically
based commodities produced by a technologically based economic system.
The concept of reverse adaptation echoes various well-established sociological
concepts, such as Weber's *iron cage of rationality*, the Frankfurt School's focus
upon *instrumental reason* and Ellul's concept of *la téchnique*. Implicit in all of these
theses is the interplay between the apparently immaterial (the ratiocinative) and
the simply material: this interplay is not suspended in the digital but rendered
increasingly complex.

Winner (1977) portrays the experience of modernity as one saturated with
the instrumental, technical values of efficiency, rationality, productivity, etc.
These instrumental norms characterize not merely the technical realm but all
spheres of life, including the industrialization of culture itself. New technologies of production in tandem with new media of dissemination generate and
exploit a novel spectrum of desires in ever more sophisticated ways and so result
in an self-generating dialectic of needs and artefacts that increases exponentially.
From this perspective, technologies do not just quantitatively extend human
capabilities – their use transforms us. There are two aspects or registers of this
transformation: first, there are *defining technologies*, which directly affect those
who encounter them and, second, there is the global effect of multiple defining technologies which, in a form of 'function creep', slowly alter the milieu.
(Winner terms this second aspect *accretional determinism*.)

These two types of determinism can be illustrated by comparing the status
of a worker on a factory assembly line with that of a company executive. When
the worker interacts with a particular machine on the assembly line his or her

physical movements will deliberately adopt a machine-like form in order to better fit with the tempo required by the machine. Charlie Chaplin's 1930s film *Hard Times* provides a vivid depiction of the extent to which factory workers had become almost literally a cog in the machine. Executives are superficially much freer in so far as their physical movements are not as obviously circumscribed by the need to adapt to the mechanical requirements of a machine. However, their conformism relates to more subtly systemic requirements. These range from the short-term pragmatic need to pay close attention to regimented timetables and computer spreadsheets, to more strategic and long-term needs such as having qualifications from an increasingly technologized education *system* in order to obtain the necessary credentials to get a job in the first place.

The 'conditioning of individuals' thus refers to a latent effect that technology has upon the individual, rather than the immediate impact of one specific artefact. It refers to the constant exposure to the pervasive influence of technological systems for which the basic notion of mechanization is inadequate. It is for this reason that the simple 'tool-use' model of technology no longer holds true in contemporary life. A tool is the facilitating means to an uncomplicated end. In contrast, technologies restructure the very way in which we interact with our environments: they mediate our experience to the extent that they can be said to create their own distinctive worlds. Winner illustrates such restructuring by comparing the qualitatively different nature of the same journey made on foot and then in a car. Not only is the former experience richer in immediate sensory terms than the inevitable distancing that takes place when a journey is mediated through a windscreen, but the experience of travel is homogenized so that, despite the greater range of destinations the motorcar opens up, more often than not one moves through a increasingly continuous space.

The argument that technology has a determinate influence upon society can be summarized as follows:

1   Technology's effects are frequently unforeseen.
2   The pace of technological change makes controlling it increasingly difficult.
3   Technology's influence is pervasive.
4   The use of technology is inherently associated with the subsequent structuring of human activity.
5   Technological developments begin to assume a momentum that is apparently independent of human direction.

It is the combined effect of all these factors that results in the idea that it is technology, above all else, that determines the nature of contemporary society. Since technology is obviously a human creation, implicit in the five factors above is the assumption that societies initially create the technologies that subsequently appear to have such deterministic effects. The key issue that theorists disagree about, however, is the extent to which, faced with the fait accompli of technologically saturated environments, human agency can be exercised.

The common position of what Feenberg (1999) terms *essentialist* writers, such as Ellul, Marcuse and Heidegger, is that technology creates a total environment. Although they do not use the term 'matrix', we suggest that their work represents an important theoretical precursor to the im/material tension of digital matters and recent representations of the Matrix. The influence of this matrix exceeds its physical limits and manifests in the apparent immaterial realm of our modes of thought and social interaction. Ellul (1963 [1954]: 4) describes this colonizing tendency of technology in terms of *la téchnique* and claims that, like Frankenstein's creature and a whole bestiary of cinematic and fictional representations, it 'has now become independent of its offspring'. Part I examines the systemic nature of the processes that are purported to drive such totalizing phenomenon as *la téchnique* whilst Part II explores their possible role in cultural production.

Chapters 1 and 2 – technics

To begin the book, we place the notion of technology's totalizing effect in the context of two theorists and their seminal twentieth-century responses to the question of modernity's technological framework: Ellul's *The Technological Society* (1963 [1954]) and Heidegger's *The Question Concerning Technology* (1977 [1954]). We choose to focus upon Ellul and Heidegger because of the key nature of their insights into the qualitatively new circumscribing nature of modern technologies. The work of both Ellul and Heidegger strongly reinforces this book's general theme that some of the most interesting key issues surrounding digital culture are the various underlying socio-technical matrices of which the digital matrix is merely the current expression. There are several reasons for the privileging of these two texts. Published originally in the same year, they might be seen as representing two parallel responses to the problem of technics, the latter purely philosophical and the former broadly socio-cultural. Taken together, we argue that they represent an important theoretical 'benchmark' for our current attempts to understand the true significance of digital technology and its enframing effects.

In his *Critical Theory of Technology* (1991), Andrew Feenberg argues that theoretical responses to the question of technology have fallen in two major categories: that of the instrumental theory of technology and that of the substantial or essentialist. By *instrumental*, Feenberg designates the common-sense notion that technologies are 'tools' that serve the purposes of their creators. Conceived thus, technology is neutral, purely instrumental, mediating without distortion or deviation the intention of those who implement it. In this reading, technology is not influenced by the agenda of the society that employs it, and nor does it posses any agenda of its own – an attitude Winner scathingly referred to as *the myth of neutrality* (Winner 1977). In contrast, the *substantive* or *essentialist* theory of technology typified by Ellul and Heidegger argues that technology constitutes an autonomous system that restructures the entire social world in its own image. Crucial to this reconfiguration (as noted above) is the role of reason or efficiency: technology is seen to arise from, and give rise to, the domination of a ratiocinative mentality.

In Heidegger, this assumes the form of the *standing reserve,* understood as the conversion of all objects of the natural world into resources for exploitation within a technological system. Similarly, in Ellul's work, this rationalization takes the form of the streamlining and general subordination of all social processes to the concept of efficiency. In both accounts, technology is seen as bootstrapping itself and its putative creators into an enframed realm where means dominate ends. It should be emphasized that neither *The Technological Society* or *The Question Concerning Technology* can in any way be taken as the final word of their authors on the subject of technology. Ellul periodically revisited the problem of technics in a series of texts in which the ideas presented in *The Technological Society* were revised in the light of social and technological developments. In Heidegger's case, we observe not so much a revision in relation to shifting socio-technical trends, but rather the further refinement of a profound ambivalence towards technology and its dehumanizing effects. Heidegger and Ellul identify a fundamental way in which technology undermines non-technological values. It does so not by simply levelling the products of the past, but rather by subtly changing the mental framework of its users: the fear is that people internalize technological values. Heidegger and Ellul identify technology per se as the source of this process, but their fears of this 'endocolonization' are perhaps even more pertinent in the context of media technologies. Rather than influencing consciousness indirectly through habits and attitudes absorbed from the use of artefacts/systems, media have, through their manipulation of communicative symbols and through their direct interface with the human sensorium, an even more intimate relationship with the psyches of their listeners and viewers.

Chapters 3 and 4 – media bias

> History is perceived as a series of epochs separated by discontinuity. Each epoch is distinguished by dominant forms of media that absorb, record, and transform information into systems of knowledge consonant with the institutional power structure of the society in question. The interaction between media form and social reality creates biases, which strongly affect the society's cultural orientation and values.
>
> (Heyer and Crowley 2003: xvi)

> For the 'message' of any medium or technology is the change of scale or pace or pattern that it introduces into human affairs.
>
> (McLuhan 1995 [1964]: 8)

The notion of *media bias* acts as an important unifying concept for the main essentialist theorists we consider in this book as they relate to digital matters. All the main theorists of Part I, Heidegger, Ellul and Kittler, emphasize the extent to which technology creates discontinuities in the nature of our experience of reality. Heidegger identifies the disjuncture as early as the emergence of distinct Western mode of cogitation, Ellul locates the crucial change as the Industrial Revolution, and Kittler contends that certain media create profound changes to the whole social environment of a particular period in time, a process that is ongoing.

The work of the Canadian Harold Innis (1894–1952) directly addresses the complex interplay between the cultural and material elements of the social communication process. In *The Bias of Communication* (Innis 2003 [1951]), he uses the concept of *bias* to describe the way in which a medium works as a nodal point for the reproduction of cultural values. This is reflected in Chapter 3's examination of Kittler's discourse networks and Chapter 4's exploration of how modern media technologies serve to disproportionately reproduce commodity values. In this manner, as Couch puts it: 'Innis . . . sought to demonstrate how the media are social environments *sui generis* that determine broad sweeping everyday forms of social consciousness and social relationships' (Couch cited in Comor 2003: 91). For Innis, *communications media* are broadly defined to include social institutions, organizations and technologies as disparate as horses, the monetary system, universities and radio. This inclusive perspective and the ability to recognize media where others would see only brute utility arose from a willingness to see media technologies as shaping environments and their inhabitants. Innis' concept of bias avoids both the naivety of an instrumental notion of technology and the excesses of technologically deterministic theories in which technological developments proceed largely independently of concerted human control:

> . . . bias directs us away from both technological and structural determinist positions precisely because its flexibility compels the analyst to recognise that, for the most part, physical or structural capacities at any given time and place are historically constructed. In Innis, such capacities are dialectically related to the intellectual and cultural capacities of human agents. As such, the bias of communication directs us toward a relatively sophisticated, critical, and materialist assessment of why we attend to the things which we attend.
>
> (Comor 2003: 105)

According to Winner's *myth of neutrality*, social choices result in social outcomes and technology's role is merely to embody and facilitate this process. The myth's notion that the choices of how and why to use a technology, rather than innate qualities of the technology itself, will be the key influence upon its subsequent social effects prompted some of McLuhan's most trenchant declarations. He argued that although 'Many people would be disposed to say that it was not the machine, but what one did with the machine, that was its meaning or message', in fact 'In terms of the ways in which the machine altered our relations to one another and to ourselves, it mattered not in the least whether it turned out cornflakes or Cadillacs' (McLuhan 1995 [1964]: 8). He is withering in his critique of the perennial failure to recognize the mediating effects of media, asserting that 'Our conventional response to all media, namely that it is how they are used that counts, is the numb stance of the technological idiot' (1995 [1964]: 18) and 'the voice of the current somnambulism' (ibid.: 11).

In McLuhan's account, the choices of the social purposes to which a technology should be applied quickly become redundant and subordinate to the requirements and demands of the technology. These 'requirements' and 'demands' refer to the extended network of technological systems that a particular technology implies and the technologically defined cultural practices that spring up in subsequent adaptation – *la téchnique* in Ellul's terms. Particular social effects will result from the adoption of a technology irrespective of the intentions of its user, and from this perspective the only neutrality that technology possesses resides in its indifference to the desires of its adopters. Thus, a railway will have a significant social impact just by virtue of its presence, regardless of what it transports. Its social effect (message) will be primarily the product of functioning (the medium): certain effects are inevitable from the moment of its first adoption. Raymond Williams took issue with McLuhan's essentialism and its assumption of an inherent grammar or logic to each particular medium of communication. Whilst McLuhan's aphorisms and sound-bites allowed him to garner a considerable media profile in the 1960s, his belief in the embedded logic of media technologies resulted in a certain fatalism and a failure to expose the social factors that allowed dominant groups to maintain their control over those technologies. For Williams this apparent apoliticism had ideological consequences since it served to disable the critique of those who controlled media to their own undemocratic ends. McLuhan's thought is ideological because in it:

> All media operations are in effect dissocialised; they are simply physical events in an abstracted sensorium, and are distinguishable only by their variable sense-ratios . . . If the effect of the medium is the same, whoever controls or uses it, and whatever apparent content he may try to insert, then we can forget ordinary political and cultural alignment and let the technology run itself.
>
> (Williams 2003 [1974]: 130–1)

Williams's critique was certainly wrong on one account, namely that 'The particular rhetoric of McLuhan's theory of communication is unlikely to last long' (ibid.: 131), and its well-intentioned humanism – 'we have to reject technological determinism, in all its forms' (ibid.: 133) – seems almost quaint in the context of hyperbolic discussions of cyberspace and the 'post-human'. Williams does, however, raise the perennial question of optimism versus pessimism in interpretations of the political implications of media technologies. Williams shares what we shall also see in Feenberg's critique of essentialism: an intellectual impatience with theories that imply a certain degree of acquiescence to media technologies (which by definition exist outside the possibility of change by direct social and political engagement). We are keenly aware of the problems that Williams raises, and while, for the most part we concur with the vision of McLuhan *et al.* of the structural effects of media technologies, we explore in the final chapter the possibility of what we term 'rewiring the matrix'. However, in contrast to Williams's vision of pure social or political realm that exists outside the technological, we argue on the basis of a qualified constructivism that meaningful political intervention has to take place within and through the technological.

Part II – living in the digital matrix: the cultural perspective

The limits of social constructivism

> The constant danger in interpreting human behaviour is to overvalue exact methods and measurable data, separated from their historical context: data, often too complex for even verbal formulation; for the very things that the conscientious historian is tempted to leave out, because of *their obscurity, their purely analogical suggestiveness, their subjective involvement, are needed to bring any richness into our judgements.*
>
> (Mumford cited in May 2003: 111 [our emphasis])

> These large tendencies hit us with effects in our deepest feelings and the ways of seeing which go with them. Indeed they frame those feelings and give them structure. This, however, is a process surely invisible to empirical research.
>
> (Inglis 1990: 151)

As already noted, Bruno Latour's influential *We Have Never Been Modern* (1993) provides a historical perspective on his work's on-going concern with establishing more flexible ways of viewing the relationship between society and technology. According to Latour, society has always been generated through its relation to artefacts, even as these artefacts are produced socially, and that, rather than conceiving of a dialectic relation between people and objects, we must think in terms of immanent networks of hybrid assemblages of humans and artefacts. Despite such recent theoretical innovations and their increasingly sophisticated understanding of the complex interrelationship between technological and social systems, there still remains a strong sense that certain aspects of these systems and their processes remain unaddressed, because accounts such as Latour's fail to engage with the specificity of media technologies and the way they determine the nature of our subjectivity. It is relatively simple to disprove the crudest conceptualization of technological determinism by pointing out that originally someone had to design the technologies that appear to dominate us. It is less easy, however, to dispel the suspicions represented in the above quotations that human agency is now constituted by structuring systems whose consequences are unconscious or at least unacknowledged. Thus, we seek to expose the latent determinism implicit in terms such as the 'Industrial Revolution' and the 'Information Revolution', stressing that these are revolutions effected by technologies: it is technology that is revolutionary and societies are what they revolutionize.

But unfortunately, given this book's main focus upon digital matters, there is not enough space to do full justice to the complexities of the debates and theories surrounding technological determinism. Suffice it to say, it is perhaps too often presented as a 'straw man' argument and, in addition, pro and anti arguments are often conducted at different registers in what can amount to at times parallel monologues. For example, Feenberg, having labelled theories that privilege technology's determining influence *essentialist*, argues 'If essentialism is unaware of its own limitations, this is because it confounds attitude with object, the modern obsession with efficiency with technology as such' (Feenberg 1999: x). He accuses essentialism of being too abstract in its treatment of technology as an autonomous realm of technique. In his mind, it overemphasizes immaterial, generic notions of technology at the expense of its material particularity – it 'disconnects the technical . . . from the experience of it' (ibid.: 1999: xii) On the other hand, however, theories that do emphasize the particularity of the material, for Feenberg, make a parallel error: 'constructivism so disaggregates the question of technology that it is sometimes difficult to see its relevance to the legitimate concerns of essentialism' (ibid.: 1999: x).

The roots of the im/material tension lie deep within the historical development of technological society. Later chapters attempt to identify the origins of this tension and show how it is greatly heightened in the contemporary world of digital matters where the im/material is now our de facto cultural environment. In this context, the notion of *the matrix* of our subtitle is crucial. The matrix here refers to the way in which the material infrastructure of technological society is informed by immaterial, but hugely powerful, aggregate forces that need to be recognized and properly understood. Failure to do so means that social constructivist theories of technology risk committing the same error they charge essentialism with: disconnecting the abstract qualities of the technical from the empirically elusive, but nevertheless very real, experience of them. Social constructivist accounts provide detailed readings of the way in which society shapes diverse technological artefacts. Useful as they are, however, their detailed examination of material artefacts tells only part of the story about technology's cultural effects. And these claims are perhaps strengthened by the fact that recent anti-deterministic theories have tended to concentrate on hardware and related processes, rather than the affective consequences of media technologies. One of McLuhan's strongest rhetorical themes is the notion that the subtlety of the consequences of media means that, like Narcissus, both individuals and cultures are highly vulnerable to falling under the spell of their reflective surfaces. He is thus contemptuous of the belief (implicitly contained within the myth of neutrality) that, supported by a strong intellectual resistance to the putative 'messages' of media technologies, an individual (or by extension a society) can remain unaffected by them. Instead McLuhan asserts that 'The effects of technology do not occur at the level of opinions or concepts, but alter sense ratios or patterns of perception steadily and without any resistance' (McLuhan 1995 [1964]: 18). In Part II we explore the cultural consequences of these media-induced changes in sense ratios that social constructivism has proved ill-equipped to address.

In Part II we perhaps interpret more literally than Jameson himself his assertion that '. . . any comprehensive new theory of finance capitalism will need to reach out into the expanded realm of cultural production to map its effects' (Jameson 1998: 143). Similarly, Hardt and Negri (2000) argue through their redeployment of Foucault's concept of *biopolitics* that the site of struggle in neo-capitalism has moved into the cultural realm. In keeping with our concern with material and cultural processes, we explore the historical roots of such a situation and, drawing on the analysis of the dialectic of reification, we examine the manner in which the interplay between technology, capital and culture produces a novel situation in which a number of previously established distinctions or boundaries are renegotiated. More populist accounts of the proliferation of digital technology have tended to address different facets of the phenomenon in discrete categories, addressing either its communicative, aesthetic or political consequences in extrinsic terms. In contrast, we are unabashedly synoptic, and draw our inspiration (if not our theory) from works such as Hardt and Negri's *Empire*. We approach the matrix in terms of a panoptic, globalized, post-Fordist capitalism. However, we argue that the full complexity of this system can be approached only through its specific effects; it is for this reason that we emphasize its cultural consequences, and so draw on a range of literary and historico-cultural material.

Chapters 5 and 6 – urban and social matrix matters

In Chapters 5 and 6, we build further upon Part I's analysis of technological enframement and its particular manifestation within the media, to explore how the abstract perception of technology's apparent autonomy is, in late capitalism, deeply imbricated within the material commodity form – an aspect of the analysis begun in Chapter 4. The fantastical properties Marx identified in commodities were developed by Benjamin in his explorations of the 'phantasmagoria' of the arcades of mid-nineteenth century Paris and in the 'lucid dream' of the newly emergent cinema. Today such phantasmagoria are increasingly aligned with physical space *in toto* as the commodification of the external environment merges and coalesces with its media representations. In this context, *digital matters* relates to the crucial role digitality plays in promoting a new form of *reification*. New commodity forms assume an increasingly informatic appearance that is im/material. We thus develop Kittler's identification of the city as an information processor to show that a crucial dimension of the digital is its ability to change whole environments into areas ripe for informationalization, so that key Marxist notions such as the reversal of relations between people and objects, commodity fetishism, etc. breach ever new thresholds.

Chapter 7 – cyberspatial matrix matters

In Chapter 7 we follow the emergence of the matrix to the point where, for some commentators, the traditional boundary between reality and the imagination is irretrievably blurred, a tradition hypostasized in fictional representations of the Matrix. J. G. Ballard, for example, argues that the ubiquity and pervasiveness of modern technology has reversed our usual ontological categories:

> In the past we have always assumed that the external world around us has represented reality, however confusing or uncertain, and that the inner world of our minds, its dreams, hopes, ambitions, represented the realm of fantasy and the imagination. These roles it seems to me have been reversed . . . the one small node of reality left to us is inside our own heads.
>
> (Ballard 1995: 5)

Ballard's comments lead us to another aspect of the analyses offered in Part II, namely the value we place upon the comments and work of creative individuals in particular novelists. We thus unapologetically use fiction (in Chapter 7 especially) as a conceptual resource. In doing so we follow McLuhan's observation that:

> The percussed victims of the new technology have invariably muttered clichés about the impracticability of artists and their fanciful preferences. But in the past century it has come to be generally acknowledged that, in the words of Wyndham Lewis, 'The artist is always engaged in writing a detailed history of the future because he is the only person aware of the nature of the present.' . . . The ability of the artist to sidestep the bully blow of new technology of any age, and to parry such violence with full aware-ness, is age-old . . .
>
> (McLuhan 1995 [1964]: 65)

For McLuhan, artists are the group best suited to observing the changes to our sense ratios that occur as a result of the impact of various technologies, since aesthetic production has often involved a sensitivity to these very ratios. Reminiscent of McLuhan's observation, in *The Logic of Sense* Gilles Deleuze (drawing on Nietzsche) offers his clinical definition of the work of art, observing that artists:

> . . . are themselves astonishing diagnosticians or symptomatologists. There is always a great deal of art involved in the grouping of symptoms . . . Clinicians who are able to renew a symptomatological picture produce a work of art; conversely, artists are clinicians . . . they are clinicians of civili-

sation . . . and it seems moreover, [this] evaluation of symptoms might only be achieved through a *novel*.

(Deleuze 1990: 237 [emphasis in original])

In this light, the novel as a form can be said to serve a diagnostic function, identifying the composition of forces, the relations of 'labour, life and language' that characterize a given epoch and offering an aetiology of the 'ills' that seize individuals and cultures alike. Part II, therefore, uses contemporary fiction to illustrate some of the key cultural impacts of digital technology. Like McLuhan and Deleuze, Kittler has stressed the diagnostic role of literature, which, in an era in which the text is deposed from its former position at the centre of Western culture, might be seen as media, however, 'pushed to their margins even obsolete media become sensitive enough to register the signs and clues of a situation. Then, as in the case of the sectional plane of two optical media, patterns and moirés emerge: myths, fictions of science, oracles . . .' (Kittler 1999: xl). Our recourse to literature is also in keeping with Baudrillard's characterization of himself as a practitioner of (the playwright and aesthete Alfred Jarry's) pataphysics (the science of imaginary solutions) and his theoretical interpretation of communication closely mirrors Ballard's view: '. . . we will suffer from this forced extraversion of all interiority, from this forced introjection of all exteriority which is implied by the categorical imperative of communication' (Baudrillard 1988: 26).

The non-empirical imaginative excess of fiction, and the cyberpunk genre in particular, is thus shown to be a potentially useful resource with which to better understand the zeitgeist of the digital age. Its theoretical pertinence and methodological suitability to the here-and-now of real life are reflected in claims that cyberpunk can be viewed as social theory (Burrows 1997), whereas 'Baudrillard's futuristic postmodern social theory can be read in turn as science fiction' (Kellner 1995: 299). Indeed, Baudrillard has argued that, given the fact that that phantasmagoria of the real (or hyperreal) exceeds the imaginative projections of science fiction, the latter has become increasingly redundant so that its golden age of vision and prophecy has passed. In this respect, we depart from Baudrillard and argue that science fiction in the form of the subgenre of cyberpunk still offers an intimation of our future as well as a perspicacious reflection of our present. Thus, we see how the imaginative excesses of cyberpunk fiction exemplify, within the context of the contemporary, the oracular role Kittler ascribes to literature in general, and so allows us to discern the emergent characteristics of what might be termed (following Kittler): 'Network 2000'.

Chapter 8 – rewiring the matrix

In the final chapter we consider the work of the Italian autonomists (Negri, in particular) and the armoury of conceptual tools they have developed in the face of theoretical and political challenge posed by the apparent triumph of a global, informatic capital. We use these concepts to examine the practical software solutions to the enframing qualities of the matrix potentially contained within the Free and Open Source software movements. Resorting to the previously used terms of optimism and pessimism, we suggest that digital matters may yet offer a hopeful strategy with which to steer the middle ground between the lacunae of essentialist and constructivist thought.

Conclusion

In this volume as a whole, we use the combined insights of its two-part structure to attempt to steer upon this theoretical middle ground and to concentrate upon the mutually reinforcing nature of the socio-technical dialectic. At the risk of appearing intractably ambivalent, we are not essentialist to the extent that we emphasize the importance of the cultural alignment between technology and its social environment, but we are convinced that the imbrication of the media technologies that culminate in the flows of digital capitalism creates a totalizing environment that, although at root a social construction, has many of the enframing qualities identified by the essentialist literature. We therefore take 'the legitimate concerns of essentialism' seriously, but we are also sensitive to the charge of dealing in immaterial abstraction at the cost of material experience. It is from this position that the full title of this volume issues: *Digital Matters: the theory and culture of the matrix*. Our basic position is that the digital's important theoretical and cultural implications cannot be fully understood without examining both its materiality and immateriality. These are not contradictory qualities but rather essential, mutually constituting elements. The poles of the technological determinism debate are ultimately about how we approach the vexed question of the relationship between the material and the immaterial: the im/material embodied in the apparent oxymoron – *digital matters*.

Part I

Theorizing the im/material matrix: technics triumphant

Part I

Uncovering the immaterial
in the material: concepts and

1   Jacques Ellul's *la téchnique*

This chapter develops our discussion of technological determinism by examining in detail the work of Jacques Ellul, particularly his central concept of *la téchnique*. Ellul's *La Téchnique ou l'Enjeu du Siecle* (literally 'Technique: the stake of the century', translated as *The Technological Society*) occupies the cusp between two technological epochs – the Industrial and Information Revolutions (Ellul 1963 [1954]: 88–9). More specifically, commentators have located Ellul's reading of technology within a constellation of texts written around the Second World War that highlight the increasing predominance of technology in all spheres of life: Feenberg's essentialists. These works include Mumford's *Technics and Civilization* (1934), Veblen's *The Engineers and the Price System* (1963 [1921]), Geidion's *Mechanization Takes Command* (1969 [1948]), Spengler's *Man and Technics* (1940), Jaspers' *Man in the Modern Age* (1978 [1932]) and the various critiques of 'instrumental rationality' undertaken by members and associates of the Frankfurt School. Ellul provides a sustained exploration of the previously encountered essentialist notion that a fundamental change has occurred in society's relationship to its technological infrastructure.

We use Ellul in this chapter and Heidegger in the next in order to examine the extent to which the anti-essentialist positions of constructivist theories still fail to fully address essentialism's key concern. At the end of this chapter we consider a critique of Ellul's position using Feenberg's critical overview of essentialism, *Questioning Technology* (1999); however, the main body of the chapter focuses on the stubborn emphasis upon a totalizing element that is an essential part of *The Technological Society* (hence the label *essentialism*). This account of technology's totalizing aspect provides us with a theoretical basis from which to understand the negative cultural consequences we explore in detail in Part II.

Although Ellul regarded himself as a philosopher, and was a theologian of considerable repute, he is perhaps best characterized (in the words of his English translator) as one of those 'gifted amateurs, who *faute de mieux* must be called philosophers' (Ellul 1963 [1954]: xvi). Langdon Winner (1977) describes Ellul's study as 'a fascinating, sprawling masterwork of autonomous technics in our time'. The sprawling quality is undeniable and presents considerable difficulties when attempting to locate Ellul's work within accepted disciplinary boundaries. Unlike Heidegger's, his theory of technology, though informed by certain philosophical presuppositions, is not inextricably intertwined within a complex of philosophical procedures or questions. In the light of this, *The Technological Society* is perhaps best regarded as a work of cultural theory *avant la lettre*, displaying in equal amounts the freedom and generality associated with that discipline. Although Ellul's conceptual framework predominantly relates to his interpretations of the abstract forces of technology, unlike the critics of essentialism, we maintain that it is an important aid with which to understand more fully the wider cultural experience of a technologically sophisticated society. For this reason, we reject Feenberg's previously cited characterization of essentialist thinking as a mode that 'disconnects the technical . . . from the experience of it'. Whilst our later focus upon Kittler is intrinsically concerned with the materiality of the media technologies that eventually culminate with the digital, we suggest that Ellul's work is a crucial contribution to a better understanding of the immaterial side of the full technological experience represented within our title phrase, *Digital Matters*.

A consequence of the cultural theory element of Ellul's work, however, is the way in which it does not feel obliged to produce analytical answers with which to escape enframement by the technologically dominant values it so effectively describes. For this reason we would group his perspective with the similarly non-philosophically grounded, *mosaic* approaches of such media theorists as McLuhan and Baudrillard. The implications of all these theorists' work are largely pessimistic in so far as they proffer no readily implemented solutions or strategies with which to counter the negative cultural consequences of technology. In Part II we shall see this pessimism fully realized in the dystopian portrayals of the digital matters of disturbing cyberspatial environments, but at this point it is to the theoretical roots of this pessimism that we turn.

Cumulative/accretional determinism

> No one can foresee the radical changes to come. But technological advance will move faster and faster and can never be stopped. In all areas of his existence, man will be encircled ever more tightly by the forces of technology. These forces, which everywhere and every minute claim, enchain, drag along, press and impose upon man under the form of some technical contrivance or other – these forces . . . have moved long since beyond his will and have outgrown his capacity for decision.
>
> (Heidegger cited in Winner 1977: 14)

In opposition to the *myth of neturality,* the deterministic effects of technology are felt in two theoretically separate, but complementary and often seamlessly interwoven ways:

1 the use of an individual artefact requires adaptive responses; and
2 additional systemic and accretional effects result from that artefact's location in a complex assemblage or networks of other technologies.

The impact of technology is thus not only felt on a case-by-case, or artefact-by-artefact, basis, it tends to be experienced in the context of large systems. Such cumulative effects combine to constitute a distinct phenomenon in themselves. At both an individual and social level, human activities partially and incrementally adapt in order to fit better with the requirements of such systems. It is the cumulative effect of many such small adaptations, rather than necessarily the dramatic effects of individual technologies, that arguably forms the most significant aspect of technology's deterministic impact upon society. Ellul, for example, uses the notion of an *ensemble* to describe this effect of technology viewed on a holistic, rather than an individual, basis:

> A whole new kind of spontaneous action is taking place here, and we know neither its laws nor its ends. In this sense it is possible to speak of the 'reality' of technique – with its own substance, its own particular mode of being, and a life independent of our power of decision.
>
> (cited in Winner 1977: 62)

Ellul develops at length his subsequent argument that this determining phenomenon he calls *la téchnique* is the defining feature of contemporary life, creating a *society of téchnique*. Dealing at this level of abstraction, it is perhaps difficult for the reader to understand exactly what is meant by these phrases. One way of providing further explanation is to compare directly the concepts of *society* and *technology*.

The term *society* is used relatively unproblematically, by academic theorists, social commentators and the lay person alike, to describe more than simply the aggregate effects of numerous individuals living together: society has a texture of its own; society is more than just the sum of its individual parts. Similarly, the agglomeration and interaction of numerous individual technologies creates a phenomenon in its own right that can be compared to Durkheim's notion of a *social fact* whereby:

> Society is not a mere sum of individuals. Rather, the system formed by their association represents a specific reality which has its own characteristics . . . To me the sociological does not consist of the addition and combination of individual actions. I believe that there is a collective reality, which is independent of the individuals.
>
> (Durkheim cited in Winner 1977: 62–3)

A strong element of the deterministic 'technology is out of control' argument, therefore, is the observation that technology is not merely used – its presence constructs environments that then have a determining influence upon the actions and lives of those that live within it. To summarize the determinist viewpoint:

1   Modern technologies are invariably more complex than a simple tool.

2 A consequence of this complexity is that the user of a technology tends to be conditioned into using the artefact in a particular way.
3 Such conditioning is in turn further conditioned by the fact that the increasingly interconnected nature of technology requires that the use of the initial artefact takes into account many other artefacts and systems of which it is but a small part.

The cumulative effect of all three factors creates a totalizing effect that is encapsulated in Ellul's notion of *la téchnique*, but before we explore this concept in detail it is worth considering this notion of technology's totalizing effects in relation to our previous discussion of optimism and pessimism.

Essentialism and the pessimism of the missing dialectic

An important aspect of the way in which Ellul's work is more cultural theory than traditional philosophy is its lack of a conventionally dialectical approach. Dialectics involves the concepts of *thesis*, *antithesis* and *synthesis*, the dynamic interaction of which implies a process of progression and development. In social theory the notion of the dialectic is that an idea meets with opposition and from this act of contradiction emerges the combined, improved outcome: the synthesis. In the Hegelian theory of history and then Marxist political philosophy, the importance of dialectics is that it necessarily implies an evolutionary process based upon an improvement in social conditions which Marx associated with the historical inevitability of the dictatorship of the proletariat. For Marx, this occurred as the necessary synthesis resulting from the thesis of the material creation of wealth by the working class and the antithesis of the class tensions created by the appropriation of this productive effort through capitalist exploitation. This socially progressive and empowering aspect of an implied dialectic is frequently also implicit in those social theorists who would nevertheless shrink from the label Marxist. Thus, contemporary social scientists tend to be predisposed to theories that offer at least some ground for optimism in terms of positive social change. To paraphrase Gramsci, their optimism of the will is met with an optimism of the intellect. In cultural theory, for example, sustained efforts are made amidst even the most heavily commodified and mediated aspects of popular culture to interpret such culture as serving independent, non-manufactured purposes by which audiences can retain their autonomy (see in particular John Fiske's body of work). The critical theorists of the Frankfurt School, by contrast, stand apart for the unalloyed darkness of their theoretical position. They are consistently accused of being unduly elitist and pessimistic in their damning indictment of both the quality of popular culture – *the culture industry thesis* – and the inherently inhuman excesses to be found in the history of Western reason – *the dialectic of enlightenment*.

The Frankfurt School's approach to the notion of the dialectic is directly relevant to our concern about the nature of human interaction with technology. Their culture industry thesis provides a vividly argued example of the tightly imbricated cultural alignment between commodity culture and mass media technologies, whilst their overarching philosophical approach, like that of Ellul, suggests that the dialectic is largely one-dimensional and unidirectional. The phrase 'the dialectic of enlightenment' is used in a somewhat ironical fashion – for the essentialist interpreters of technological culture, the history of Western culture illustrates one overwhelming trend: the dominance of *la téchnique*. Their combined pessimism of the will *and* intellect means that they tend to be criticized for their lack of optimism as much as for any analytical weaknesses, so that Feenberg, for example, feels able to assert 'This approach leaves me sceptical, not because it affirms the existence of social pathologies linked to technology, but because it forecloses in principle any serious action to address them' (Feenberg 1999: ix). Thus, an immediate stumbling block for at least some people's encounter with the work of essentialists is likely to be the pessimistic, non-solution-orientated nature of their technologically totalizing message.

The theoretical basis of this pessimism is to be found in the manner in which Ellul's dialectic differs from those of Hegel and Marx in one fundamental aspect. His conception of the dialectic is non-teleological: it does not imply a necessary progression towards a discernibly improved end. Thus, while he concurs with Hegel and Marx in the assertion of the absolute primacy of contradiction, contradiction for Ellul does not imply any form of sublation within a higher synthesis: there is no 'negation of the negation'. As a result, Ellul does not subscribe to a dialectics of 'ascent' in which we would witness the ultimate absorption of contradiction in the triumph of *geist*, or in the negation of class conflict in the form of a fully realized communist society. Instead, in his study of technology, Ellul posits a model in which contradiction is immanent and incapable of self-transcendence, and in which the elimination of contradiction results not from a new-found synthesis but from the ultimate triumph of a disproportionately contradictory force: *la téchnique*. Thus, Ellul's history of technology does not reflect an orderly progression of thesis, antithesis and synthesis. Rather, it offers an image of a process of continually redistributed but only partially sustained contradiction: society and technology exist in a fundamental opposition but the latter consistently tends to subsume the former without the contradiction ever being totally resolved. The situation only 'evolves' to the extent that this unequal and contradictory relationship is recast under different determinant historical circumstances.

Again, in distinct contrast to Hegel and Marx, rather than being the Holy Grail of the polity, the end of dialectics for Ellul is a source of deep disquiet since it suggests victory for a single term. Indeed, *The Technological Society* was composed in fear and trembling in the face of what John Boli-Bennet, in a detailed analysis of Ellul's 'absolute dialectics', describes as 'the impending eclipse of dialectics' (Boli-Bennet 1980: 191). The technological society that Ellul explores is one in which contradiction is increasingly impossible, not through any form of *aufgehoben* (dialectical annihilation), but through the total diminution of one of its contradictory terms: the human or social. The end of the dialectic in Ellul's terms illustrates two important features of digital matters: (i) the difference between the matrix and the Matrix; and (ii) the rise of immanence in digital matters.

The difference between the matrix and the Matrix

Appreciation of the matrix rests upon a recognition of the determining qualities of technologies that, although couched in theoretical terms, is ultimately derived from direct or inferred observation of their material social effects. The Matrix, in contrast (especially in its more febrile fictional renderings presented in Chapter 7's account of cyberpunk), has lost its moorings, or frame of reference, within the material. The continued importance of the physical is generally glossed over in the various rhetorical flourishes of hi-tech boosterism. Thus, the New Economy may still be based upon the material exploitation of disadvantaged groups in the global economy, but these human and social needs are displaced by the dominant rhetoric of technological imperatives. Whilst such rhetoric is a political weapon (in the same sort of ideology-by-default way with which, as we saw, Williams charged McLuhan), Ellul's work demonstrates in sharp relief the extent to which such strategies, rhetorical or not, are still reinforced and supported by deeply insinuated mental and social processes: the digital Matrix is the most recent culmination of the matrix.

The rise of immanence in digital matters

It is interesting to note in relation to our theme of optimism and pessimism the position taken in a number of recent works that deal with the political aspects of digital matters. Lash (2002) explicitly, but also Dyer-Witheford (1999) and Hardt and Negri (2000) more implicitly, seem to accept the all-encompassing, totalizing nature of the new informational social and economic global order. Hence, the notion of *immanence* for Lash arguably goes further than the totalizing tendency of the essentialists:

> . . . the rise of the information order, of the media society, explodes the binaries, explodes the 'difference' between instrumentality and finality. It explodes this pervious transcendence into a more general immanence, and indifference of information and communication flows. Information and communication are neither instrumentalities nor finalities: information and communication build networks, they make connections. Information and communication are now – in what is no longer an industrial society, but now primarily a media society – prior to both instrumentality and finality.
>
> (Lash 2002: 68)

Lash *et al.* share some of the totalizing elements of the essentialist approach in their consistent argument that there is no longer an outside to the new informational order. In contrast to pessimistic, essentialist interpretations of technology's effects, however, this group of theorists more optimistically promotes the on-going feasibility of political strategies that can subvert such totalization in a digital age. They also claim that the Information Revolution represents a further qualitative change to that originally marked by its industrial namesake. We will keep returning throughout this book to the importance of the purported qualitative change that has occurred within the Information Revolution since it is self-evidently crucial to a full understanding of digital matters. What needs emphasizing at this point, however, is the importance of the conceptual links between the two revolutions. If the Information Revolution is a further development of trends that originally occurred in the Industrial Revolution, then the exact nature of these original trends needs attending to, and we revisit Ellul because of the relatively untapped relevance of his critique of the Industrial Revolution to these roots of digital matters. In addition, although radically different in tone and political message from Ellul's pessimism, the work of Lash *et al.* can be interpreted as owing an unacknowledged debt to Ellul the essentialist and the intrinsically immanent nature of his *la téchnique*.

La téchnique

> The term technique, as I use it, does not mean machines, technology, or this or that procedure for obtaining an end. In our technological society, technique is the totality of methods rationally arrived at and having absolute efficiency (for a given stage of development) *in every field of activity*.
> (Ellul 1963 [1954]: xxv [emphasis in original])

In the words of Daniel Cerezuelle, Ellul's 'reflections on technology are of a sociological order. His analysis of technology and its relationship to society does not claim to reveal clearly the universal essence of technology, but more its role and function in a well defined historico-cultural context, that of modernity' (Cerezuelle 1979: 176). As will become apparent, however, Ellul's reflections in establishing a clearly delimited 'historico-cultural context' do implicitly represent a universal theory of technology, making it difficult to bracket off his sociological observations from the analytical presuppositions with which they are underwritten. His basic thesis is that contemporary Western civilization is falling increasingly under the dominion of what he terms *la téchnique*. By '*la téchnique*' Ellul means not only technology in its most concrete forms but also the forms of subjectivity and social organization that are the inevitable result of a society whose infrastructure is technological. Although Ellul's term *la téchnique* is chosen with the intention of encompassing a wider range of activities than those normally regarded as technological, he is emphatic that technique begins with the machine. It is the emergence of mechanization that ushers in the technological society. However, Ellul claims that the image of the machine is no longer sufficient to encapsulate the broader sense in which technology has slipped free from human control: 'technique has now become independent of its offspring' (Ellul 1963 [1954]: 4).

La téchnique, then, is not simply technology but an ineluctable process that begins with the progress of mechanization but assumes further complexity and invasive qualities in the realm of digital matters. It describes the reduction of the individual and society to functions that can be restructured to better suit the demands of the machine (*reverse adaptation*). Once these demands have been met, technique sets about reconfiguring those elements of society formerly outside of the machine. Ellul describes technique as *the ensemble of means* that operate in a technological society, which include:

1   economic technique: economic practices whose purpose is to facilitate technological progress;
2   the technique of organization: managerial practices that ensure the smooth integration of man and machine;
3   psychological/human technique: the technological environment determines human behaviour.

It is the sum total of these three techniques – the economic, organizational and psychological – and their function in single ensemble that characterizes *la téchnique* in terms that prefigure Lash's claims for the informational immanence of digital matters:

> Technique integrates everything. It avoids shock and sensational events. Man is not adapted to the world of the steel; technique adapts him to it. It changes the arrangements of this blind world so that man can become part of it without colliding with its rough edges . . . when technique enters into every area of life, including the human, it ceases to be external to man and becomes his very substance.
>
> (Ellul 1963 [1954]: 7)

It could be argued that if technique has so escaped its material confines and arrogated to itself that which was formerly 'outside', then does its own status not begin to seem problematic or unstable, in short, is it a symptom or cause? Ellul's response is emphatic – technique is the *primum mobile* – thus he can confidently declare that 'it is useless to rail against capitalism. Capitalism did not create our world: the machine did' (ibid.: 1963 [1954]: 5). Again, this rather prefigures radical theories of the digital order such as those of Lash (2002) and Dyer-Witheford (1999), which advocate the political strategy of working within the system because there is no longer an outside from which to bring it down. In Ellul's framework, this loss of a transcendent perspective occurs not with the information revolution but at the time of the Industrial Revolution. Capital is merely midwife to the machine, and the machine qua technique will eventually result in capital's demise – though without coinciding with the emergence of utopia. In order to fully appreciate the scope of Ellul's conception of technique, we must first briefly examine the prehistory he provides in *The Technological Society* before its full-blown realization in modernity. A prehistory that in keeping with an 'absolute dialectics' is one in which technique's totalitarianism was forestalled or held in abeyance by social values – but only until the advent of the Industrial Revolution.

The prehistory of *la téchnique* and the origins of digital flows: static and mobile techniques

Ellul's prehistory of *la téchnique* provides a useful illustration of the theme of technology's mobility and flux that constitutes a major theme in Part II. He makes the controversial proposition *that the origin of technology is to be found in magic,* which constitutes the first technology, i.e. the first attempt to influence, control and master the external environment through a set of procedures:

> Magic clearly displays the characteristics of primitive technique, as [Andre] Leroi-Gourhan indicates when he says that technique is a cloak for man, a kind of cosmic vestment, in his struggle to survive man interposes an intermediary agency between himself and his environment . . .
>
> (Ellul 1963 [1954]: 25)

Alestair Crowley famously defined the practice of magic as 'the science and art of causing change in conformity with Will' (Crowley 1929: xii), and this definition provides us with the means of understanding Ellul's equation of primitive technology and magic. Technique is the ensemble of procedures that enable the modification of the external environment in accordance with human needs. However, Ellul argues that immaterial 'magical' technique and 'material' artefactual technique, while confused in origin, ultimately diverge. In the case of magical technique we observe a phenomenon that is static in two senses. First, by virtue of the fact that magical procedures, once stabilized, are rarely modified, the ancestors or gods must be propitiated in a manner that has always been, and deviations from ritual order threaten to bring in their train want and privation: 'strict adherence to form is one of the characteristics of magic' (Ellul 1963 [1954]: 24). In contrast, material technique tends, in and of itself, to evolve. For example, the benefits of a modification of a given tool are readily apparent to all who employ it and consequently are readily adopted. Second, magical technique is static in the sense that it is restricted by the specificity of its location: magical techniques are the possessions of a given group in a given context and cannot easily be transposed or adopted by another group.

One consequence of this is that magical techniques (unlike material techniques) do not survive their endemic context: 'when a civilisation dies, it transmits to its heirs its material but not its spiritual apparatus' (ibid.: 1963 [1954]: 26). Conversely, material technique is characterized by a twofold freedom that allows its development and diffusion – that of modification or invention in the act of use and that of relative cultural independence. It is this freedom to evolve and diffuse that ultimately results in technique's triumph in the modern era, as well as ensuring the gradual elimination of magic from humanity's technical repertoire. Paradoxically, magic is immaterial but based upon a circumscribed material environment, whilst the material basis of technology only serves to give it an immaterial independence from a static material environment. In the digital matters of Part II, we trace how, over time, this freedom that technology's inherently mobile properties give it from static tradition reaches a disorientating level of autonomy to the extent that socio-technical flux becomes something to be mastered by those with semi-magical affinities to the informational flows of cyberspace. For example, in a seminal early piece about cyberspace, 'Crime and Puzzlement', John Perry Barlow is fearful before meeting what prove to be a harmless group of hackers that they are 'digital brujos about to zombify my soul' (Barlow 1990: 47), and in Gibson's *Neuromancer* trilogy there are explicitly magical/mystical Voodoo spirits deep within the Matrix.

In the case of Ancient Rome, Ellul finds a quite different relation to technology from that found with magic. It is one that offers an intimation of the future domination by technique described in Postman's (1993) schema as *technopoly*: the uncontrollable and inextricable relation between technology and social organization. In Ellul's account, the demands of the Roman state required the adoption of an 'ensemble' of technical means. However, to the extent that the demands of the state were paramount, in Rome technique did not become autonomous (Ellul 1963 [1954]: 29–32) and so it still qualified as a technocracy rather than technopoly (technocracy being defined by Postman as a society that contains potentially technopolistic technologies rather than simple tools, but which succeeds in subordinating them to social purposes). Thus, the Middle Ages, according to Ellul, saw the effective suspension of technical development, which is attributed to the restraining influence of Christianity and its elevation of otherworldly pursuits over the exploration and manipulation of the material world – again, technocracy's control over technological expansion. This trend continued into the Renaissance, which, despite a release from the constraints of Christian theology, did not pursue the development of technique in and for itself – a state of affairs that Ellul attributed to a belief in 'universalism' (ibid.: 1963 [1954]: 39–40). Despite the radical disparity of the cultures and epochs addressed in Ellul's history of premodern technics, Ellul argues for a set of common characteristics or, more accurately, limitations that prevented the emergence of an autonomous technique and so preserved dialectical freedom:

1   In every society up until the advent of the Industrial Revolution, technique operated in limited number of social domains and was employed in particular determinant circumstances and its uses were embedded in a non-technical belief system – it was always subordinate to social relations and 'functioned only at certain precise and well defined times: this was the case in all societies before our own' (ibid.: 1963 [1954]: 66).

2   Since technique was called upon only in circumscribed circumstances, it remained limited in power. Given its limited area of application there was no incentive to develop its capacities or effectiveness. Technique served to maintain non-technical social structures, its function being not to innovate but to preserve: 'man tended to exploit to the limit such means as he pos-

sessed and took care not to replace them or create other means as long as the old ones were effective' (ibid.: 1963 [1954]: 67).

3   Preindustrial technique exhibits cultural specificity. Embedded in the particulars of a given culture, inseparable from a nexus of non-technical practices, the opportunities for the diffusion of techniques were forestalled: 'Geographically there could be no technical transmission because technique was not some anonymous piece of merchandise but bore the stamp of a whole culture' (ibid.: 1963 [1954]: 69). Here, cultural difference functioned as a prophylactic that prevented the diffusion of techniques outside their parent cultures. The result of these limitations was that technique and humanity remained on equal terms; humanity preserved a freedom of choice in regard to the technical – a freedom which, Ellul believed, modern man has forgone.

The Industrial Revolution as the origin of digital matters

What does the phrase 'the Industrial Revolution broke out' mean? It means that sometime in the 1780s, *and for the first time in human history, the shackles were taken off the productive power of human societies,* which henceforth became capable of the constant, rapid, and up to the present limitless multiplication of men, goods and services.

(Hobsbawm 1975: 28 [our emphasis])

In the light of Ellul's prehistory of technology, the Industrial Revolution assumes the status of a singular event, a unique caesura in human history that determines all that follows in its wake. From the outset Ellul acknowledges that the ultimate cause of the Industrial Revolution must remain indeterminate, that the reason why, in a century and a half, a process should have taken place that resulted in a social structure radically different to any that had preceded it will remain an enduring enigma (Ellul 1963 [1954]: 44). Nevertheless he proposes five factors that taken together might account for this epochal transformation:

1   The first is what he terms 'the slow maturation of technical means', namely the existence of a latent set of techniques awaiting appropriate conditions for their systematic implementation. It is 'this enormous sum of experiments, of apparatus and inquiries' that constitutes the reservoir of potential technical solutions to be drawn upon in the process of industrialization. However, for the latent history of techniques to become an autonomous force we must look beyond technological and it is within society that Ellul locates the other forces implicated in the emergence of industrialization.

2   Thus, the second condition is that of population expansion, arguing that an increase in population demands the implementation of means to satisfy the material needs of a burgeoning population, this in turn further increasing the development of technology.

3   The third condition is that of a determinate economic condition, one in which 'the economic milieu must combine in two apparently contradictory

traits: it must at once be stable and in flux' (ibid.: 48), a contradiction we will examine in greater depth in Part II's treatment of the flux upon which the informational flows of digital matters are premised.

4   The fourth condition – 'possibly the most decisive' and allied to the third – is that of the plasticity of the social milieu. This plasticity is dependent upon the suspension of previous social prohibitions and the deterritorialization of social groups. For instance, the disappearance of 'sovereign power' (to borrow Foucault's terminology), the emergence of the bourgeoisie and the uprooting and displacement of previously fixed populations might be considered examples of the sort of changes that favour the development of social plasticity. Part II explores this plasticity in terms of the social flux of the wider cultural environment of digital matters and the widespread sense of the deterritorialization and social dislocation it creates.

5   The fifth condition (inseparable from the fourth) is the emergence, within this context of radical social plasticity, of groups of individuals who understand the potential for gain that arises from the application and expansion of technology under these conditions. This self-serving embrace of the potential of technology can be carried out by the state, though it is historically associated with the bourgeoisie, whom Ellul regards as a technical caste, and from whose ranks are drawn both those responsible for technical innovation (engineers, scientists and inventors) and those who implement and turn these techniques to the creation of profit. Temple, writing on Ellul's treatment of the bourgeoisie in *Metamorphose du Bourgeois*, states: 'he maintains that the bourgeoisie gained ascendancy through their use of the new means of production, through their adherence to technique . . . They succeeded so well that they ceased to exist as a separate class. What has finally arrived is the embourgeoisement of a whole society . . . [in this] technique itself has emerged triumphant' (Temple 1980: 235). In Part II we discuss figures such as the *flâneur* and the cyberpunk, who, as prototypical explorers of the Information Revolution, can be viewed as a further development of the bourgeois caste's origins in the Industrial Revolution.

These then are the five factors that Ellul believes were responsible for the emergence of *la téchnique* and, while individual factors may have appeared before in previous eras, it is their co-presence that results in the emergence of a technological society. Taken together, these factors are sufficient to abrogate technique from the cultural limitations that hitherto held it in check. Furthermore, while the ultimate cause of this unique conjunction of forces may prove elusive, its consequences are much easier to identify.

The characteristics of autonomous technique

The synergistic operation of technique in the Industrial Revolution is well attested, as Bruce Mazlish observes of the emergence of the textile industry in late eighteenth- and early nineteenth-century England:

Its ramifications were what economists call backward and forward linkages. Backwards they led to the cultivation of cotton by slaves . . . whose pickings were then ginned mechanically by the invention of Eli Whitney. Forward they led to a developing chemical industry, spurred on by the new requirements of bleaching and dyeing. And on all sides, they led to increased demands for bulk transportation, first provided by the canals, as well as for coal to power the mills and for iron to serve as material to build the machines formerly made out of wood. *The interlocking nature of the Industrial Revolution is perhaps its most striking feature.*

(Mazlish 1993: 61–2 [our emphasis])

It is this interlocking, this process of recruitment and incorporation, which for Ellul marks the emergence of modern technique. *The Technological Society* proposes a further five characteristics or functions that produce (and are produced by) the increasing ubiquity of technique. Furthermore, each of these elements exacerbates or spurs on the development of the others. It is for this reason that Ellul's conception of technique is (at least in *Technological Society*) autonomous and apparently irreversible. Ellul begins by asserting the total artificiality of contemporary technical phenomena. Technique is in every sense opposed to nature; to compare technique to nature, to compare man and machine, is fundamentally misguided, as 'the world that is being created by the accumulation of technical means is an artificial world and hence radically different from the natural word' (Ellul 1963 [1954]: 79). This absolute contradistinction between technique, man and nature cannot be overstated and is a vivid illustration of not only Ellul's 'absolutist' conception of the dialectic but also the dualist real world/simulated neo-gnostic theme of popular representations of the Matrix.

Technique, which leads men out of nature and into artifice, is for Ellul the product of the deification of rationality. Technique is a product of the application of reason, and reason's efficacy, its self-evident superiority to other modes of apprehending the world, is attested to by technique's triumph (Temple 1980: 225). *The deification of rationality* is an important phrase. It points directly to the issue of how human creations can nevertheless appear to produce inhuman, artificial consequences. This is why Ellul is an important theorist of the matrix who, although essentialist, does not deny the social element of technological determinism. Instead, he provides a detailed analytical framework to account for the alienating properties of technology without denying, at root, that human intention originally lies behind such subsequent alienation. Ellul's framework thus provides a coherent conceptual approach to the matrix to inform the imaginative popular representations of the Matrix. This is a theme we discuss in the next chapter, using Heidegger's notion that technology represents a withdrawal from reality and, more than this, a tendency for society to be more and more unconscious of that withdrawal. According to Ellul, this process of rationalization exhibits five characteristics, the combined effect of which creates the dominance of an artificial matrix to circumscribe human action and facilitate withdrawal's natural and predominantly unconsciously accepted spread:

1   technical automatism;
2   self-augmentation;
3   'monism';
4   universality; and
5   autonomy

Technical automatism

By technical automatism, Ellul refers to the tendency (which is basically synonymous with the previously encountered concept of *reverse adaptation*) for technical systems to select 'the best possible means' – that is to say, the most efficient procedure for the implementation and maintenance of given technical operation. This process, once initiated, is self-determining – efficiency is judged in terms of the technical. Within the sphere of the technical, the choice between different procedures or operations becomes automatic – even when choices are still carried out by human beings – because such choices are made within the criteria instituted by technique. Here the human becomes nothing other than that component of the technical system whose purpose is to carry out judgements on the efficiency of individual components or procedures with regard to the overall efficiency of the technical system.

Self-augmentation

Self-augmentation equates with Winner's (1977) notions of *technological momentum/drift* and *accretional determinism,* and describes the tendency for technique to evolve incrementally, through the build-up of modifications, which tend towards the perfection of a given ensemble. This process is simultaneously human and inhuman: human to the degree that modifications emerge and are incorporated only through the actions of humans; inhuman to the degree that these modifications tend towards the production of an ensemble whose purpose and design is far beyond the intention and comprehension of its human 'components'. Moreover, the modifications produced in this manner are of much greater significance than those that emerge from the actions of a putative 'inventor':

> The accretion of manifold minute details, all tending to perfect the ensemble, is much more decisive than the intervention of the individual who assembles the new data, adds some element which transforms the situation, and thus gives birth to a machine . . . that will bear his name.
>
> (Ellul 1963 [1954]: 86)

The alienating effects of this cumulative accretion, increasingly immune to conscious control, is what produces the inhuman element of the ensemble we term a matrix. This is the theoretical basis of the popular representations of a Matrix run by artificial intelligences.

Ellul proceeds to argue that the oft-observed phenomenon of the simultaneous discovery of a given technical modification by unrelated researchers bears witness to this process of self-augmentation. Technique, in its progress towards greater and greater integration, requires the discovery of certain new principles and means – in this regard 'scientific discoveries are . . . governed by technique' (ibid.: 86). This movement of self-augmentation can be expressed in two 'laws', namely that:

1   within a given society, technical progress is irreversible; and
2   technical progress occurs in a 'geometric' rather than 'arithmetic' manner (ibid.: 88) [a process that we shall see aesthetic intimations of later in Gibson's definition of cyberspace as geometrically receding lines of light – 'bright lattices of logic' (Gibson 1984: 4)].

For Ellul, technical progress once embarked upon cannot be reversed; technique at any stage of its development tends inherently towards development – not towards any final goal or outcome, but always towards integration or augmentation. Technique, in and of itself, cannot be subject to any reversal: it can only progress. (Of course, such a 'law' of technique is strictly dependent upon the recognition that modern technique is radically different to any form of technics that has preceded it.) Ellul's second 'law' of technique's self-augmentation problematizes the first. Thus, while progress is irreversible and inevitable, the manner in which this progress unfolds is unpredictable. This is a major determining feature of the out-of-control characterization of technology that we shall see in Part II as the cause of either great concern or excitement, which adds to the perception that human agency becomes compromised by its self-augmentation. Technical breakthroughs in one field may have unforeseen and far-reaching effects upon other areas of technical activity. Technical innovations may emerge whose application extends across the entire technical sphere (e.g. computerization) and which radically alter individual technical activities. Thus, the manner in which technique develops is both certain (it will develop) and unpredictable (the manner and speed of this development is subject to the 'butterfly's wings' effect of chaos theory).

Monism

Through the concept of monism, Ellul addresses the underlying unity of all technical phenomena. For Ellul, under technique there can be no (plural) techniques. Technical operations cannot be approached as heterogeneous collections of procedures whose origins and applications remain local or specific. Under technique, all techniques partake and express a shared logic – there is 'thoroughgoing unity which makes the technical phenomenon a single essence despite the extreme diversity of its appearances'. Here the medium is the message – all technology testifies to technique, it is a univocal phenomenon: 'its parts are ontologically tied together; in it, use is inseparable from being' (Ellul

1963 [1954]: 95). This ontological univocity means that technique is always a use; it is never put to use. Rather, technique in its use bespeaks a certain use of things. As a result there can be no 'good' use of technique and there is no part of the technical order that might function as opening to another use of technique:

> It is a 'method of being used' which is unique and not open to arbitrary choice: we gain no advantage from the machine or from organization if it is not used as it ought to be. There is but one method for its use, one possibility. Lacking this it is not technique . . .
>
> (ibid.: 97)

This technical monism is embodied in the concatenation of technical process, the interlocking of procedures, industries, transport, temporalities, etc. into one overarching system, a system whose function is the maintenance and perpetuation of technique (ibid.: 111–16). Again, we would suggest that this theoretical account of one overarching system provides a theoretical ground for understanding the impressionistic import of the Matrix in its fictionalized, digital forms.

Universality

Ellul's fourth element in the dominion of technique is that of universalism, technique being self-augmenting and marked by a tendency to incorporate or sublate its components in interconnected ensembles that of necessity must expand their field of operations. This occurs both intensively – the life and activities of the individual in the technological society becomes an ever-expanding site for the implementation of technique – and extensively – technique operates via a sort of neo-colonialism in which the more technically accomplished nations control and dictate to those who are 'underdeveloped'. Cultures are sacrificed in the name of efficiency, Western civilization – which is first and foremost a technical civilization – becomes the source of all values and other cultures are judged in terms of their proximity to this technocratic norm:

> . . . the alleged corruption of the Chinese and Islamic civilizations depends solely on the criteria by which they are judged. In the making the objection, we are in effect judging solely on the basis of technical criteria.
>
> (ibid.: 125)

Universalism is the death of culture(s), as we shall see in the specific manifestations of Part II, where the alliance of technique and capitalism serves to extinguish more traditional social life worlds in the rush to urbanism. It is important to note, however, that there occurs both death *of* those cultures that refuse or are unable to embrace technique and death *within* those cultures that have given birth to this monstrous offspring. As Leonard J. Waks in his discussion of Ellul observes, this process of Westernization cannot be seen simply in terms of the conquest or conversion of other cultures to an Occidental technics since 'even traditional western ethical concepts of individuality, freedom, and so forth, collapse under the burden of a civilization by and for technique' (Waks 1989: 106).

Part II explores this process within the context of the West's experience of both the Industrial and Information Revolutions. The pervasiveness of technique's dominance is attested to in the fate that befalls even the work of art (in which one might hope to find resistance to technique's overpowering influence). Ellul argues that art exhibits, in post-war culture, a thorough 'subordination to the technique which has extended its power over all activity, and hence over all culture'. This trend is supposedly reflected in modernist art's celebration of the 'machine age', and in the emergence of electronic music, which is transformed 'by means of techniques which were not originally musical techniques, that is, neither musical methodology nor instrument construction' (Ellul 1963 [1954]: 129). For Ellul, the work of art contains nothing in it that could resist or meliorate the progress of technique.

Autonomy

Ellul's final characteristic refers not to an agency-driven characteristic of individualism but rather to a particular form of individualism that is the net result of the interaction of the characteristics outlined above (Boli-Bennet 1980: 182). Thus, for instance, with reference to technique's universalism, Ellul notes that this universalism in no way fosters communication between individuals. Rather, technique specializes, it atomizes, to such a degree that individuals cannot communicate with each other about their function in a technological society (their specialization precluding easy explanation). Technique's universalism thus produces the atomization of individuals, and these monadic subjects can be co-ordinated only by a system that encompasses and distributes their specializations. This isolating effect felt as a result of the five factors explains key features of the M/matrix. For example, we are not aware of portrayals of the Matrix that involve a strong sense of communality and sophisticated social structures. Society is invariably presented in terms of widespread dislocation and breakdown, where the Matrix is a realm of retreat since the real world is largely broken and uninhabitable. Individuals operate within dystopian settings as lone figures, or at best within small subcultural groups that have banded together in order to compensate for widespread social anomie. In this regard, the atomization of individuals confirms both technique's omnipresence and its autonomy. For Ellul such autonomy is the essence of technique: it is the subordination of forces outside of technique to the dictates of technique, dictates that ensure its continued proliferation. Technique is determined by nothing outside of technique, the minor vicissitudes of human politics, the ephemeral changes of culture are without consequence in this vision:

> Technique elicits and conditions social, political, and economic change. It is the prime mover of the rest . . . external necessities no longer determine technique. Technique's own internal necessities are determinative.
>
> (Ellul 1963 [1954]: 134–5)

Implications of Ellul's theories of technique: the social fact of the matrix

Having provided a general outline of Ellul's thesis regarding the emergence and characteristics of a society in thrall to technique, we are now in a position to consider the broader implications of his work for digital matters. Two interrelated factors are immediately apparent:

1   *Technology's true significance lies beyond its immediate use.* Ellul is unrepentedly 'macro' – for him the true nature of the technological society cannot be found through the analysis of everyday practices, individual cultural documents or any given technical object. Ellul's emphasis upon the macro points to a fundamental aspect of technology crucial to our understanding of digital matters. In a technological society, a human actor is subject to the a priori enframement of various processes before the material effects of particular artefacts ever circumscribe them. We explore the philosophical implications of this in depth in the next chapter with Heidegger's account of technology's alienating properties and then add both perspectives to the more media-specific analysis of Kittler. This gives us a fuller sense of the totalizing aspects of technology, the early origins of which Ellul's analysis explicitly highlights but which are seen to their fullest extent in Part II's account of the im/material cultural context of the digital.

2   *Technique is totalitarian and the myth of neutrality is exactly that: a myth.* Technique cannot be understood in instrumental term; it is not a neutral tool that does man's bidding – its tendencies and consequence are the result of the socio-political context in which it is deployed. Instead, technique is its own society, its own politics: in short it is totalitarian and 'cannot tolerate aberrant activities'. Technique's totalitarianism can be uncovered only through an examination of society as a whole. In this regard, Ellul is resolutely Durkheimian; as he himself put it: 'I explicitly take a partisan position in a dispute between schools of sociology. To me the sociological does not consist of the addition and combination of individual actions. I believe that there is a collective sociological reality, which is independent of the individual' (Ellul 1963 [1954]: xxvi). It is this that underpins his notion of the 'ensemble' which is a distinctive entity in itself: 'it is possible to speak of the 'reality' of technique – with its own particular mode of being, and life independent of our power of decision' (ibid.: 93).

From the above detailed account we can see how Ellul provides a somewhat fundamentalist, albeit internally consistent, interpretation of the a priori futility of hopeful engagement with technological systems to achieve humane ends. Ellul thus labours under very different premises to the line of thinkers whose approach we have crudely summarized as 'constructivist' (Feenberg 1999: 10–12, 75ff.), in particular Bruno Latour, who has identified Gabriel Tarde as the precursor or forefather of certain aspects of his project – a figure held in contempt by Durkheim. Perhaps allied to this belief in the determinative power of collectively generated social 'facts' is Ellul's belief in the unitary, self-contained status of man, technique and society. Such an approach exists in clear contrast to Latour, who, rather than chose or grant agency to a single factor, instead attempts to construct a model that is distinguished by its multifactorial polyvalence: society is made up of human/technological hybrids. For Ellul technique is a thing in itself, as is man; they are not formed through or reducible to sets of relations, but always retain their essential quiddity. Consequently, the only relations that can exist between them are dialectical. Ellul's commitment to an absolute dialectic means that technique cannot be seen in terms of a multiplicity of elements even though it is born from the conjunction of a multiplicity of factors – a pessimistic essentialism that makes other theorists uncomfortable.

Feenberg's anti-essentialist model – the optimism of democratic rationalization

> If essentialism is unaware of its own limitations, this is because it confounds attitude with object, the modern obsession with efficiency with technology as such . . . Yet constructivism so disaggregates the question of technology that it is sometimes difficult to see its relevance to the legitimate concerns of essentialism.
>
> (Feenberg 1999: x)

Before moving on to consider Heidegger's more philosophical interpretation of similar themes, we look in this section at Feenberg's syncretic critique of essentialism. This is necessary because a major element of digital matters and their im/material tension is the apparent paradox that the material is determined by the abstract. The essentialist framework as we have presented it through Ellul's work deals directly with this tension. In the above quotation Feenberg accuses essentialism of conflating attitude with object and efficiency with technology. We would argue that this description of essentialism is more accurate than the conclusion drawn from it. Essentialism may well have limitations but the conflations it carries out are a deliberate part of its theoretical agenda rather than perspective-inhibiting oversights. We have seen in detail how Ellul does indeed equate 'attitude with object, the modern obsession with efficiency with technology as such'. This is why his theoretical project is so illustrative of digital matters and aspects of the matrix: he gives a powerful account of the insidiously invasive effects of technological usage, effects that the following chapters of Part I build upon further with later specific emphasis upon the media technologies of which digital matters are, as we have stated, but the culmination.

In a second unjustifiable charge, Feenberg accuses essentialists of artificially separating out the technological from the social: 'Essentialist dualism cuts across the lifeworld of technology . . . and disconnects the technical as such from the experience of it . . . Technology as a total phenomenon thus must include an experiential dimension' (ibid.: xii). A simple response here is that essentialism's conception of technology as a total phenomenon is designed for the express purpose of addressing more fully the experiential dimension that Feenberg himself admits tends to be lost in the constructivist project and its excessive disaggregation of the technological. In keeping with our prior discussion of Ellul's absolute dialectic and its implicit pessimism, we suggest that Feenberg is motivated less by any basic faults in the essentialist project and more by its failure to match the proactive optimism of his model of *democratic rationalization* with which he seeks to counter technological determinism: 'I do not see how one can come up with a similarly positive program from the essentialist standpoint' (ibid.: xiv). We accept the fact that essentialism lacks a similarly positive programme but maintain our position that pessimism in the face of a perceived problem of technology simply does not constitute prima facie evidence that the theory is wrong. For his part, Feenberg offers a model for understanding technological change that attempts to incorporate in a two-level framework the strengths of both the essentialist and constructivist approaches. It contains the notions of primary and secondary *instrumentalization*. The former refers to macro-level themes similar to those addressed in essentialism, whilst the latter, like constructivism, focuses upon the realization of technical processes in objects and networks that operate within social contexts.

First, primary instrumentalization consists of four basic categories that deal with the relationship between technical objects and human subjects in terms similar to those used by Ellul at the beginning of this chapter:

1   *Decontextualization.* There is a prior need before inclusion within a technical system to remove an object from its original context and grounding in a particular place and time. [This is very similar to Benjamin's notion in his famous 'Work of Art' essay (Benjamin 1973 [1935]) of the removal of aura by the mechanical reproduction of images.]
2   *Reductionism.* Following on from decontextualization, here the particular qualities of individual objects are removed for smooth functioning within technological systems (reverse adaptation), a process that is an integral part of our next chapter's treatment of Heidegger's works, in particular his matrix-constituting notion of enframement.
3   *Autonomization.* Technology serves to isolate and insulate the subject from the full impact or experience of his/her actions. As McLuhan (1964) points out, when technologies serve to extend human capabilities there is a concomitant loss of experience. The car extends the ability of one's feet, but one loses the sensation of the ground that one previously walked upon.
4   *Positioning.* To get the most out of a technical system the individual has to position him- or herself in the strategically most useful place – the technological matrix leads to cultural extinction as those elements of society formerly outside of the machine are reconfigured to adopt the best position.

Secondary instrumentalization then reintroduces the element of social values and interests to the otherwise determining qualities of primary instrumentalization's technological processes. It consists of:

5   *Systematization.* Decontextualized technical objects need to be reassembled into systems to appear natural. The combinations and connections required to do this have a large social component.
6   *Mediation.* The seamless and apparently natural embedding of objects into systems is aided by the aesthetic and cultural qualities objects have beyond their immediate functionality.
7   *Vocation.* This specifies the effects reverse adaptation has upon the subjects who use objects. McLuhan (1964) in this context suggests that users become part of a servo-mechanistic loop with their artefact of choice, as with, for example, the Native American's canoe and the executive's clock.
8   *Initiative.* Subordinated to the technical control of systems, users can still show initiative to re-engineer artefacts for their own purposes as illustrated, for example, by hackers and hacktivists (see Taylor 1999; Jordan and Taylor 2004; Harris and Taylor 2005).

For Feenberg, essentialism's fault is its fetishization of technology. Drawing the parallel with Marx's theory of commodity fetishism, Feenberg argues: 'The fetishist perception of technology similarly masks its relational character: it appears as a non-social instantiation of pure technical rationality rather than a node in a social network. Essentialism theorizes this form and not the reality of technology' (Feenberg 1999: 211). In Part II we add to essentialism by using it as a theoretical base from which to explore the very reality of technology that Feenberg claims it ignores. We have seen how, according to Ellul, capitalism is a symptom of *la téchnique* as the *primum mobile*, so, in his terms at least, it would be inaccurate to give equal weight to both. For our part, however, we explore their combination in the *cultural alignment* that is created between commodity society and technology to produce the matrix of digital matters. In Feenberg's model he offers the notions of *isomorphism* and *concretization* to describe our notion of cultural alignment: 'isomorphism, the formal congruence between the technical logics of the apparatus and the social logics within which it is diffused' (Bidou cited in Feenberg 1999: 89) and 'Concretization is the discovery of synergisms between the functions of technologies and between technologies and their environments. Here the functionalization of the object is reconciled with wider contextual considerations through a special type of technical development.' (Feenberg 1999: 217).

The fundamental disagreement between essentialists and their opponents centres upon the extent to which they believe primary or secondary instrumentalization dominates the society–technology relationship, and this may account for our previous characterization of the debate over technological determinism as one which tends to occur in the form of simultaneous monologues taking place largely in parallel realms. Feenberg's model is vulnerable to the charges that it largely reinvents the wheel and offers optimism in place of realistic assessment. With regard to the former charge, the synergisms he wishes to highlight are already an integral part of *la téchnique* and our later essentialist-inspired account of its subsequent development into a social matrix of digital matters. Returning to the theme of optimism and pessimism from the beginning of the chapter, his categories of secondary instrumentalization do not seem to threaten unduly the dominance of primary instrumentalization. Looking at each in turn:

- *Systematization*. The fact that the systemic combinations and connections have a large social component does not adequately detract from the remaining fact that subjects still have to exercise their agency in predefined, enframing, matrices.
- *Mediation*. The aesthetic and cultural qualities that objects have beyond their immediate functionality are still subordinate to the primary effects of functionality. In addition, mediation can work in both directions. For example, cars have social values over and above their immediate role in transportation (conspicuous consumption etc.) but society is mediated far more by the physical impact of the various technological systems required for the car to function (oil supplies, road networks, etc.) than the car, as a technology, is mediated by the aesthetic values of its users.
- *Vocation*. It is difficult to see how becoming part of a servo-mechanistic loop is particularly empowering (see below).
- *Initiative*. Although our own work has shown how subjects within technological systems can still show initiative to re-engineer artefacts for their own purposes, as illustrated, for example, by hackers and hacktivists (see Taylor 1998, 1999; Jordan and Taylor 2004; Harris and Taylor 2005) and Free/Open Source software, which we look at in detail in Chapter 8, there is also good evidence to suggest that various forms of resistance to enframement are rather piecemeal and marginal and are frequently co-opted and reversed themselves by the combined effects of our revised factors 5–7.

Conclusion – cultural alignment and capitalism

A significant part of our approach is to add Ellul's brand of essentialism to our examination of capitalism's cultural alignment with media technologies. It must be acknowledged that this goes against Ellul's original aims. For Ellul capitalism is a symptom of technique's emergence, and capitalism can be correctly understood only when it is seen as an epiphenomenon of the onward march of technique. Here we see a clear demonstration of the 'either/or' logic that permeates Ellul's thinking (Feenberg 1990: 8) and whose ultimate source is his theological commitment in an absolute contradistinction between the mundane and the transcendent which avoids Lash's retreat into immanence: 'for Ellul the manifold contradictions of sociological reality derive from the theological dialectic in which man lives' (Boli-Bennet 1980: 190). In Ellul's thought there can be no interplay between technique, society and capital, no possibility of placing sets of relations before their terms. Consequently, the choice is stark – one is either for technology or against it: 'The individual is faced with an exclusive choice, either to use technique according to the technical rules, or not to use it at all' (Ellul 1963: 98). We now see how in the work of Heidegger a similarly stark proposition awaits those with optimistic designs for technological society.

2 Martin Heidegger and enframement

Heidegger represents modern technology as radically different from the one other model of technical action he recognizes, premodern craft. He emphasizes the reduction of the object of modern technology to a decontextualised, fungible matter cut off from its own history. This reduction is value charged, or more precisely in Heideggerian terms, it brings 'value' into being by cancelling the intrinsic potentialities of the object, which craft respected, *and delivering it over to alien ends.*

(Feenberg 1999: 16 [our emphasis])

Heidegger's doctrine of the thing is a puzzling combination of deep insights and idiosyncratic esotericism.

(ibid.: 194)

The first of the above quotations gives an excellent summary of the significance of Martin Heidegger's work for *digital matters*. Whilst Ellul identified the Industrial Revolution as a tipping-point in the qualitative transformation of technology into an autonomous force, Heidegger makes a much earlier historical distinction between craft and later forms of production. The way in which he explores technology's ability to cancel an object's intrinsic potentialities provides the basis for Part II's emphasis upon the replacement of traditional life worlds with the anonymous flows of technology that accompany the rise of the city as a large-scale prototype for the digital m/Matrix. Of particular relevance to Part II's treatment of popular representations of the Matrix is the above notion that the essence of physical objects (and by extension reality) is handed over to alien ends: a major theme of the Matrix trilogies of both William Gibson and the Wachowski brothers. In the previous chapter we quoted Feenberg criticizing essentialism's failure to fully recognize the experience of technology as it is lived. Here, Feenberg's charge is that Heidegger's work is marked by an 'idiosyncratic esotericism'. We would argue that this is an inevitable consequence of avoiding the pitfall of constructivism we also quoted from Feenberg, where he claimed that it tended to disaggregate the question of technology too much. In other words, it would seem that essentialists, in Feenberg's eyes, are rather caught between a rock and hard place. They need to pay more attention to technology as it is lived, but when they attempt to do full justice to its aggregate qualities they are vulnerable to the charge of esotericism. Despite Feenberg's misgivings, in this chapter we present Heidegger as a crucial theorist for the theme of digital matters and their im/materiality quality because of the way his analysis does attempt the difficult combination of close attention to both the material qualities of things and the abstract qualities of more general technological processes. Even Feenberg has observed that 'Heidegger is no doubt the most influential philosopher of technology in this century', noting:

> it is the very authority of Heidegger's answer to 'the Question' that has blocked new developments . . . If we want to acknowledge the possibility of alternative modernities, we will have to break with Heidegger.
>
> (ibid.: 183)

Part II of this book builds upon this analysis of Heidegger's phenomenology (in particular the themes of *withdrawal* and *forgetting*) to explore some of the cultural expressions of life in the Information Revolution of advanced capitalism and to ask whether substantively different and alternative modernities are in fact possible within its totalizing environment of enframement.

The status of technology in Heidegger's thought has been the site of considerable controversy and debate, much of which is beyond our present purposes. Of particular frustration to many potential readers is the linguistically slippery nature of many of the phenomenologically specific terms used by Heidegger. Trying to keep such terms to a manageable level, we therefore confine our analysis of Heidegger to the account of technology he offered in his 'later' work [after the supposed *kehre* (turn)] and in particular in his 1954 essay *The Question Concerning Technology*. This purported *kehre* or *turn* in Heidegger's work relates to a shift in emphasis from *doing* in his earlier work to *dwelling* in his later work (approximately post 1930). He paid sustained attention in this later period to the problems of being-in-the-world with other people (*Mit Sein*) and the issue of what constitutes a technological *environment* understood in its deepest and most invasively psychological/existential sense. His work thus offers some crucial insights into this book's central focus upon living in a contemporary world in which two different types of matrices exist simultaneously: one consisting of physical artefacts and the other essentially immaterial but hugely influential matrices made up of trends, processes and powerfully underlying, but largely unquestioned values that profoundly shape and control human agency.

Whilst major theoretical and methodological differences exist between Heidegger and Ellul, we argue in this chapter that in many ways their readings of technology are compatible – at least with regard to technology's apparent autonomy and the difficulty of locating any mode of resistance to its infiltration within all aspects of human life. We have seen how Ellul's account of technology was informed by his commitment to a certain absolutist conception of the dialectic, and likewise in this chapter we encounter an analysis of technology inextricably bound to an overarching philosophical perspective. But whereas Ellul's philosophical 'position' constituted little more than a rather pessimistic qualification of Hegel and Marx's dialectics, Heidegger's philosophy is much deeper. As a result, when examining Heidegger we cannot separate the problem of technology from what he believed was the problem of philosophy – that is the question of Being or, more precisely, the question of the being that asks itself the question of Being (*Dasein*). Heidegger's entire philosophical corpus is a response to this question and the question concerning technology arises within the context of this primordial question of Being.

For Heidegger, philosophy cannot commence until the question of Being has been raised, and any attempt to address this question reveals that Being is a far more mysterious entity than has hitherto been acknowledged. Being, we discover, is not so much an entity as a complex admixture of disclosure and withdrawal; it is a process of difference and is always posed in terms of difference (Deleuze 1998: 64–6). For example, there is a famous ontic/ontological distinction put forward in *Being and Time*. It relates to the difference between beings (the world of subjects and objects) and *Being* as the ultimate ground that each being presupposes but is always less than (Heidegger 1962: 21–35). In other words, as part of the basic paradox of existentialism and of a kind with Sartre's discovery of meaning's basis in nothingness, objects and people gain their identity only in terms of what they are not – a greater reality of which they can inevitably only ever constitute but a small part. There is also the difference between Being's *historality*, which is the unacknowledged past that is inevitably 'at hand' whenever we raise the question of being in the present, and its equally inherent and inevitable *futurity* – the certain yet radically indeterminate fact that each being will cease to be (beings die) (Stiegler 1998). In its very essence, Being is thus inescapably made up of tensions or torsions relating to the part/whole, past/future. The task of a philosophy that asks itself the question of Being is to be rigorously faithful to this 'double articulation' (*the existential analytic*). Indeed, this articulation or torsion comes to replace traditional categories such as subject, object and consciousness.

In Ellul's approach, humanity's attempt to manipulate objects backfires. Subjects become subordinated to objective processes and the interaction produces a mental approach that replaces Heidegger's tension with a technical matrix that is all-encompassing and circumscribing – essentially offering a fake solution to the existential analytic. Feenberg's schema from the previous chapter is an attempt to provide a balance between subjects and objects, but it is disproportionately based upon a predetermined need for solutions (arguably he is guilty of an essentially instrumentalist approach – despite his opposition to essentialism). In Heidegger's work, the existential analytic is an inevitable feature not only of human existence but also of the existence of objects with which humans share the world, and produces a questioning that Heidegger seeks to follow wherever it leads. This questioning reveals that 'the essence of technology is by no means anything technological'. This provocative statement sets the tone for Heidegger's analysis – in declaring the essence of technology as non-technological he challenges conventional conceptions of technology which, whether they celebrate or decry it, cannot approach technology's essence. Worst of all these traditional conceptions is that of technology as neutral (in Feenberg's terms the instrumental theory of technology and in Winner's the *myth of neutrality*), whereby the technological is seen simply as a tool that effects a predetermined end.

The shift in emphasis between Heidegger's earlier and later periods marked an increased attention to the notion of *openness to being* and how this is undermined by technology. Whilst to some readers this may sound excessively dramatic and poetic, this was exactly Heidegger's intention, and any such response from a reader provides a small, but nevertheless revealing, hint of the type of mindset a technologically saturated society tends to inculcate and which Heidegger sought to highlight. He explicitly contrasts the values inherent in poetry (*poiesis*) with those of technology and its tendency to treat the world as a standing reserve (*bestand*) where resources are to be exploited rather than related to in terms of their own inherent qualities. The notion of the standing reserve is well illustrated by all four of Feenberg's processes of primary instrumentalization. It represents the presence in the human mind of an abstract, immaterial cerebral framework that has profound material consequences. Loyal to Being's torsion, *The Question Concerning Technology* begins by asserting the primacy of questioning which, in and of itself, 'builds a way'. It is through questioning that the 'essence' of technology is to be uncovered. Questioning here refers to a return to first principles: all must be sacrificed to the act of questioning – both the apparent terms of the question and any tentative solutions. It is only by carrying questioning to its highest power that the essence of technology can be encountered and the possibility of what Heidegger terms a 'free relation to technology' established (Heidegger 1977 [1954]: 3).

Authentic production as bringing-forth: *poiesis*

The fact that the digital construct of the cyberspatial Matrix is presented in popular culture as an inhabitable environment represents an attempt to give expression to technology's otherwise abstract but immensely powerful totalizing causality. For Heidegger, as for Ellul, technology as it is commonly understood merely hypostatizes the logic of technics and so (as in *la téchnique*), when approaching the question, we must recognize that:

> The manufacture and utilisation of equipment, tools, and machines, the manufactured and used things themselves, and the needs and ends they serve, all belong to what technology is.

> (ibid.: 4)

Technology can never be a mere means since its existence is dependent upon certain ends, which are themselves fully techno-logical. Thus, to see technology as an instrument is wholly insufficient; instead 'we must ask: what is the instrumental itself?'. The instrumental suggests that which is adopted for a purpose, that which effects a particular change. The tool as instrument is, at the most basic level, that which effects a change in the external environment. By extension, the instrumental is that which causes and thus 'wherever instrumentality reigns, there reigns causality' (ibid.: 6). If we are to understand the nature of the instrumental we must understand what causality is; through this understanding we open a way into the essence of technology. To do this Heidegger considers the most venerable philosophical theory of causality: the Aristotelian doctrine of the four causes. To illustrate this fourfold causality, Heidegger offers the example of the causes involved in the production of a sacred chalice for a ritual or religious purpose. According to Heidegger's understanding of Aristotle's doctrine of formal causes, the chalice may be seen as consisting of:

1   *causa materialis* – the matter out of which the chalice is formed;
2   *causa formalis* – the form imposed on this matter;
3   *causa finalis* – the purpose for which this matter is formed (the ritual); and
4   *causa efficiens* – that which effects the forming of this matter (the silver-smith).

For Heidegger this fourfold causality conceals a deeper cause or truth. It is not sufficient simply to observe the nature of these causes – instead their inter-relation must be appreciated, since it is this interrelation (or rather its absence) that will enable us to approach the essence of the technological. The critical point is that the four causes all belong 'at once to each other'; thus, the chalice is 'indebted' to the silver out of which it is fashioned. At the same time the vessel is 'indebted' to the form of the chalice; likewise, the vessel, in as far as it is fash-ioned for a purpose (that of ritual use), is 'indebted' to that purpose. Similarly, the silversmith as that which effects the manifestation of the chalice is indebted to these causes, as they are in turn in debt to him. Heidegger employs the term 'poiesis' to describe the co-implication or 'bringing forth' of formal causes and argues that this co-implication is primary in relation to the Aristotelian fourfold formal causes. This revealing or bringing forth is the ground that conjoins the four causes: 'The modes of occasioning, the four causes, are at play, then, within bringing-forth' (ibid.: 11).

Through bringing forth, an entity is brought into presence. It is this that constitutes what Heidegger termed 'poiesis' and which characterizes authentic production or what Heidegger described as *techne* (ibid.: 12–13). *Techne* describes a mode of production in which man, tool and final product are equally involved and equally brought forth. For Heidegger this mode of production was com-mensurate with an era in which Being was understood and expressible – an understanding he believed the thought of the pre-Socratics bore witness to, thus representing a philosophical golden age before Plato's inauguration of metaphysics. In the case of latter-day technological production it is precisely this poietic mode of production that has been forsaken, a loss coterminous with the inability to address the question of Being (Zimmerman 1990: 222ff.). It is this perspective that enabled Heidegger to make declarations such as the following:

> The limitless domination of modern technology in every corner of this planet is only the late consequence of a very old technical interpretation of the world, [this] interpretation is usually called metaphysics.
>
> (ibid.: 166)

Being can no longer be discerned because of the triumph of metaphysics – that is to say the positing of static, unitary definitions of Being over those of Being as co-production or 'indebtedness'. This history of the gradual occultation of Being by metaphysics is 'the essence of technology that is by no means anything technological'. Technology is a consequence of this history of Being's decline and fall, its declension, and thus the history of the emergence of technology is the history of Being's withdrawal. Latter-day technology is marked by what Heidegger termed *Gestell* (generally translated as 'enframing'). Enframing is what occurs when production is no longer a site of poiesis, i.e. one in which entities disclose themselves in co-production, but instead a realm in which entities are challenged forth for a particular task, that is to say converted into a 'standing-reserve' (*Bestand*) – objectified resources to be employed by technological man.

Before continuing, it is important to emphasize how what may appear to some readers to be the construction of abstruse philosophical categories is in fact of fundamental importance to the tension of the im/material, which in turn is the foundation upon which digital matters rest. What Heidegger is emphasizing here is the way in which, as soon as we move from *techne* to technology, an increasingly immaterial perceptualization of matter paradoxically creates ever more powerful material consequences. The organic interdependency of the fourfold Aristotelian network of causes is replaced by the abstracted, denuded, decontextualized matrices and networks of technological enframement. Digital technology's ability to function on the basis of virtuality is thus merely the current point we have reached in an on-going historical process. In digital matters:

1   *Causa materialis* does not exist beyond the actual physical infrastructure of the digital networks or ultimately does so only within the enervated form of binary electrical impulses – *decontextualization* is dominant.

2   *Causa formalis,* form, is imposed by the *reductionism* of the system. The abstractness of the binary form privileges informational flow as the dominant form.

3   *Causa finalis,* ritual, is replaced by tautologically justified circulation. For example, we trace in Part II how flows first dominate people in the newly emerging and rapidly accelerating urban environments and, then, those flows are hypostasized in the informational flows of digitality. In both cases they are enjoyed as ends in themselves by the *flâneur* and cyberpunk respectively. *Autonomization* removes such figures from ritualistic involvement.

In his essay 'The Work of Art in the Age of Mechanical Reproduction', Walter Benjamin (1973 [1935]) argued in favour of the positive political implications of the death of ritual through the effects of photography's mechanical reproduction of images. For theorists such as Heidegger and later Baudrillard, and in the dystopian elements of the Matrix, the loss of ritualistic, symbolic activity is perceived much more negatively.

4   *Causa efficiens,* the craftsmanship of the silversmith, is replaced by the *positioning* of the hacker/cyberpunk. Again, whilst there are arguments that claim the potential survival of poiesis in such forms as hacktivism (see Taylor 2005), the positioning of certain potentially technologically empowered groups such as hackers can also be seen as an ultimately flawed, poor substitute for substantive human agency (see Taylor 1998), although in Chapter 8 we assess the attempts of the Free/Open Source software movements to offer a positive alternative.

For Heidegger, technology's reduction of the fourfold network, rather than *bringing forth* objects into the word, *challenges* entities by reducing them to mere stock for an ulterior purpose. This is the fundamental characteristic of modern technology:

> This setting upon that challenges forth the energies of nature is an expediting . . . and in two ways. It expedites in that it unlocks and exposes. Yet expediting is always itself directed toward furthering something else, i.e. toward driving on to the maximum yield at the minimum expense. The coal that has been hauled out in some mining district has not been supplied in order that it may simply be present somewhere or other. It is stockpiled; that is, it is on call, ready to deliver the sun's warmth that is stored in it. The sun's warmth is challenged forth for heat, which in turn is ordered to deliver steam whose pressure turns the wheels that keep the factory running.
>
> (ibid.: 15)

This challenging determines all relations; thus, 'the field that the peasant formerly cultivated . . . appears differently than it did when to set in order still meant to take care of and maintain' (ibid.: 14–15). Whereas the peasant's activities were marked by a care for seed and soil, the mechanized food industry sets upon the land as so much stock to yield so much product.

Perhaps the best known of Heidegger's examples of this setting upon the natural so that it functions as stock is that of the Rhine when used as a source of hydroelectric power. For Heidegger this pressing into service of natural phenomenon fundamentally alters its nature and man's relation to that phenomenon. Thus, the Rhine becomes a reserve of power to be summoned by man as and when it is required. Heidegger emphasizes the chasm that separates this manner of approaching entities from that of 'bringing forth' or poiesis by comparing the Rhine 'as dammed up into power works' with ' "The Rhine" as uttered out of the art work in Holderlin's hymn by that name' (ibid.: 16).

As a work of art, Holderlin's *The Rhine* was brought forth out of co-production, whereas as a source of hydroelectric power the Rhine is subjected to a violence that reduces it to so much raw capacity for the production of that power. Heidegger's purpose here is to stress the distance that exists between the river as the site of genuine mutual unfolding of elements of Being and the river as something *challenged forth* for its capacity to generate power. Such challenging forth cannot be regarded simply as one relation amongst a multiplicity of possible relations; there is a mutual exclusivity between these two modes of addressing nature. In seizing the river as source of power, man's relation to the river is irrevocably altered and, for Heidegger, this is one instance of that greater loss of Being that technological enframing brings in its train. The damming of the Rhine is not an event that occurs to an entity outside of man and that leaves man's nature unaffected; rather, man, in pressing the river into service, presses himself into service. Both man and river are enframed and challenged forth as standing reserve. This is where Heidegger and Ellul's approaches come together – enframement and *la téchnique* describe essentially the same invasive power the immaterial has over the material – the culture-colonizing tendencies we explore in more detail in Part II.

The signless cloud of the media matrix – the hand and the typewriter

In his study of Parmenides, Heidegger offers, in the form of a short meditation on the status of the typewriter, a cogent example of the particular manner in which media technologies press their users into service. He begins by asserting the hypothesis that *Homo sapiens* is characterized by his possession of two unique attributes – the hand and language: 'the hand is, together with the word, the essential distinction of man . . . the hand holds the essence of man, because the word as the essential realm of the hand is the ground of the essence of man' (Heidegger 1992: 85–6). Only the human has the hand and only the human has language; in this regard, the hand is the prerequisite of language just as language is that of the hand. It is this interrelationship that distinguishes the hand from any of its apparent precursors – 'no animal has a hand, and a hand never originates from paw or a claw or a talon' – because 'the hand sprang forth only out of the word and together with the word' (ibid.: 86). Man's relation to the hand is, in keeping with the nature of authentic production outlined above, not one of ownership but one of co-production or indebtedness; man, hand and language are *brought forth*. This poietic relation of man and hand is demonstrated in handwriting, which can be seen as the site of this bringing forth. The typewriter corrupts or occludes this relationship as 'it tears writing from the essential realm of the hand'. Furthermore, the typewriter, being, as Heidegger puts it, 'an "intermediate" thing' that occupies the middle ground between tool and machine, demonstrates vividly (because of this intermediate status and its proximity to those activities and faculties associated with the 'bringing forth' of man) the manner in which technology engulfs the true being of man.

In Heidegger's eyes the typewriter turns the word itself into something other, which 'no longer comes and goes by means of the writing hand, but by means of the mechanical forces it releases'. Handwriting as the site of the co-production of man, language and hand is replaced by typing, which always involves the mediation of technology. But mediation is never neutral – the typewriter is no mere instrument; instead, the activity it mediates is irrevocable altered, as is the entity that carries out this activity: 'Therefore, when writing was withdrawn from the origin of its essence, i.e. from the hand, and was transferred to the machine, *a transformation occurred in the relation of Being to man*' (ibid.: 86 [our emphasis]). This transformation, whose origins Heidegger locates in the West's rediscovery of print, shares the same logic of challenging forth described above – it is characterized by a pressing into service of elements that previously revealed themselves. Thus, type is 'set' so that it can be 'pressed'; this ordering results in a range of technologies that mechanically order language. This ordering reflects Heidegger's fundamental thesis that Being consists in a simultaneous process of concealment and disclosure:

> The typewriter veils the essence of writing and of the script. It withdraws from man the essential rank of the hand, without man's experiencing this withdrawal appropriately and recognising that it has transformed the relation of Being to his essence. [Thus] the typewriter is *a signless cloud*, i.e. a *withdrawing concealment in the midst of its very obtrusiveness.*
>
> (ibid.: 86 [our emphasis])

Again, what may appear as a rather abstruse discussion of the particular artefact, the typewriter, goes straight to the heart of digital matters. Heidegger uses this evocative phrase, 'signless cloud', to describe the way in which media technologies have subtle, unacknowledged effects as a paradoxical consequence of the very openness of their operations. This is reminiscent of McLuhan's notion that the medium itself is the message – but this basic fact tends to be disguised by the fact that the medium's content acts like:

> . . . the juicy piece of meat carried by the burglar to distract the watchdog of the mind. The effect of the medium is made strong and intense just because it is given another medium as 'content'. The content of a movie is a novel or a play or an opera. The effect of the movie form is not related to its program content. The 'content' of writing or print is speech, but the reader is almost entirely unaware either of print or of speech.
>
> (McLuhan 1995 [1964]: 18)

Yet, to the degree that the typewriter is an 'intermediary thing' we are, in its emergence, able to glimpse something of the perdition of Being that it produces. In the case of industrial technology this loss is harder to observe, and in the case of digital technology harder still, owing to the totality of its concealment of Being. Thus, for Heidegger, the ultimate fate of language torn from the hand and pressed into the service of the machine was to be found in the computer:

The structure and performance of mainframe computer systems [*Großrechenanlagen*] rests on the techno-calculative principles of this transformation of language as saying into language as a mere report of signal transmissions. What is decisive for our reflection lies in the fact that it is from the technological possibilities of the machine that the instruction is set out as to how language can and should be language. The kind and character of language are determined according to the technological possibilities of the formal signal transmissions which execute a sequence of continual yes–no decisions with the highest possible speed . . . The kind of language is determined by the technology.

(Heidegger [1998] cited in Feenberg 2000: 448)

The advent of the tablet personal computer's rapprochement of handwriting and the machine may attempt to regain some of the computer's poietic deficit but, owing to the gap in bringing forth that still exists as a loss of the much more organic properties of paper and ink, the deeper substantive point still stands. In Claude Shannon's information theory, for example, communication is defined in terms of that which can be quantitatively processed. There is simply no room for the qualitative subtleties and ambiguities of more complex human communication. Language here is no longer the site of Being's unconcealment in the work of the hand, but instead a set of technologically overdetermined commands that order the work of both man and hand. Here Being's retreat into the 'signless cloud' of the typewriter becomes complete, and in the computer Heidegger identifies the presence of *the Danger* of the loss of Being: a process we can now see instantiated within the technology of *virtual reality*. Thus, while in the intermediary status of the typewriter it was still possible to puzzle the disappearance of handwriting; with digital technologies language itself has become an ordering, 'a mere report of single transmissions' rather than the realm of poetry or love.

At this point it is again interesting to note that Feenberg (1999) criticizes essentialist thinkers for analysing technology too abstractly and thereby losing the significance of the meaning attributed to it within social environments. Feenberg illustrates his point by referring to the way in which a house is more than just a concatenation of technologies but is actually rich with symbolic cultural associations. In this context, his previously cited criticism that essentialism 'disconnects the technical . . . from the experience of it' (ibid.: xii) is somewhat ironic given that Heidegger once described language as 'the house of being' (Heidegger 1993 [1947]). Contra Feenberg, we would argue that the essentialists do not ignore the full life world experience of technology but, rather, they demonstrate the full extent of that experience by showing how such life worlds are irreparably damaged by technology. This is the significance of Heidegger's analysis of the typewriter and computer. To keep with the image of the house, Being is rendered homeless, while technological enframing becomes the squatter.

Enframement's eclipse of Being – cybernetics

Having considered the nature of authentic production (that of the craftsman) and its relation to Being and the 'case study' of the typewriter, whose intermediary status allowed to us witness Being's occlusion, we are now in a better position to consider Heidegger's work in relation to the Information Revolution and the extreme nature of the opportunities opened up by digital matters for the further entrenchment of humanity with the all-encompassing technological environment of the matrix. In his observations upon the typewriter, Heidegger notes that:

> This 'machine' operated in the closest vicinity to the word, is in use; it imposes its own use . . . This situation is constantly repeated everywhere, in all relations of modern man to technology. Technology is entrenched in our history.
>
> (Heidegger 1992: 85)

It is the extent to which technology is figured in our history that holds the key to an understanding of Heidegger's vision of technology, and to appreciate this we must return to the key concept of 'enframing'. Enframing, we are told, 'is the gathering together that belongs to that setting-upon which sets upon man and puts him in position to reveal the real, in the mode of ordering, as standing reserve (Heidgger 1977 [1954]: 20).

We need to unpack this admittedly dense proposition: enframing is a way of articulating Being; it is Being expressed under determinate circumstances. Enframing is marked by its tendency to articulate Being as a whole; it addresses itself to all entities and assesses them according to a single rubric (or, for our purposes, matrix). In doing this, enframing 'sets upon' not only entities external to man but man himself. In enframing, man enframes himself and in doing this enframes Being. Within the context of technology this results in the conversion of all beings to the status of 'standing reserve', i.e. stable units possessed of abstract quantities and qualities (the *decontextualization* and *reductionism* of Feenberg's primary instrumentalization) ripe for further manipulation by the technological mindset (*la téchnique*). Enframing as the essence of technology 'starts man upon the way of that revealing through which the real everywhere . . . becomes standing reserve' (1977 [1954]: 24). However, implicit in enframing, and, by extension, the essence of technology, is the notion of what Heidegger terms 'destining' (*Geschick*). To enframe is 'to start upon a way'; by enframing Being in technological terms, humanity sets out upon a particular path.

Technology as enframing 'destines' humanity to history. It is this that constitutes technology's greatest threat, because the history of technology precludes recognition that history itself is technological, that is, an 'enframing' of Being. Put crudely, humanity cannot apprehend the enframing of technology because apprehension itself is an instance of enframing; humanity is always 'in the frame': 'Where Enframing holds sway, regulating and securing of the standing-reserve mark all revealing. They no longer even let their own fundamental characteristic appear, namely, this revealing as such' (ibid.: 27). Another way of thinking about this would be by considering Ellul's eclipse of the dialectic through the supremacy of the technological model. In Ellul and Heidegger, the potentially contradictory elements of human agency and technological method are surpassed by the invasiveness and pervasiveness of the latter. For Heidegger, this totalizing, pervasive nature of the process prevents recognition that it is occurring at all. The apparent construction of all beings, and consequently Being itself, as a standing-reserve led Heidegger to the conclusion that human-ity was now in the presence of the gravest of dangers, or what he succinctly describes as the Danger. By this he meant not simply the withdrawal of Being in presence of technology but the forgetting of Being in this presence. Deleuze, in a commentary on Heidegger's *The Question Concerning Technology,* eloquently articulated the nature of the Heideggerian Danger:

> It is not enough to oppose Being to its forgetting or withdrawal, since what defines the loss of Being is rather the forgetting of forgetting, the withdrawal of the withdrawal, whereas withdrawal and forgetting are the manner by which Being shows itself, or is able to show itself.
>
> (Deleuze 1998: 93)

The Danger is not Being's withdrawal, since withdrawal or concealment is what Being is; rather, it is the withdrawal of this withdrawal, i.e. the presence of beings as self-sufficient. It is this that constitutes the Danger, and a further danger to be added to Heidegger's is the ease with which the technological means that facilitate the withdrawal from withdrawal are seen as enjoyable ends in themselves. In Part II we address this particular aspect of the Danger in terms of the enjoyment of the informational buzz within the cyberspatial Matrix of the hacker/cyberpunk.

For Heidegger the Danger was embodied in the emergent discipline of 'cybernetics' and information technology, in which enframing becomes autono-mous, and systems regulate themselves through their own feedback:

> Upon [this ordering circuit] rests the possibility of self-ordering, the auto-mation of a system of movement. In the cybernetically represented world, the difference between automatic machines and living things disappears. It becomes neutralized by the distinctionless process of information. The cybernetic world project 'the victory of method over science' makes pos-sible a completely homogenous and in this sense universal calculability, i.e., controllability of the lifeless and the living world. In this uniformity of the cybernetic world, even man gets trained.
>
> (Heiddeger cited in Zimmerman 1990: 200)

Heidegger's observation on the danger of cybernetics parallels his observa-tion on the computer and its effect on language. In both the loss of Being is total

– humanity has become enslaved to a fully realized metaphysics, embodied in the form of an autonomous technics. This alarming claim that 'In the cyberneti- cally represented world, the difference between automatic machines and living things disappears' is the central focus of the cyberpunk literature we examine in Part II, in which we see how fiction has put imaginative flesh on the philosophi- cal bones of Heidegger's Danger. While much of the Heideggerian (and to a lesser extent Ellulian) analysis is couched in philosophical terms, more practical or at least culturally orientated examples can be found in Part II's more recent cultural theories, specifically the notion of *the hyperreal*.

Letting be: the Danger of furniture

Is Being lost forever to technological man? Heidegger's answer to this question is fraught with ambiguity – 'The essence of technology is in a lofty sense ambiguous. Such ambiguity points to the mystery of all revealing. . .' (Heidegger 1977 [1954]: 33) – and hinges upon the Danger. As already stated, the Danger is that of the *withdrawal of the withdrawal*; yet, to the extent that withdrawal is the manner in which Being shows itself, i.e. Being as withdrawal, then the Danger contains within it the possibility of salvation, as the lines of Hoderlin famously quoted by Heidegger have it: 'But where the danger is, grows/The saving power also' (ibid.: 28). Put simply, the saving grace present in the Danger of technology is that of Being's withdrawal. This, of course, appears frustratingly paradoxical. How can Being's eclipse, the great Danger and perdition, represent any form of salvation? Heidegger's answer is that technology as the site of Being's departure is at the same time Being's revelation; since Being is characterized by its departure, it is the ever-retreating horizon of our experience. Technology, to the extent that it is involved in this withdrawal, offers the opportunity to grasp Being.

However, the question remains as to what the saving power means in terms of our actual relation to the technological. Is Heidegger suggesting that the grave danger that technology presents somehow offers us the chance to grasp the essence of technology? Does the possibility of grasping the essence of technol- ogy represent the possibility of an escape from the technological and a return to that poietic mode of revealing that characterized authentic, artisanal produc- tion? On one level it would appear that this is not the case; certainly Heidegger, like more optimistic theorists of the matrix who emphasize digital information's immanent nature, is clear that there is no 'outside the technological' (ibid.: 38), no future that does not involve technology. Rather, the saving power is the rec- ognition of the enframing that brings about our dependence on technology. If this is understood (via a rigorous fidelity to the question of the technological), then we may begin to apprehend beings as something other than mere stock in a standing-reserve, this in turn allowing the possibility of a 'free relation' to tech- nology. This 'free relation' Heidegger described as *gelassenheit* (usually translated as 'releasement' or 'letting be'). Yet it is difficult to understand what the concrete consequences of this releasement might be for a technological society, if 'letting be' is to be understood in terms of an escape from technology – the careful cultivation of those aspects of our being that fall outside enframing.

In Part II, we explore 'letting be' in terms of various ways of accommodating with the technological flows that result from the enframement of any traditional notions of a life world that has continued apace since the Industrial Revolution. The nearest emblematic figures such as the *flâneur* and the cyberpunk get to a free relationship with technology is their excessive identification with the technology-inspired flows of the city and the Matrix respectively. It is unclear how such forms of 'letting be' are particularly empowering; but in activities such as hacktivism and Free software/Open Source production (see Taylor 2005; Harris and Taylor 2005) we attempt to at least suggest some optimistic aspects to Heidegger's belief that there is no outside to the technological. Heidegger places his hope in the work of art as the site of possible redemption from the violence that a technological mode of apprehension performs upon Being. Thus, in the conclusion of the essay Heidegger argues that:

> There was a time when it was not technology alone that bore the name techne. Once that revealing that brings forth truth into the splendour of radiant appearing was also called techne. Once there was a time when the bringing-forth of the true into the beautiful was also called techne. And the poiesis of the fine arts was also called techne.
>
> (Heidegger 1977 [1954]: 34)

At this point it is hard for many commentators not to accuse Heidegger of a reactionary idealism in this conclusion – his evocation of an Ancient Greece in which technology and art were a single entity invokes a prelapsarian age before art and technology were sundered. Benjamin's seminal 'Work of Art' essay, although finding the positive rather than the negative implications of technology's social effects, reinforces Heidegger's conclusions. Benjamin suggests that the proliferation of images made possible by the photographic process of chemical–mechanical reproduction represents a point at which the quantitative increase in images leads to a qualitative change in their nature. This matches Ellul's identification of the Industrial Revolution's increase in output as marking a qualitative change in the human–technology relationship, and Benjamin uses it to argue that the advent of photography and its mechanical reproduction of images represents the death of the traditional conception of art.

> To an ever-greater degree the work of art reproduced becomes the work of art designed for reproducibility. From a photographic negative, for example, one can make any number of prints; to ask for the 'authentic' print makes no sense. But the instant the criterion of authenticity ceases to be applicable to artistic production, the total function of art is reversed. Instead of being based on ritual, it begins to be based on another practice – politics.
>
> (Benjamin 1973 [1935]: 226)

Benjamin recognizes the tendency of technology's ability to strip away authenticity but proceeds to make a positive political interpretation of this reduction. Art is now freed by photography's impact from its hierarchical and ritualistic role to produce images that can empower rather than dominate the masses. In stark contrast, Heidegger believed that only art in its refusal of utility 'may expressly foster the growth of the saving power' that protects humanity from the Danger of withdrawal.

Heidegger would appear to condemn from the outset the possibility of the saving power being somehow found in the technological (Feenberg 1991: 8). This impression is reinforced by other instances of 'letting be' in Heidegger's writings, which is always presented in terms of the artisanal, in the form of authentic craft. Consider in this light the following passage:

> One can object that today every village cabinetmaker works with machines ... [Such objections fall] flat, because [they have] heard only half of what the discussion has to say about handicraft. The cabinetmaker's craft was chosen as an example, and it was presupposed thereby that it would not occur to anyone that through the choice of this example is the expectation announced that the condition of our planet could in the foreseeable future, or indeed ever, be changed back into a rustic idyll ... However it was specifically noted that what maintains and sustains even this handicraft was not the mere manipulations of tools but the relatedness to wood. But where in the manipulations of the industrial worker is there any relatedness to such things as the shapes slumbering in the wood?
>
> (Heidegger in Zimmerman 1990: 162)

Although Heidegger here clearly acknowledges the impossibility of returning the planet to the conditions that preceded the depredations of a technological society, he nonetheless believes that certain practices remain the site of possible recuperation. The 'shapes slumbering in the wood' act as a trope for the four-fold network that is lost in the technological process. In Chapter 7, the Matrix of fictional imagination (especially Smith's notion of 'The Gap') is shown to be full of slumbering shapes of a much more disturbing sort that this time act as emblems, not for our organic affinity with the fourfold network of natural objects and processes, but rather for the deep anxieties the Matrix represents in its *gap* between its technologically enframed world and Heidegger's ideal of a technologically unadulterated Being.

Heidegger could be accused of a certain fetishism of craft production in arguing that the relatedness to the wood of the modern cabinetmaker who uses machine tools is somehow superior to that of the manipulations of industry. The forms that the cabinetmaker reveals are said to slumber in the wood, yet it is unclear as to when a form slumbers and when it is pressed upon matter. The part of the process that Heidegger privileges is 'the relatedness to the wood'. The hands-on approach to wood, even mediated by machinery, still confronts the aura of the wood directly. Mass-produced cabinets are not totally aura free because they are made of originally auratic material (even mass-manufactured pieces of wood retain the individual characteristics of their tree's whorls and burls), but their authenticity is deeply submerged within the mass production matrix from which they are 'challenged forth'. Heidegger's example of cabinet-making raises interesting questions regarding the position of an object with respect to the broader existential background from which it derives its individuality. It intimates the existence of a matrix underlying the social use of objects that prefigure its much more explicit development in the digital Matrix. Thus, it is perhaps not as surprising as it otherwise might be that Jean Baudrillard, an arch-theorist of the Matrix, whose book *Simulations* makes a guest appearance as a prop in the first *Matrix* film (a hollowed-out copy is used to store computer disks), addresses the existential issue of furniture in his *The System of Objects* (1997).

In a similar fashion to Heidegger, Baudrillard uses furniture as an exemplum of a lost authenticity that in digital matters reaches a much higher peak. He contrasts traditional and mass-produced furniture, showing how furniture handed down from one generation to the next stands in a different relationship to concepts such as aura and authenticity than mass-produced furniture, designed as it is as part of a preordained matrix that follows the commerce-inspired modish trends of the interior design industry:

> Whereas the old-fashioned dining-room was heavily freighted with moral convention, 'modern' interiors, in their ingeniousness, often give the impression of being mere functional expedients . . . The modern set of furniture, serially produced, is thus apparently destructured yet not restructured, nothing having replaced the expressive power of the old symbolic order.
>
> (Baudrillard 1997: 17)

The loss of symbolism Baudrillard highlights relates to the Being-denuded nature of Benjamin's life world in which aura is eviscerated. It is a direct consequence of mechanical reproduction and the serial nature of mass-produced objects that are set apart from the craft objects that Heidegger seeks to privilege. To *position* oneself effectively within a matrix of seriality requires the requisite amount of reverse adaptation:

> First of all man must stop mixing himself up with things and investing them with his own image; he will then be able, beyond the utility they have for him, to project onto them his game plan, his calculations, his discourse, and invest these manoeuvres themselves with a sense of a message to others, and a message to oneself. By the time this point is reached the mode of existence of 'ambient objects' will have changed completely, and *a sociology of furnishing will perforce have given way to a sociology of interior design*.
>
> (ibid.: 25 [emphasis in original])

In a section entitled 'Man the Interior Designer', Baudrillard proceeds to describe the effect upon the individual of such positioning as one in which 'instead of consuming objects, he dominates, controls and orders them. He discovers himself in the manipulation and tactical equilibration of a system' (ibid.: 27). Echoing Heidegger's fourfold analysis of the chalice and Feenberg's call for essentialists to pay more attention to the cultural *mediation* of objects, Baudrillard argues that objects such as furniture have – over and above their practical functionality – 'a primordial function as vessels, a function that belongs to the register of the imaginary' (ibid.: 27). Again matching Feenberg's selection of the house as an example of an object that reflects more than simply technical values (Feenberg 1999: xi), Baudrillard argues that psychologically receptive objects reflect a natural form of Being: 'They are the reflection of a whole view of the world according to which each being is a "vessel of inwardness" and relations between beings are transcendent correlations of substances' (Baudrillard 1997: 28). In contrast, and in response to Feenberg's call to pay attention to the lived experience of technology, for Baudrillard:

> . . . the project of a technological society implies putting the very question of genesis into question and omitting all the origins, received meanings and 'essences' of which our old pieces of furniture remained concrete symbols; it implies practical computation and conceptualization on the basis of a total abstraction, the notion of a world no longer given but instead produced – mastered, manipulated, inventoried, controlled: a world in short, that has to be *constructed*.
>
> (ibid.: 28–9 [emphasis in original])

We suggest that this is a succinct summary of Heidegger's distinction between the *bringing forth* of being in the fourfold network of causes and *challenging forth* it is replaced with the rise of the networks of technology we shall shortly explore in detail via the work of Kittler. We would highlight here Baudrillard's use of the word 'computation' to describe the positioning required from the human user. It demonstrates the link between the matrix of serially produced objects and the cyberspatial Matrix of which it is a hypostasization.

In the particular case of 'Man the Interior Designer', the reverse adaptation required from the subject to exist within the world of serial objects applies to the specific case of furniture but, by extension, it becomes the standard mode of behaviour with which to approach all technological artefacts that now appear as serial parts of a totalizing technological whole rather than individual aspects of Being. (Baudrillard cites in support of his position Barthes' similar analysis of the reverse adaptations required in the act of driving a car.) The distinction created between Being and industrially produced serial existence creates an important *gap,* which, as we have pointed out, is a notion that constitutes an explicit conceit of the cyberpunk novel *Spares* (Smith 1996) that we address in Chapter 7. The industrially produced furniture Baudrillard highlights is predesigned to fit the pre-existing values of an interior design industry and is emblematic of the essential nature of all commodities. The essence of these objects derives not from their individual manufacture or consumption as unique objects but from their relationship to a wider matrix of other commodities from which they derive their meaning. Baudrillard distinguishes between the closed structure of the bourgeois dining room and the freer functional environment of the fashion-driven industrially produced furniture and points out:

> Somewhere between the two, *in the gap* between integrated psychological space and fragmented functional space, serial objects have their being, witnesses to both the one and the other – sometimes within a single interior.
> (Baudrillard 1997: 19 [our emphasis])

Baudrillard's example of modish furniture technologically produced to fit a preplanned consumer framework helps us see how the rather abstract-sounding danger of 'the withdrawal of withdrawal' assumes a much more material form as symbolically loaded family heirlooms are transformed into objects of an industrial process that enframes and *systematically* removes symbolic elements from our life world, introducing a gap of im/materiality between traditional Being and technologically mediated existence. The Heideggerian conceptualization of Being may appear excessively abstruse and philosophical, but it speaks directly to what is fundamentally different about technological Being and what lies at the crux of digital matters and their im/material tension. Thus, in the remaining chapters of Part I we trace how the media technologies preceding the digital have promoted a powerful and excessive form of positive identification with the Danger represented by withdrawal from Heidegger's fourfold network. We use Friederich Kittler's work to show the mediation of withdrawal by various media technology networks and how, like Heidegger, Kittler treats the digital as the latest development in the on-going technological mediation of withdrawal. Part II, meanwhile, explores the social and cultural manifestations of withdrawal in terms of excessive identification with the fragmented functional space of the m/Matrix: Being is not so much let go of as jettisoned with enthusiasm.

Conclusion: Ellul and Heidegger – united in pessimism?

For Ellul, Heidegger and Baudrillard, technology cannot be neutral since its material components always already testify to something beyond themselves. Allied to Ellul's belief in technology's autonomy is Heidegger and Baudrillard's conceptualization of technology as a self-determining system that coerces its human components into roles they must play within this system. Both Heidegger and Ellul also apparently reject as futile any attempt on behalf of society to influence the direction of technological development. As Heidegger wrote: 'No single man, no group of men, no commission of prominent statesmen, scientists, and technicians, no conference of leaders of commerce and industry, can brake or direct the progress of history in the atomic age' (Heidegger 1976 [1966]: 52). This apparent inability of society to influence the direction of its own technological development is in part, for both Ellul and Heidegger, the result of the predominance of certain mode of thinking which, adopting Adorno's phrase, might be described as 'instrumental rationality'. Nonetheless, there remain crucial differences between the accounts of technology offered by Ellul and Heidegger. Firstly, they profoundly disagree in their accounts of history of technology and the status of this history. Thus, in Heidegger we discover a history of technology that stretches from Ancient Greece to the present day and is essentially a long, slow history of error and decline. Most significant of all is his devaluation of crucial socio-historical moments in the emergence of technology, most notably the rise of science in eighteenth-century Europe and the cataclysmic changes of the Industrial Revolution. In Heidegger these major points of historical bifurcation are nothing other than superficial effects of the hidden history of metaphysics's growing dominion. By contrast, Ellul's account is far more historically nuanced and places great emphasis on the Industrial Revolution as the turning point in humanity's relationship to technology. Following on from this is the difficulty, in the case of Heidegger's argument, of determining exactly at what point *techne* or authentic production ceased and technology as enframing emerged. While it is clear that such a transition did occur, we cannot locate a time or epoch in which this change occurred. In contrast, Ellul is clear that it is within the Industrial Revolution that technological innovation breaks with earlier culturally bound forms of technology, i.e. mechanization.

We have already touched upon the significant difference that exists between Ellul's dialectical framework and Heidegger's existential analytic but we have not yet explicated its consequences for their understanding of technology. Put simply, Heidegger's theoretical methodology results in profound ambiguity and puts into question every term it employs. Thus, while his declarations suggest that no human institution has the power to delimit technology, this is not because he shares Ellul's essentialism. For Ellul, technology is a force like Frankenstein's creature: unfettered and abroad, spreading its chaos and confusion. In contrast, in Heidegger's account we cannot be sure where agency lies. Certainly, technology at first glance appears autonomous; however, this autonomy is brought into question by the assertion that the history of technology is the history of metaphysics. The problem here is the degree to which this history is the way in which Being chooses to show itself. If technology is an expression of Being rather than an expression of human power or capabilities, then it is highly unlikely that it will be easily transformed by human agency. Thus, we must consider the differing prognosis that Ellul and Heidegger offer for the technological society. In both we find a strong case presented for the need to cultivate something outside of technology and the forms of thought that it engenders. In Heidegger the art work bears the weight of these ambitions; it is in the realm of the aesthetic that he believes an alternative to the values fostered by technology is to be found. Ellul, by contrast, has no faith in the redemptive power of aesthetics; it is not the aesthetic that he calls for but rather divine intercession, making his account somewhat more pessimistic. The iron determinacy of his dialectic offers little scope for alternatives. At least Heidegger's very conception of technology contains within it the possibility of alternative relations to technology, even if Heidegger himself became increasingly pessimistic about humanity's ability to avail itself of this opportunity.

In both Ellul and Heidegger's accounts the difficulty of thinking outside of the all-encompassing rationality of the technological is repeatedly emphasized. In Heidegger we find ourselves victims of enframing to such an extent that we become blind to its presence (the Danger). In *The Technological Society*, *la téchnique*'s qualities of rationality and efficiency are thoroughly internalized. In both cases every new development in technology is seen as consolidating this mode of thinking and so there is a cumulative progression of technological networks that precludes the recovery of the fourfold network of Being's authentic bringing forth. In the case of Ellul this leads to a deep-seated pessimism about the future of humanity in the face of technology's relentless and self-augmenting progression and Ellul (at least when wearing his theologian's hat) argued that the redemption for mankind lay in the intercession of divinity in mundane affairs – not perhaps the most practical solution to the problem of technology in an advanced secular society. In Heidegger, too, we find an emphasis upon redemptive power – in his case art – but to understand his reservations about the limitations of its saving power one need only consider the title of his 1966 *Der Spiegel* interview 'Only a God can save us' (Heidegger 1976 [1954]).

Heidegger's thought is criticized for what is seen as a retreat from the complications of his own thought into a world that, in Feenberg's acerbic summary, has about it the ' . . . reek of volkish nostalgia for the good old days of thatch roofed huts, silver chalices, quill pens, humble jugs, wooden shoes, and suchlike trappings of the elitist anti-modernism of right wing German intellectuals in the Weimar and Hitler period' (Feenberg 1999: 230). Critics also tend to take exception to Heidegger's insistence on pushing back the emergence of technology to an epoch before the appearance of modern science or any form of industrialized technology. If the limitless domination of modern technology is simply the late consequence of a very old interpretation of the world, then the distinction between what is truly poietic production and what is an inauthentic *setting upon* becomes highly problematic. More helpfully, Ellul's model of technological domination singles out the Industrial Revolution as a jumping off point for technology's uncontrollable pervasion, and in the next two chapters we build upon this notion of a point of exponential growth and qualitative change to highlight the specific role played by media technologies in the creation of the technological alternative to Heidegger's key concept of the fourfold network of Being: the im/material gap that generates digital matters.

3 Friedrich Kittler – Network 2000?

> But the world, mind, is, was and will be writing its wrunes for ever, man, on all matters that fall under the ban of our infrarational senses.
>
> (James Joyce, *Finnegans Wake,* 1939: 20)

As we pointed out in the Introduction, the mainstream success of the Wachowski brothers' movie trilogy has ensured that the notion of the Matrix has strong pop-culture connotations. In the preceding chapters, by way of contrast, we have drawn upon various theorists of technological change in order to emphasize the richer conceptual depth that can be found within the m/Matrix distinction. In this chapter we prepare for Part II's focus upon the cultural implications of these rather pessimistic theories of technological change. We expand upon the issues of the previous chapters using the insights of German media theorist Friedrich Kittler, whose impact has yet to be fully felt in cultural studies. His work is a dense and detailed mediation on the interface between media and culture, combining the erratic insights of McLuhan with the theoretical rigour of French post-structuralism.

In keeping with our focus upon degrees of theoretical optimism and pessimism, we explore the extent to which Kittler's theories might be seen as deterministically granting an agency to technical media. However, whilst it may be accurate to describe Kittler as a determinist, the theoretical presuppositions that guide his thinking result in far more complex conception of determinism than that found in Ellul. This is not least because Kittler's concern is media determinism as opposed to the generalized technological determinism we have predominantly discussed thus far. Kittler's interpretation of the media leads us to a determinism that shapes thought itself, even modes of thinking that aim to expose determinism. Coupled with his focus upon media determinism is his concern with materiality, with 'matter' or the hardware of communication. For Kittler the digital is not weightless, but simply a new distribution of the materialities of communication. In this regard, Kittler's theory offers an alternative to a vision of the digital as an immaterial escape from the confines of the physical into an unlimited realm of virtuality. However, given the fact that the originality of Kittler's media theory begins with the way he has fused and transformed the theories of others, we will start by considering some these key influences.

'Media determine our situation': Kittler's radicalization of McLuhan and the implications for digital matters

McLuhan's thought, partly as a result of the extraordinary prominence he attained in the 1960s, has been mistakenly treated as little more than a celebration of new media. This image of McLuhan belies a deeper ambivalence, and Kittler's work can be seen as drawing on these darker implications. We can identify four points of contact between Kittler's media determinism and that of McLuhan:

1   a prioritization of media over their message;
2   a belief in the absolute determinate capacity of media both historically and within our current epoch;
3   a belief that war is mother of techno-medial invention;
4   a recognition of the centrality of the body in relation to media.

The medium is the message

McLuhan's slogan suggests that the consequences of a medium qua medium are greater than any putative message they might transmit. The content of any given medium is always an antecedent medium: writing's content is speech, printing's content is writing, radio's content phonography, cinema's content photography, and so on. Crucially for our purposes, with the advent of digital media, Kittler argues we have arrived at an over-arching medium whose content is that of all preceding media.

Media determine culture

This prioritization of medium over message leads to a concern with the structural effects of different media, since the absence or presence of a given medium is far more significant than its apparent content. For McLuhan, media (rather than their messages) determine the ratios of man's senses and the structure of human societies; thus, he argues that the emergence of the phonetic alphabet effects a cultural revolution: in substituting 'an eye for an ear' it frees man from 'the tribal trance of resonating word magic and the web of kinship' (McLuhan 1995 [1964]: 86). Likewise, the invention of movable type ushered in an entire 'galaxy', one of whose components was a certain expression of man, understood as a rational linear thinker, while, as the 'first uniformly repeatable "commodity"', printed matter provided a new paradigm for production (McLuhan and Fiore 1967: 50). Similarly, the global village was a direct result of the emergence of new non-textual media that replicated the modalities of those senses that had been exiled by the triumph of print, offering an omnipresent immersion rather than a discrete sequence. Thus, for McLuhan, the attention deficit often imputed to the young was simply a clash between different media-determined sensory regimes: the linear processing of an older generation born in a primarily textual age and the immersive sensibility of youth inculcated in a multimedia matrix. Thus, media are matrices that determine the nature of their epoch 'by altering the environment, [media] evoke in us unique ratios of sense perception . . . when these ratios change, men change' (ibid.: 8).

War is the mother of techno-medial invention

Kittler, in solidarity with Paul Virilio and McLuhan, identifies war as major stimulus to technological development, building on the latter's claim that: 'all technology can plausibly be regarded as weapons' (McLuhan 1995 [1964]: 344). The emergence of the computer and the internet's original development within military contexts and the apparent fusion of media and war (see Virilio 2002) provide further evidence of this vector.

The locus of corporeality

The progression of epochs is determined by that of their media, but these media themselves are externalizations, 'outerings' of the human body. Although this thesis can be traced back to the nineteenth-century philosopher of technology Ernst Kapp, McLuhan's formulation of this thesis has achieved the widest currency: 'all technologies are extensions of some human faculty – psychic or physical, the wheel an extension of the foot, the book an extension of the eye, clothing, an extension of the skin, electric circuitry, an extension of the central nervous system' (McLuhan and Fiore 1967: 41). McLuhan, however, remains too anthropocentric for Kittler, who rejects the simplicity of unidirectional externalization of man in the form of technological prostheses. His position is rather that contemporary media technologies are 'apparatuses that no longer reflect the performance of the peripheral sensory organs, [but] rather imitate the command centres themselves' such that 'independent thoughts are cerebral software, *Geist* refers to every possible combination of data, and culture the play on the keyboard of the mind' (Bolz [1990] in Griffin 1996: 712).

The key issues to emphasize here as part of our discussion of digital matters are:

- *Media are matrices that determine the nature of their epoch.* The digital medium within Kittler's framework is an *über-medium*. It is the logical extension of a long process whereby media evolve, absorbing their predecessors as content. The comprehensive way in which the digital has achieved this makes it a particularly strong example of *enframement*.
- The digital represents the advent of *an experience of omnipresent immersion* rather than the discrete sequences promoted by the printed word and closely allied to economic developments such as assembly-line production. Technologically inspired enframement becomes an integral, subtle part of a culture through a process of *cultural alignment* or *social embeddedness*, wherein communication and commerce become blended to create a complex process of mutual reinforcement at the most fundamental cultural level. We trace the roots of this process in the next chapter and see in Part II how this

conflation of communication and commodification is greatly heightened by its enframement in the communicational flows of first the city and then the digital medium for which the city can be conceptualized as a precursor.

- *Independent thoughts are cerebral software and culture is a play on the keyboard of the mind.* McLuhan emphasized the manner in which electronic media represented an extension of our central nervous system. There are intimations of technology's more profoundly invasive power in McLuhan's descriptions of man becoming a servo-mechanism of his artefacts like the Native American with his canoe and the executive with his clock. Kittler further develops notions of the determining aspects of technology by suggesting that the human is simply the product of the cultural software that is run on its neurological hardware.

From the above we can see the extent to which Kittler represents a radicalization of McLuhan. This has its origin in Kittler's appropriation of a number of themes from poststructuralist thought, and it is to his treatment of this tradition that we must now briefly turn.

Poststructuralism and Foucault: episteme as media matrix

Kittler adopts much from McLuhan, but this borrowing is in turn transformed by a detailed engagement with a constellation of ideas drawn from poststructuralism. This gives Kittler's project a far greater rigour and theoretical complexity than McLuhan's more intuitive approach. In order to explore systematically this hybridization, we will take each of Kittler's major influences in turn and identify what he draws from their projects, and how they are fused together to provide a unique framework for discussing the im/material impact of the digital. Kittler has offered the following definition of his central term 'discourse network': 'The term . . . designates the network of technologies and institutions that allow a given culture to select, store, and process relevant data' (Kittler 1990: 369). The concept has its origin in the archaeological phase of Michel Foucault's thought, and can be seen as a technologically supplemented version of Foucault's own notion of an *épistème*. In works such as *The Order of Things* (1994 [1970]) and *The Archaeology of Knowledge* (1972), Foucault developed the thesis that the status of knowledge in a given epoch was determined by the nature of global 'discursive formations', which dictated the relationship between words and things. These formations were characterized both by their relative stability, often lasting for one or more centuries, and by the rapidity of their alternation. (Foucault noted that it often takes no more than a mere thirty years to consign to history a discursive matrix that has proved serviceable for a century.) What is critical for Foucault, and more importantly for the use Kittler makes of his thought, is the radical 'exteriority' of these epistemes. The epistemes of Foucault's archaeology are described in terms resonant of a particularly sophisticated form of enframement as 'anonymous field[s] whose configuration defines the possible position of the speaking subject' (ibid.: 122) as well as the knowledge such a subject produces or possesses.

Furthermore, epistemes are not overarching structures that determine from an external or transcendent point the production of knowledge, or the order of words and things; rather, they are produced alongside the specific ordering of a given field of enquiry. A consequence of this exteriority is that the structure and nature of a given episteme can only be known retroactively: 'man ... can be revealed only when bound to a previously existing historicity' (Foucault 1994 [1970]: 330). It is only when the individual fields that make up a given discursive formation *have been emptied of their apparent truth by the passage of time* that the hidden contours of the episteme or discursive system under which they were formulated are revealed. Similarly, for Kittler, it is only in retrospect that the characteristics of a given matrix can be discerned. Consequently for Kittler: 'Understanding media – despite McLuhan's title – remains an impossibility precisely because the dominant information technologies of the day control all understanding and its illusions' (Kittler 1999: xi). Kittler is perhaps a little unfair to McLuhan since the latter was aware of the difficulties of assessing new media environments as they were emerging. Thus, for example, he described the way in which media forms tend to reveal themselves to our fullest understanding only when they are in the process of being supplanted by new forms:

> Just before an airplane breaks the sound barrier, sound waves become visible on the wings of the plane. The sudden visibility of sound just as sound ends is an apt instance of that great pattern of being that reveals new and opposite forms just as the earlier forms reach their peak performance.
>
> (McLuhan 1995 [1964]: 12)

It is from this position that Kittler has refused to discuss the characteristics of our contemporary discursive formation, on the basis that we are so immersed within that we cannot articulate its conditions with any objectivity.

As a result of this reluctance, Kittler inherits Foucault's fraught commitment to a discontinuity between epistemes. Foucault argued that the transformations in the structure of the subject of knowledge that occur simultaneously across disparate fields could not be attributed to their progressive, internal evolution. Thus, rather than the steady development of a given question over time (i.e. those of language, economics and biology) we observe an abrupt recasting of knowledge under the conditions of a new episteme. Similarly, rather than an ideal continuity, Kittler's discourse networks are figured in terms of breaks or ruptures: 'the historical adventures of speaking do not form a continuum and so do not constitute a history of ideas. They are marked by breaks that in a single stroke can consign entire discourse networks to oblivion ...' (Kittler 1990: 177). The influence of these networks determines not only what is spoken but also who speaks; in other words, concepts such as 'man' or 'meaning' carry the imprint of the networks under which they are formulated. Media, as the 'outside' of discourse, are apparent only in their eclipse and so cannot be approached in terms of transhistorical continuity; each in relation to the unspeakable scene of a contemporary discursive network must perforce appear discontinuous.

Kittler both adopts these Foucauldian positions and moves beyond them. He argues that Foucault's 'archaeology' unconsciously articulates the conditions of our own network, because only under the conditions of technological media does the idea of a discontinuous history arise:

> Only media technologies allow for the conception of a structure which itself emerges from stochastic disorder, instead of philosophically representing ontological or subjective orderings, which means to continue to write a metaphysics . . .
>
> (Kittler 1997: 140)

Foucault unwittingly introduces the caesuras that define technical media 'into historical methodology itself' (Kittler 1999: 117), and in the 'white, paradoxically atemporal crack in which one sudden formation replaces another' (Foucault 1972: 166) – breaks whose cause in Foucault remains notoriously mysterious – Kittler identifies the transmodulation of discourse networks as induced by changes in media. In this fashion Kittler asserts, in place of an enigmatic thought of the outside, an empirical positivity. It is media that determine who we are and what we mean; therefore, to trace the evolution of man and meaning is to trace the evolution of media. Foucault never departed from the text, therefore he could not see the effects that rival media had upon its sphere; Kittler, by embracing the positivity of media, is able to observe their silent registration in the realm of the written.

Derrida: technics and writing

Into this quasi-Foucauldian framework, Kittler inserts a problematic he derives from Derrida, namely the concept of logocentricity, or the privileging of speech over writing. Kittler argues that this problematic (so assiduously traced by Derrida) can be illuminated or contextualized through a consideration of media technology, that the 'supplement' 'gramme' and the concept of 'writing' through which Derrida deconstructed the concept of 'presence' can be focalized through an analysis of technical media. Thus, in *Discourse Networks 1800/1900* (1990) Kittler explores the manner in which a certain form of phonocentricity was assembled through the convergence of a range of practices in nineteenth-century German territories and suggests that it is the conditions of the media matrix of 1900 that lie behind Derrida's interrogation of the question of writing, and his attempt to free it from its fallen secondarity, its supplementary status to a prior 'full' speech. In seeming confirmation of this reading, Derrida (1976), in *Of Grammatology*, makes a number of pronouncements, declaring the deconstructive project to be the product of the 'closure of a historico-metaphysical epoch', a response to a 'dislocation' of a 'system' and 'the ineluctable world of a future which proclaims itself at present' (Derrida 1976: 4). Most significant is Derrida's declaration that 'a certain sort of question about the meaning and origin of writing . . . merges with a certain type of question about the meaning or origin of technics' (ibid.: 8). This question is that of the meaning of writing, first as the supplement of a full speech that exists prior and involate and, second, as this question is rearticulated by the contemporary problematization of the relationship; consequently the question of writing:

> . . . merges with the history that associated technics and logocentric meta-physics for nearly three millennia. And now it seems to be approaching what is really its own *exhaustion*; under the circumstances – and this now more than one example among others – of this death of the civilisation of the book . . . this death of the book undoubtedly announces (and in a certain sense has always announced) nothing but the death of speech (of a *so-called* full speech) and a new mutation in the history of writing, in history as writing.'
>
> (ibid.: 8)

While the cause of epistemic breaks remained enigmatic in Foucault's archaeology, Derrrida clearly grants technology a role in the exhaustion of the Guttenberg galaxy, identifying this as a stage of history conceived as writing, of writing as the cause of history and history as the history of writing. Kittler's novelty resides in the unprecedented level of historical data that he brings to bear upon this thesis, combining the cultural detail of Foucault's archaeology with the conceptual wager offered by Derrida's grammatology.

Lacan's psychic apparatus

After Foucault and Derrida, the third major influence on Kittler's theoretical framework is the psychoanalytic theory of Jacques Lacan. As he did with Derrida and Foucault, and demonstrating why he is so important to our consideration of *digital matters*, Kittler offers a material supplement to the abstraction of Lacan's thought. His basic argument is that Lacan as an interpreter of Freud renders explicit the hidden technological a priori of the Freudian unconscious. Thus, for Kittler, Lacan was the first psychoanalytic theorist to embrace the constitutive role of technological media in the formulation of the unconscious, to recognize that media represent the 'unconscious of the unconscious'. The recognition of the relation between psychoanalysis and technical media can be seen in Walter Benjamin's 'Work of Art' essay, and its claim that film transformed routine perception:

> Our taverns and our metropolitan streets, our offices and furnished rooms, our railroad stations and our factories appeared to have us locked up hope-lessly. Then came the film and burst this prison-world asunder by the dyna-mite of the tenth of the second, so that now, in the midst of its far-flung ruins and debris, we calmly and adventurously go travelling.
>
> (Benjamin 1973 [1935]: 238)

These ruins are those of our formerly unified perceptions, which are now broken up into subroutines, quantified by the technologies of the image and their 'interruptions and isolations . . . extensions and accelerations . . . enlargements and reductions'. As a result the camera is said to 'introduce us to unconscious optics as does psychoanalysis to unconscious impulses' (ibid.: 238–9). Thus, Benjamin compares cinema to Freud's *Psychopathology of Everyday Life* (2002 [1901]), after which formerly inconsequential verbal slips become windows that open onto the machinery of the unconscious:

> This book isolated and made analysable things that once would have gone unnoticed in the broad stream of perception . . . film has brought about a similar deepening of apperception.
>
> (ibid.: 237)

But while Benjamin offers an analogy between psychoanalysis and cinema, Kittler argues that Lacanian psychoanalysis embraces technical media as its ground. That is to say, the terms of psychoanalysis are a direct acknowledgement of its ambient discourse network – its media matrix.

According to Kittler's reading, Lacanian psychoanalysis approaches 'consciousness [as] the imaginary interior view of media standards' (Kittler 1997: 132), a position that recalls McLuhan's observation that a person is a temporary constellation of mediatically determined sensory ratios. For Kittler, this understanding was implicit in Freud's notion of the 'psychic apparatus' and his attempts to construct a model of memory that could account both for the ever fresh receptivity of the sensorium to novel impressions and its ability to permanently store such impressions, a conflict between random-access memory and read-only memory (ibid.: 133). What separates Freud and Lacan is the emergence of media that can not only receive or transmit and store data, but can also process it. Implicit in Lacanian psychoanalysis (according to Kittler) is the belief that consciousness can be broken down into three functions: reception/transmission, storage and calculation/processing. More importantly, these three functions can, as a result of computation, be replicated in technical media, thus:

> . . . Freud and Lacan are separated by the computer. Under high-tech conditions . . . psychoanalysis no longer constructs psychic apparatuses (if they are still psychic) merely out of the storage and transmission media, but rather incorporates the entire technical triad of storage, transmission and computation.
>
> (ibid.: 135)

In Kittler's model, enframement at the cerebral level occurs by means of this technical triad.

Thus, Kittler adopts and adapts the themes he draws from all these thinkers into a remarkable framework for understanding technological media. He combines the structural vision of the archaeological Foucault, a Derridian concern with the question of writing, a Lacanian vision of the psyche as a media system and a McLuhanite belief in media determinism, in a grand synthesis, locating this constellation of ideas at the level of 'historically specific machineries', such that these themes, born of different thinkers operating in disparate fields, assume 'the anonymity of an episteme' (Wellbury in Kittler 1990: xi). This is a significant phrase, for in as much as Foucault *et al.* are folded into a single party, their projects express the contours of a general discourse network. Indeed, the eruption of a distribution of problems across a range of authors may be seen in terms of a episteme that writes itself through these thinkers, so that (to adopt Derrida's comments on Freud) 'a relationship to itself of the historico-transcendental stage of writing was spoken without being said, thought without being thought: was written and simultaneously erased . . . *was represented*' (Derrida 2001: 288). In this manner media determinism is liberated from question of its direct reception: we do not have to consume the output of modern media, even in the apparent preserve of the archive and the text our shared situation registers itself. The effects of the processes of enframement that have been developed in earlier chapters extend their effects far beyond those who explicitly engage with these technologies, penetrating into the very depths of the psyche and into every area of cultural production.

Discourse networks

The theoretical synthesis supplied above is essential to an understanding of Kittler's project, but it would be erroneous to see Kittler's work as merely the skilled exegesis of others' thoughts. Kittler's reworking is uniquely his own, and it is the specificity of his work that we now emphasize. His writings may be roughly divided into two phases: first we have the substantial body of his own theory as it is offered in his *Discourse Networks 1800/1900* (1990) and *Gramophone, Film, Typewriter* (1999) (originally published in German within a year of each other in the mid-1980s); second, we have a number of essays written in the past fifteen or so years that extend this theory within the context of the Information Revolution brought about by the personal computer and its networking in the form of the internet. At this point, rather than descend into the welter of historical and cultural data that is Kittlerian 'media science', it would be helpful to gain a sense of the framework in which this material is placed. As a literary critic, Kittler's concern is with cultural production: the manner in which cultural artefacts register and operate within their informatic milieu. While we cannot offer a detailed discussion of Kittler's reading of various cultural products, we can offer an outline a broad outline of the two major discourse networks and identify their major points of contrast.

The discourse network of 1800

In keeping with Kittler's techno-medial determinism, the discourse network of 1800 represents a historically specific information processor. Described as a 'technology of the letter' it is an abstract machine whose product is readers of a particular strain; those engineered to respond to the poetics of German Romanticism. The components of this network include: educational reforms; gender roles; the structure of family; the functions and functionaries of the state; and the materials of communication. These elements operating in concert constitute an information system of 'senders', 'data' and 'addresses' that produces a specific form of subjectivity. This subjectivity finds its clearest expression in the 'aural hallucination' experienced by the reader of Romanticism, i.e. the experience of the mute voice of the bard which, according to Kittler, each reader of Romanticism hears in a textually induced reverie. This voice, as opposed to the actions of the reader or the marks on the page, is seen as the source of sense. Romantic poetics displaces this voice's origins, constructing its practitioners not as senders but as mediators of a speech whose origins lie elsewhere – in nature conceived as the 'Great Mother'.

For Kittler this experience is technically determined by the technology of the letter – it is the local product of a global system. The core component of this network was a series of changes in the 'materiality' of elementary acculturation techniques introduced around 1800, which served, through the introduction of 'alphabetized' learning, to make mothers the primary educators of their children. Children were taught to associate letters with sounds, to learn writing and speech at the same time. This scene of primary instruction participates in a 'large feedback loop' that couples the most intimate experience of the reading subject with the operations of an entire discursive field (Kittler 1990: 53). Foremost amongst these was the state, which dictated the institution of the mother as educator. In assuming control of education, the state assumed a new status; it became:

> A state that reaches beyond its own laws and punishments to grasp the modern possibility of universal discipline must necessarily form a pact with that most universal and 'indispensable class of civil servants' know as teachers.
> (ibid.: 59)

This is the bureaucratic state, which controls the operations of reading and writing because they are indispensable to its very functioning – a power exercised via the text must produce 'alphabetized' readers and writers. Mothers became the Other of the state, its complementary pole. This reflected a certain cleavage in the operations of writing since 'there was no place, in a system of polar sexual difference where the two sides of the system could be written down'. The discourse network of 1800 defined man (the product of alphabetization) as he who writes – 'the sole determination of man is to inscribe' (Schlegal in Kittler 1990: 63), and woman as she who inspires writing. In this manner the sexes 'remained separated by the abyss that divides speech from writing' (Kittler 1990: 63). Kittler dubs this system the *'Muttermund'* (a term that in German recalls both the mouth of the womb and the mouth of the mother) and within the context of the broader themes of this discussion we should be alert to the resonance of this term. Kittler is describing a matrix, a circulation of data whose apparent locus is the mother qua instructor, and the term matrix resonates with its roots in the Latin 'mater' and its subsequent associations with the womb. The *Muttermund* is at once a precursor of the matrix as we understand it (that is a pervasive informatic system) and recalls the earlier functions that are absorbed or co-opted in the technological matrix, in particular reproduction, which becomes the generalized reproducibility of information first recognized by Benjamin. (As we noted in our Introduction the master disc from which gramophone records were reproduced was also called the 'matrix'.)

In Network 1800 man wrote and woman read or inspired. Thus, we have, on the one hand, the Great Mother as muse and the legions of daughters and mothers that consumed the texts written by male authors, who were denied access to the status of author – both the outside and the centre of textuality – and, on the other hand, the male author who inscribes the virgin page with his phallocratic stylus, who knows himself through the act of inscription. This leads to an emphasis, within the governmental and authorial components of this discursive matrix, on handwriting. Civil servants as the end product of the educational reforms that placed the Mother at the heart of the induction into the symbolic were individuals whose status was guaranteed by the production of handwriting. Handwriting was the avatar of a unified psyche – it was indivisible, continuous: 'the organic continuity of . . . writing materialized the biographical-organic continuity of the educated' (ibid.: 84). Continuous handwriting, to the extent that it involves the recomposition of letters learnt individually, captures the occultation that characterizes the discursive complex in general, in that it conceals letters learnt discretely within a continuous flow.

This brief summary of the network of 1800 might seem curiously literary or pre-technological, bearing little relation to the avowed theme of the digital matters of the matrix. But Kittler's point is that this is a matrix. The readers and writers, senders and addresses, of Romantic poetics are media determined – they are nodes in a network that extends from the 'interior' of the subject to the structure of the state. These discursive practices should be understood as seizing an entire social field: from the education of children to the position of women, to the affairs of state and modes of textual production. As such we cannot ascribe a determinate status to any individual component of this system; the network of 1800 must thus be understood in systematic rather than genetic terms, as made up of 'interlocking circuits rather than simple causes' (ibid.: 60), in other words, the kind of assemblage of incorporeal information and material components that we have called the matrix. For Kittler there is not an outside to the matrix; if something as seemingly naturalized as Romantic poetics can be traced as a system then discourse networks do not allow something that could not become enframed. Humans are, and have always been, terms in a system of information processing. Under the influence of technics and war, the system of senders and addresses that is Network 1800 is both fractured and concretized on silicon in microscopic dimensions.

The discourse network of 1900

Kittler's belief in the materiality of communication means that his focus is upon hardware, on the medium rather than the message, and his account of the evolution of the matrix is almost exclusively devoted to questions of media and hardware rather than any message they might transmit. We have noted above the 'blind spot' that is a fundamental presupposition of Kittler's media analysis, understood as the impossibility of describing the discourse network under which we labour since networks can only be explored retroactively. Implicit, then, in Kittler's account of the discourse network of 1900 is its eclipse by the 'Network 2000'. Given this, we might briefly dwell on the features of this new mediascape as presciently described by Kittler. Writing in 1985, Kittler approaches the network to come through a vision of the mass installation of fibreoptic cables: Network 2000 promises a 'writing scene' that represents the convergence of previously separate media within a single digital über-medium. In transmitting all possible messages, fibreoptics will bring to an end the world of plural *media* – radio, television, cinema, post, print etc. – all will circulate via a single *medium*:

> The general digitisation of channels and information erases the differences among individual media. Sound and image, voice and text are reduced to surface effects, known to the consumers as interface. . . . Inside the computers themselves everything becomes a number: quantity without image, sound, or voice.
>
> (Kittler 1999: 1)

The end of media is in the digital; their convergence reduces the characteristics of earlier media to surface effects, retained only by virtue of their familiarity. Media (plural) are comforting anachronisms that conceal the reality of their subsumption in a common digital matter. 'With numbers, everything goes': both in terms of the loss of separate media and in terms of hitherto undreamt of possibilities of algorithmic manipulation. This brave new world brings into focus the discourse network it replaces, one based not on convergence but on differentiation. The media of 1900 begin with separation, the 'thematization' of individual sensory streams. The sense perceptions subsumed in 'eyewash' had to first be arrested: before transmission and calculation there was first storage.

Unlike the writing of 1800, which was determined by sense, the new media of Network 1900 stored noise, in other words data that had no relation to the sense a subject might locate within it. For instance, phonography 'emptied out words by bypassing their imaginary aspect (signifieds) for their real aspect (the physiology of the voice)' (ibid.: 246). The separate media of 1900 are, at their inception, methods of storage, and what they store is time: understood as the evanescent *real*. Prior to the gramophone's deterritorialization of writing or the *graphie*, time could not be captured directly but only symbolically:

Texts and scores – Europe had no other means of storing time. Both are based on a writing system whose time is (in Lacan's term) symbolic . . . all data flows, provided that they really were streams of data, had to pass through the bottleneck of the signifier.

(ibid.: 4)

Kittler maps the media that break with the signifier in terms of Lacan's 'methodological distinction' between the *symbolic*, the *real* and the *imaginary*, arguing that in the discourse network of 1900 machines no longer solely replicate the actions of muscles (as in industrial technology) but take over the operations of the nervous system (as McLuhan observed). Machines move from thermodynamics to information, dealing not only with a material real but also with the symbolic (ibid.: 16). Thus, it is technical media that reveal the symbolic qua symbolic, and thus permit the Lacanian distinction. Kittler develops this theme by arguing that his trinity of media:

1   gramophone;
2   cinema; and
3   typewriter

corresponds respectively to the Lacanian trinity of the:

1   real;
2   imaginary; and
3   symbolic.

Gramophone

The gramophone holds a privileged place in Kittler's media history because as a medium it inaugurates the storage of the real. Indeed, Kittler's claim is stronger: the real (as opposed to the imaginary and the symbolic) has its proper birth with the advent of the gramophone. The gramophone is identified with the real in this way because, for the first time, time or signal is imprinted directly on to matter; matter becomes a storage medium in and of itself, not as the recipient of abstract symbols or discrete units (e.g. the photograph), but as a medium that records the real in its passing. It is the first stage in the process that will result in digital matters. For Kittler the media of 1900 dissolve the unity of a subject that heard itself speak and saw itself write. The new media are characterized by their disjunction or absolute separation, abstracting separate sensory channels from a previously unified sensorium and technically implementing them. The fragmentation of the subject is nowhere clearer than in the components of the recording process, in which the gramophone (which initially both recorded and reproduced) can be seen as an artificial ear and mouth. Phonography implies the technical reconstruction of the apparatus of speech and audition, albeit in a manner far cruder than the original. This interplay between signal and noise effects music as a form of information phonographically stored. The gramophone not only recorded and replayed music but, in time, allowed the production of music, introducing the concept of pure noise as a potential sonic material. Thus, in 1923 Moholy-Nagy suggested that the gramophone could be turned from 'an instrument of reproduction into a productive one, generating acoustic phenomena without any previous acoustic existence by scratching' (Moholy-Nagy cited in Kittler 1999: 46). Music would thus issue no longer from a subject or its instruments but from the very medium of its storage. This situation might be seen as recalling Ellul's statement that under *la téchnique* music is transformed 'by means of techniques which were not originally musical techniques, that is, neither musical methodology nor instrument construction' (Ellul 1963 [1954]: 129), but for Kittler this is not a subordination, nor a perversion, but simply a redeployment of elements.

Kittler's mediaology traces a movement from storage, to transmission, to calculation or manipulation, in which (following McLuhan) one medium acts as the content for another. In the case of the gramophone we see its trace of the *real* transposed into radio, because 'the continuous low frequencies of records are ideal for the amplitude and frequency modulation known as broadcasting' (Kittler 1999: 94). This movement from storage to transmission introduces a crucial theme largely absent in *Discourse Networks*: that of the role of *war* in the evolution of media. Mechanical war (tank, aircraft and submarine) required wireless communication, and the modulations of the real uncovered by the gramophone were seen as far more flexible in terms of real-time communication than Morse code – the initial content of military radio. In time, in what Kittler argues is the common logic of all electronic media, 'an abuse of army equipment' turned the wireless communications systems of warfare into a medium for the distraction of bored soldiers and later for the distraction of civilian populations. Thus, Kittler traces innovations such as stereophony (developed as a means of co-ordinating the Luftwaffe's aerial bombardment) and magnetic tape (developed so as to allow real-time storage of radio communications in combat) to the demands of communication in advanced warfare. Originally the gramophone as the medium of the real bore witness to a strict separation of data streams, but in its capacity as medium that both read and recorded (as it then did) it heralded the arrival of calculation or processing. This capacity is clearest in magnetic tape, which: 'like the paper strip of the universal machine . . . can execute any possible manipulation of data because . . . equipped with recording, reading, and erasing heads, as well as with forward and reverse motions' (ibid.: 108).

Cinema

If the gramophone equates to the Lacanian real, then cinema is the medium of the imaginary. This equation is explained by the technical conditions of the medium. While the gramophone traced the real in real time, cinema begins with deception: a succession of static images are projected in rapid succession, fooling the eye and inducing the illusion of continuous movement. To capture the visual as a direct trace, that is to say in the manner of phonography, is beyond the capacities of our technology given that 'optical data flows are two-dimensional' and 'consist of high frequencies . . . [that] outpace (unbelievably) today's electronics'. As a result, optical data cannot (as yet) be directly recorded, and as 'a medium that is unable to trace the amplitude of its input data' (ibid.: 119), cinema necessarily owes its origins to cuts, samples and selections. This truth applies to all forms of moving image, from cinema to television to the digital technologies of today. All are composed of excerpts and selections, whether it is the twenty-four frames per second of traditional celluloid or the various bit/time ratios of the animated electronic image. In this fashion, cinema both breaks up and recombines the subject of the previous discourse network (which it must be stressed was itself entirely media determined), and as a result it was initially accompanied by an experience of shock or confusion on the part of those who encountered the moving image (we will consider this 'shock' in Chapter 6). The body image, which corresponds to the illusion of a unitary subject, does not survive its cinematic replication; film 'liquidates the fund of stored images in . . . [the] psychic apparatus' (ibid.: 150). This is not because media distort or disfigure in the act of recording but because the 'trace detection' of mechanical media exposes the components sublated within the self-present subject of 1800. Media reveal an assemblage of disparate traces that are (initially) difficult to subsume under the sign of a single self. In this respect they preclude the (illusion) of interiority or inner life that preceded them.

Typewriter

The typewriter is of particular interest since it focalizes the stakes involved in the transition from discourse network to discourse network. Kittler equates the typewriter with the Lacanian register of the symbolic (i.e. the sign or text), and the typewriter stands as the avatar of this sphere's transformation. In our brief summary of the characteristics of Network 1800 we noted the relationship of handwriting, the state and gender. Men, whose presence as subjects was sanctioned by their handwriting, participated and presided over a textual network. Authors stood as the noble representatives of this network, but its routine processing was carried out by an army of unglamorous scribes and 'computers', who carried out with pen and paper the editing and replication of documents (tasks that are now delegated to software). These are the preterite clerks of Dickens's fictions or Melville's *Bartleby the Scrivener*, whose world disappeared with the emergence of the typewriter. Kittler relates how the typewriter, greeted largely with indifference by the processors of Network 1800, recruited its operators from a previously underemployed pool of dexterous young women. The secretary's appearance, as the twentieth century knew her, in the workplace was commensurate with that of the typewriter.

As a technology, the effects of the typewriter were in keeping with the general characteristics of the new network, that is to say it participated in an uncoupling, a discretization of the unified subject of 1800. Handwriting, whose continuity was the outward expression of the biographical continuity of the writing subject, is replaced by a mechanical transposition. The word is mechanized, the symbolic passes through the machine, a passage that results in the destitution of the terms of the previous network. By way of illustration, Kittler cites Heidegger's meditation on the typewriter, in which he argued that 'when writing was withdrawn from the origin of its essence, i.e., from the hand, and was transferred to the machine, a transformation occurred in the relation of Being to man' and thus was a powerful instance of enframement: 'this "machine" operated in the closest vicinity to the word . . . imposes its own use' (Heidegger cited in Kittler 1999: 199–200). The grim determinism and contempt for agency that directs much of Kittler's thinking is clearly revealed in this context. Thus, unlike Heidegger's faith in the originary status of handwriting, such that the 'typewriter *tears writing from the essential* realm of the hand [our emphasis]', as we have seen, handwriting was the product of earlier network rather than an essence. Similarly, the emergence of the secretary and the no-longer pseudonymous women writer bears witness not to women's emancipation, but only to a shift in networks, recalling G. K. Chesterton's sly observation that 'women refused to be dictated to and went out and became stenographers' (Chesterton cited in McLuhan 1995 [1964]: 228).

Kittler identifies a number of other transformations born of the mechanization of the symbolic, arguing, for instance, that modernist literary poetics are in no small part a result of this discretization of the word. Most important, however, is the fate of the typewriter in the field of battle, which introduces the increasingly central theme of war as the prime catalyst in the evolution of media. Kittler revels in an inhuman techno-genetic dynamic in which: 'technical media don't arise out of human needs, as their current interpretation in terms of bodily prostheses has it [i.e. contra McLuhan], they follow each other in a rhythm of escalating strategic answers' (Kittler 1999: 121). McLuhan, while recognizing (like Benjamin at the end of his 'Work of Art' essay) that war is 'a process of achieving equilibrium among unequal technologies' (McLuhan 1995 [1964]: 344), still subordinated this process to a vision of the 'outering' of the human body in which weapons are 'extensions of hands, nails, and come into existence as tools needed for accelerating the processing of matter' and the informational warfare of modern warfare is a consequence of the extrusion of the nervous system. But for Kittler this processing of matter is apparently self-catalysing.

While we cannot here address, in the detail it warrants, the role this processing plays in Kittler's media theory, we can offer some illustration of this theme through a consideration of the role of typewriter in war as it is figured in *Gramophone, Film, Typewriter*. McLuhan, in a short discourse on the typewriter, noted that 'an army needs more typewriters than . . . artillery, even in the field, suggesting that the typewriter fuses the functions of the pen and sword' (ibid.: 228) and Kittler takes this insight and runs with it. His theory hinges upon a recognition of the centrality of communications in warfare and that the evolution of the technical media of 1900 was accelerated by the great conflicts of that century. Communications as a strategic advantage mean that media enter into the strategic escalation of military hardware. Thus, Kittler's account of the evolution of the typewriter merges with his history of communications in warfare, which pass through three stages that correspond to the three main functions of any media system: storage, transmission and calculation or processing, hence Kittler's formula: 'Storing/transmitting/calculating, or trenches/blitz/stars. World wars from 1 to n.' (Kittler 1999: 243).

In this light, the deterritorialization of the typewriter in the field of war has its origins in the trench warfare of the First World War, in which both sides found themselves at the mercy of an information bottleneck. Once infantry left the relatively centralized space of their lines (linked to central command by the rudimentary transmission technology of fixed telephone lines), they entered into no-man's land, where 'only the thinnest line of communication remained open: soldiers running back and forth from one side to the other of no-man's land' (De Landa 1991: 73). This black hole produced siege warfare on a monumental scale, the obscene spectacle of thousands of young men sacrificed in the pure noise of no-man's land, whose net result was the rearrangement of lines at a snail's pace: 'in the absence of portable wireless communications, the Western Front swallowed massive amount of troops' (1991: 73). Solutions were needed, and were found in the development of transmission media that would banish once and for all the bottleneck, via the application of the real of the gramophone to the modulations of radio waves. But radio came at cost – as a broadcast medium it was inherently 'leaky'. To fulfil its military potential, radio had to be made secure, and the solution to this problem was found in the Enigma machine. Its inventor Arthur Schrebius, after unsuccessfully approaching the German military and diplomatic services, began to market his *Chiffriermaschinen* for commercial use in the early 1920s. Able to produce encrypted documents automatically, Schrebius's machine represented a modification of the typewriter. In the earliest models it was possible to utilize the Enigma as a conventional typewriter, even in the middle of producing an enciphered text (Kruh and Deavours 2002: 3), and the 'ciphering typewriter' exploited at its most basic technical level the effects on written language that Kittler identifies as a result of the typewriter: the reduction of writing to the production of spatially designated and discrete signs. Thus, a technology that allowed the individual to automatically produce spatialized and discrete writing was adapted to produce automatically enciphered text – a typewriter within a typewriter so to speak.

What the Enigma granted the German military was the ability to exploit the transmission technology of radio while ensuring that their transmissions would remain indecipherable to all but their intended recipients. The Enigma squared the circle, allowing narrowcasts to be broadcast. This security, in turn, facilitated *blitzkrieg* – the massive synchronized mobilization of land, air and naval forces, coordinated by encrypted radio transmission, and able to direct their combined force to devastating effect. To quote:

> The lightning war . . . because it depended on the most advanced transmission media, had to return to simple and most underrated of storage media.

Systematically it operated by means of typewriters that . . . didn't simply print, in a bi-univocal relationship, the letters that had been typed. Instead, by means of five alphabetic rotors and an electrical switch-board (whose start positions had to be redefined each day), any input text was translated into two hundred million mathematically possible and seemingly randomized outputs.

(Kittler 1997: 124)

However, to the extent that Enigma was a machine it remained theoretically possible to crack its codes using other machines, and it was precisely this that occurred in Bletchley Park or 'Station X' under the guidance of the father of the digital computer, the brilliant Alan Turing. What Engima and Station X provided was the impetus to transform Turing's Universal Discrete Machine (originally proposed as a solution to an abstruse mathematical problem) into a working technology. For Kittler, Turing's machine can be seen as a elaboration of the typewriter:

All it works with is a paper strip that is both its program and its data material, its input and its output. Turing slimmed down the common typewriter page to this little strip. But there are even more economisations: his paper machine doesn't need the many redundant letters, ciphers, and signs of a typewriter keyboard; it can do with one sign and its absence, 1 and 0. This binary information can be . . . scanned by the machine. It can then move the paper strip one space to the right, one space to the left, or not at all, moving in a jerky (i.e., discrete) fashion like a typewriter, which in contrast to handwriting has block caps, a back spacer and a space bar.

(Kittler 1999: 18)

This 'typewriter' implemented in the form of valves and paper strips provided the means to crack Enigma and gave birth to the digital computer, which increasingly defines the digital matters of the twenty-first-century.

The digital matters of Network 2000

We have seen how the grand convergence of Network 2000 has its origins in a war that for Kittler was won by a strategic escalation of media, wherein an army based on storage and transmission media was defeated by one able to implement calculative media (a similar theme is explored in 'Dracula's Legacy', his highly imaginative account of the role played by media in the tracking down of Count Dracula' see Kittler 1997: 50–84). In doing this, the three conditions of any medium (storage, transmission, calculation) were satisfied: functions that previously were distributed between individuals and their materialities of communication could, for the first time, be implemented in a single medium that could read and write itself. And, as is well known, the computer's association with military necessity was to continue in the form of ARPANET – the precursor of today's internet: in this fashion, 'the war to end all wars leads to the medium to end all media' (Winthrop-Young 2000: 830). Thus, the digital matter that enwombs us is an immanent record of this conflict between different media. But what lies behind this process? Given that Kittler repeatedly signals his contempt for man, and his structural position precludes any possible inventiveness on the part of a prior subject, it would seem that technology, as in the work of Ellul, has its own agency, and that war provides this agency with the conditions most propitious to its own self-augmentation. As Winthrop-Young puts it, in Kittler: 'war appears to operate much like life itself; it engages in the continuous extraction of information, it uses that information to devise protocols for the further gathering of information and the subsequent extraction and processing of material flows' (ibid.: 848).

As we have previously stated, Kittler's belief in the absolute determinate capacity of media precludes anything but their retroactive description; as the technologies that determine what we can say, we can say anything only about those technologies that no longer determine what we say. As a result, he has ruled out the possibility of providing an account of the contemporary techno-medial situation along the lines of those 1800 and 1900. This does not mean that he has remained silent on the subject of contemporary conditions, but merely that he has refrained from providing a synoptic analysis of our current state. Indeed, over the last fifteen or so years, Kittler has produced a series of essays which direct themselves precisely to the problem of contemporary mediascape. These have partaken of the general determinacy, even paranoia, that charac-terized his earlier work. His first target has been that of the proliferation of interfaces, whether windows, menus, interactive media, etc. For Kittler, these represent seductive surfaces that serve to conceal harsher realities. Thus, Kittler talks of a loss of writing, of a situation in which we no longer understand what our writing can do: to write (i.e. to word process) is to set in motion a fractaline chain of code whose substrate is simply the voltage difference that marks 0 from 1. This substrate is enveloped and accessed by a series of levels of code, whose outer face for so-called man are the words that dance across the screen.

For Kittler, modern computing, as a result, is not a democratic agora of free expression, but an elaborate simulation whose purpose is to disempower its users. At the heart of this strategy of occultation Kittler sees the US military and the giants of the software industry. The former he sees as withholding technical innovations from general knowledge for their own strategic purposes; the latter as shutting out 'end-users' from the mechanisms of the machines they employ. For Kittler, there is no software but only hardware: software is a manufactured illusion that shuts out users from their own hardware. Thus, through a process of systematic 'information-hiding', the software industry has deprived its customers, without consultation, of a range of freedoms in favour of user-friendliness and greater programming ease. Software functions as a veil of Maya, an illusion in which we are ensnared, which conceals reality and serves the interests of its creators. It is a betrayal of the universality of Turing's machine since, according to Kittler, it serves to obscure the recognition that a Turing machine can in principle solve any computable problem. Instead of reflecting this intrinsic condition, software exalts the algorithm over hardware: 'by identifying physical hardware with the algorithms forged for its computation, [it] has finally gotten rid of hardware itself' (Kittler 1997: 152). According to Kittler, programming languages in concealing hardware operate in a manner analogous to 'one-way functions' in cryptography (as used in public key systems such as PGP (or 'pretty good privacy'). One-way functions are mathematical operations that are significantly easier to compute in one direction (the forward direction) than in the opposite (inverse) direction; thus, they serve to hide 'an algorithm from its result' (ibid.: 151).

In Kittler's somewhat paranoid account, software emerges as a vast cryptographic enterprise whose necessity is not technical 'but rather, like all cryptology, has strategic functions' (ibid.: 158). This strategy's rationale is economic – by separating an algorithm from what it can do, software serves to maintain the phantom of creators or authors. Upholding these fictions, via the juridical concept of intellectual copyright, ensures the continued economic benefits of software development, which is nothing more than accessing the resources of hardware: 'precisely because software does not exist as a machine independent faculty, software as a commercial or American medium insists on its status as property all the more' (ibid.: 151). This strategy has two functions: first, to ensure that software enjoys the status of intellectual property and exists as a bounded commodity rather than a collective endeavour; second, to create subjects such as those 'under' Microsoft, who 'did not simply fall from the sky, but had to be produced like all of their media-historical predecessors . . .' (1997: 158). Software conspires to create 'end-users', to erect coded boundaries between users and creators – a manoeuvre of the same strategic import as those that created the readers of 1800 and the spectators of the twentieth century. For Kittler, this situation is the product not of technical necessity but rather of power (though his suspicion of human agency renders the loci of this power problematic): '. . . these layers . . . , like modern media in general, have been explicitly contrived to evade perception. We simply do not know what our writing does' (ibid.: 148). From this position Kittler has become an advocate of the Free/Open Source software movement we explore in detail in our final chapter, arguing that 'we should attempt to abandon the usual practice of conceiving of power as a function of so-called society, and . . . attempt to construct sociology from [a] chip's architecture' (ibid.: 162). Digital matter encodes power, which resides within the construction of technology itself, and any attempt to contest the terms of the matrix must engage with this level of power.

Conclusion

Kittler's thought is an important contribution to the question of the pervasive and insidious impact of hidden technological infrastructures. It further develops the notion of technological determinism. Its unique contribution is the manner in which it concentrates on media technologies, and places them rather than technology in general at the centre of the matrix. Kittler demonstrates how changes in media networks result in the transplantation of elements of the human sensorium to technology and how this technology comes to constitute a pervasively invasive network of digital matters. We become surrounded by a matrix of concretized formerly human functions, recalling Heidegger's total enframement of the human: a totalizing reproduction of ourselves. What sets Kittler apart from the accounts we have examined thus far is his absolute refusal to talk in terms of the loss or the eclipse of any prior condition. From a Kittlerian perspective, the lamentation of an Ellul is merely quaint; there are only ever information systems whose increase in complexity does not entail any loss. In addition, Kittler's account stresses the materiality of communication – it emphasizes how the digital is material and involves a complexification of matter rather than its transcendence. Thus, it provides a useful corrective to accounts that celebrate the supposed immateriality of the digital. In Kittler's vision, society is a material media matrix, not in the sense of a society ruled by simulation or spectacle, but rather at the deepest structural level. The question remains of what the role of human beings becomes in this scenario: are they redundant, little more than fuel cells, as in *The Matrix*, or is there a point at which the aims of technology and those of humanity converge?

4   The commodified media matrix

This study rests upon the assumption that each medium has a specific nature which invites certain kinds of communications while obstructing others.

(Kracauer 1965: 3)

Patrick Geddes said that the road destroyed the Greek city-state. But writing made the road possible, just as printing was later to pay for the roads of England and America ... Swift silent reading came with the macadamized surfaces of the printed page ... Ultimately the medieval clock made Newtonian physics possible ... Movable type was already the modern assembly line in embryo.

(McLuhan in Moos 1997: 129–31)

In this chapter we look at the notion of the mechanical reproduction of images, and in particular photography, in order to highlight the early stages of the distancing effects of media technology whose latest expression is that of digital matters. In order to examine the cultural effects of concepts such as Heidegger's *withdrawal* or *forgetting,* we examine the real consequences of media technologies. In the Introduction we encountered the notion of media bias and the concept of the society–technology dialectic or *cultural alignment*. The above two quotations relate directly to the role the media play in this alignment. In the first, Kracauer asserts the inherent tendency of each particular medium to promote some forms of communication over others. In the second quotation, McLuhan provides a dramatic example of Kracauer's assertion, illustrating how easily the notion of media bias can appear as essentialist technological determinism. Of particular interest to us, however, is the last sentence, in which he highlights the basic nature of the cultural alignment involved in media bias. A key part of movable type's profound impact upon Western culture is the subtle, culturally aligned way in which its outputs (books) reinforced the emergent social climate of capitalism, representing as they did examples of both a new medium and one of the earliest commodity forms. We show in this chapter how, in turn, the advent of photography marked a newly ambiguous relationship between the materiality of reality and the immaterial yet totalizing nature of the media representations that prefigure the immersive media-generated environments explored in Part II.

In this chapter, and in Part II as a whole, we analyse the mutual reinforcement that takes place between media technologies and commodity values. Here we trace a similar process in relation to photography to further illustrate the society–technology dialectic of Mumford/Williams/Innis encountered in our introduction. It is also a useful addition to Ellul's totalizing dialectic – to his identification of the industrial revolution as a key point for Western culture's departure into technique and to Kittler's theory of discourse networks and the way in which particular media technologies both determine and are determined by their epoch. However, we choose the example of photography to illustrate the specific role of capitalism in the media matrix that these two thinkers marginalize.

In his seminal 'Work of Art' essay, Walter Benjamin (1973 [1935]) describes the way in which the quantitative increase in the number of images produced by photography, and later film, led to a qualitative change in human perception, which may be taken as a local example of McLuhan's assertion that the true significance of a medium is the change in the scale and pace it brings to human affairs. The authenticity that Heidegger sees threatened by the various negative tendencies of technology (enframement, standing reserve, the Danger of withdrawal, etc.) represents for Benjamin, in contrast, an opportunity to facilitate the emancipation of the working classes from their enthralment to traditional forms of art and a political order that draws upon this tradition to ensure its continuance. According to Benjamin, Fascism used reified and mythical visual forms to rally the people to its political cause; it adopted the technologies of reproduction but used them as means of mass-producing a reactionary aesthetics, rather than allowing these technologies to produce a new, democratic aesthetic. Heidegger's notion of authenticity can thus be easily misappropriated for exploitative purposes (and Heidegger infamously became a member of the Nazi party). From Benjamin's perspective, the threat to authenticity or *aura* (defined as an object's or an environment's unique point in place and time) is a positive development. Rather than art, which relies on an aesthetic indifferent to, or in denial of, real relations of productions, reproducibility brings art and politics into direct confrontation. An art expunged of aura is, for Benjamin, by definition, a political art.

Of particular interest in the present context is Benjamin's notion of the *optical unconscious*, which he uses to describe the camera's ability to provide a range of images unavailable to the naked eye. For the first time in human history, for example, people could see the corona of droplets created by pouring milk or the precise movements of the legs of a galloping horse. Experienced by human beings at first hand, reality is suffused and inevitably coloured by subjective impressions, assessments and interpretations. This synthesis of direct experience, memory and subjective response conceals the particularity of immediate sense data. Photography removes such ambiguities and doubts. It provides an objective slice of time and space: the camera 'never lies'. It provides a surfeit of visual information with the paradoxical result that its technical loyalty to the reality it depicts produces more, not less, distance between that reality and our understanding of it. Thus, prior to the mechanical reproduction of images, our understanding of the world around us, although based upon abstract notions such as 'truth', or filtered through the imaginative narrative structures of various art forms, was predicated upon the mutual interdependence of the world and our representations of it. This interdependence has always previously been safeguarded by the fact that our representations were obviously just that: imperfect imitations. A process that began with photography, however, replaced this interdependence of the world and our representations of it with representations that are capable of becoming the basis of their own frame of reference and largely independent of external reality – the media matrix (a theme we pursue in more depth in Chapter 6).

Circulation for its own sake – the origins of the digital flow

> By decentring the authority of embodied perception and destabilizing the customary relationship between presence and absence, the camera has induced a crisis at the border between 'representation' and 'reality', affecting all contemporary experiences of time, space and memory . . . The ability to witness things *outside all previous limits of time and space* highlights the fact that the camera doesn't just give us a new means to represent experience: it changes the nature of experience and redefines our processes of understanding.
>
> (McQuire 1998: 1–2 [emphasis in original])

In McQuire's above claims for the importance of photography he provides: (i) an illustration of the photographic form of Heidegger's withdrawal; (ii) an important development of Ellul's emphasis upon the crucial significance of industrial production techniques; and (iii) a sense of the disjuncture that Kittler suggested exists between epochal networks. The last point relates to how technologies of mechanical reproduction, such as the printing press and photography, embody the roots of the 'gap' that media technologies introduce to our experience of reality. The shared significance of print, photography and the assembly line is their ability to produce qualitative change through the quantitative increase in the output of their reproductions. As McLuhan argued, the significance of a medium is the change in pace and scale it brings to human affairs, and the mechanical reproduction of communication creates the conditions necessary for a manipulable gap between a thing being represented and the representation (the signifiers and the signified) and the profound cultural consequences of that gap.

In societies prior to the advent of mechanical production, such signs served explicit social purposes and received their meaning by an explicit institutional sanction; they represented non-arbitrary relationships between people or institutions. The Bible, for example, was an object of veneration located specifically within church buildings, maintaining a closely maintained physical link between the word of God and the house of God. Meaning stemmed from the powerful forces that ensured a firm bond between the signifier and the signified. Thus, 'the signs are anything but arbitrary. The arbitrary sign begins when, instead of linking two persons in an unbreakable reciprocity, the signifier starts referring back to the disenchanted universe of the signified' (Baudrillard 1983: 84–5). The mechanical reproduction of communication first seen with the printing press therefore provided an early and dramatic example of the new quality of abstract mobility that was now introduced into human affairs by the conjunction of individualizing technologies and incipient capitalist production techniques. Mass-produced bibles broke the feudal bond of 'unbreakable reciprocity' between the sinner and the Church by promoting the Protestant hermeneutic relationship to the word of God. As a continuation of reproducibility introduced by the printing press, the camera offers another example of the technologically induced cultural and epistemic breaks that mark the beginning of modernity:

> The mechanical reproduction of the book not only changed its material characteristics, but significantly altered the social relations of meaning . . . the camera has vastly accentuated this condition by producing a multitude of signs without anchorage or home.
>
> (McQuire 1998: 49)

Signs are liberated from the fixed relationships they were subject to in a symbolic culture; thus, the significance of photographic images does not rely on the institutional authority. Photographic images speak largely for themselves. They are free to circulate and, crucially, in terms of our concept of cultural alignment, this makes photographic images the perfect accompaniment to a commodity culture premised upon an analogous circulation of commodities whose value, as Marx points out, through tautologically emerges from their exchange. Some of the most imaginative explorations of photography's self-generating rationale can be found in fiction. For example Italo Calvino, in his short story 'The Adventure of a Photographer', portrays the way in which:

> The line between the reality that is photographed because it seems beautiful to us and the reality that seems beautiful because it has been photographed is very narrow . . . You only have to start saying of something: 'Ah, how beautiful! We must photograph it!' and you are already close to the view of the person who thinks that everything that is not photographed is lost, as if it had never existed, and that therefore in order really to live you must photograph as much as you can, you must either live in the most photographable way possible or else consider photographable every moment of your life. The first course leads to stupidity; the second, to madness.
>
> (Calvino 1985: 43)

In his novel *White Noise,* Don Delillo (1985) echoes Calvino's notion of a photographic delirium in which everything in life becomes the site of its own photographic replication. In a moment of exquisite satire, the novel's main characters visit 'The most photographed barn in America', a sight for which they are prepared by numerous exclamatory signs emphasizing its status, while the barn itself is equipped with a car park, prepared elevations that provide a position to ensure the best photo-opportunity and stalls selling postcards and slides of the barn. This emblematic scene leads one of them to observe that:

> 'No one sees the barn,' . . . 'Once you've seen the signs about the barn, it becomes impossible to see the barn . . . We're not here to capture an image, we're here to maintain one. Every photograph reinforces the aura. Can you feel it, Jack? An accumulation of nameless energies . . . Being here is a kind of spiritual surrender. We see only what others see. The thousands who were here in the past, those who will come in the future. We've agreed to be part of a collective perception. This literally colors our vision. A religious experience in a way, like all tourism . . . They are taking picture of taking pictures . . . What was the barn like before it was photographed? . . . What did it look like, how was it different from other barns, how was it similar to other barns? We can't answer these questions because we've read the signs, seen the people snapping the pictures. We can't get outside of the aura. We're part of the aura. We're here, we're now.' He seemed immensely pleased by this.
>
> (ibid.: 12–13)

It is a combination of the proliferation and nature of these signs that creates our contemporary 'disenchanted universe of the signified' and fundamentally challenges not only the traditional status of art as Benjamin identifies in his 'Work of Art' essay but, more significantly, traditional patterns of meaning. The sheer number of images and concepts circulating with the advent of mechanically reproduced media means that 'we find ourselves increasingly surrounded by mental configurations, which we are free to interpret at will. Each is iridescent with meanings, while the great beliefs or ideas from which they issue grow paler' (Kracauer 1965: 9). This is part of the 'subtle' brand of media determinism that emphasizes the ecological effect of a medium's social presence. With words such as 'surrounded', Kracauer portrays a surfeit of content, which causes a proliferation of meanings that relativize and overwhelm traditional symbolically based beliefs. This is the origin of the perception of the lived experience of modern media as one of immersion in flows such as Lash's concept of immanence, which forms a major element of Part II's focus upon the essential continuity between the flows of the urban city and the communicational flows of the cyberspatial Matrix.

Both Kracauer's and Benjamin's analyses of the significance of the photographic image highlight the way in which the radically new visual perspectives afforded by the technical conditions of the medium are commensurate with a transformation of individual and collective perspectives, such that: 'modern photography has not only considerably enlarged our vision but, in doing so, *adjusted it to man's situation in a technological age'* (ibid.: 9 [our emphasis]). Here, Kracauer identifies the crucial manner in which photography *aligns* human perception with the ambient technological system, and this alignment implicitly involves (to adopt Heidegger's terminology) a *withdrawal* from, or forgetting of, earlier modes of perception. In Benjamin we find a more developed account of this thesis. Thus, he notes how 'the manner in which human sense perception is organised, the medium in which it is accomplished, is determined not only by nature but by historical circumstance . . .' (Benjamin 1973 [1935]: 224). The apperception inaugurated by the new technologies was one based on the 'universal equivalence of things', a commutability that is identical to that of the commodity. Media technologies are devices of inculcation; they prepare the sensorium for the environment of technological capitalism:

> Film serves to train humans in those new apperceptions and reactions conditioned by their interaction with an apparatus whose role in their lives increases daily. To make the human [enervation] to the monstrous technological apparatus of our time is the historical vocation in which film has its true meaning.
>
> (Benjamin cited in Caygill 1998: 107
> [Caygill's parentheses])

In identifying this process, Kracauer and Benjamin could be said to provide an example of the way in which media technologies realize Heidegger's Danger. Photography and film serve to align their users into an environment which, as we shall see in Part II, is itself aligned with the commodity form: the mechanical reproduction of images results in a enframement of interiority that parallels the conversion of the external world into a standing reserve brought about by technology.

This change of perspective brought about by technological media affects our perception of things. No longer are immediate-sense data the measure of the phenomenal; instead, those dimensions revealed by Benjamin's 'optical unconscious' become increasingly integrated into our perception of what things are. To quote Kracauer:

> we are moving about with the greatest of ease and incomparable speed so that stable impressions yield to ever-changing ones: bird's-eye views of terrestrial landscapes have become quite common; not one single object has retained a fixed, definitely recognizable appearance.
>
> (Kracauer 1965: 9)

This transformation finds its echo in the way that traditional value systems are themselves fragmented or dissembled within the context of technological capitalism:

Given to analysis, we pass in review, and break into comparable elements, all the complex value systems that have come to us in the form of beliefs, ideas or cultures, thereby of course weakening their claims to absoluteness.

(ibid.: 9)

Here again, the key elements of Kracauer's and Benjamin's analyses converge, with the latter providing a similar account of the media's potential to undermine traditional views when he describes how, freed by mechanical reproduction from the limits of tradition, the masses confront the social world with renewed vigour:

Thus, for contemporary man the representation of reality by the film is incomparably more significant than that of the painter, since it offers, precisely because of the thoroughgoing permeation of reality with mechanical equipment, an aspect of reality which is free of all equipment . . . Mechanical reproduction of art changes the reaction of the masses towards art. The reactionary attitude towards a Picasso painting changes into the progressive reaction towards a Chaplin movie.

(Benjamin 1973 [1935]: 236)

For Benjamin, the disjuncture that photography and film bring to traditional ways of seeing – their 'thematization'– to use Kittler's terminology, has great socialist potential. In his 'Work of Art' essay he argues that this potential resides in the way it brings previously rarefied art forms either directly into the view of the masses, in the case of cinema, or literally into their hands, in the case of photographically illustrated magazines and newspapers. The fact that commonplace activities could, for the first time, be analysed in the minute visual detail afforded by the *optical unconscious* was thus enhanced by the mass reception of this technologically induced decline of aura, creating nothing less than a culturally aligned, historically new way of seeing. For his part, Kracauer argues that the camera's novel ability to record reality in objective fragments was well adapted to, first, a cultural atmosphere that valued scientific proofs and images and, second, as we shall explore below, a social environment of emergent industrial capitalism:

Photography was born under a lucky star in as much as it appeared at a time when the ground was well prepared for it. The insight into the recording and revealing functions of this 'mirror with a memory' – its inherent realistic tendency, that is – owed much to the vigor with which the forces of realism bore down on the romantic movement of the period. In nineteenth-century France the rise of photography coincided with the spread of positivism – an intellectual attitude rather than a philosophical school which, shared by many thinkers, discouraged metaphysical speculation in favor of a scientific approach, and thus was in perfect keeping with the ongoing process of industrialization.

(Kracauer 1965: 5)

The practical means of mass producing images were readily provided by this 'ongoing process' but, at a cultural level, another crucial factor in the alignment of the technical and social was that new technological means of seeing were increasingly conceived as veritable signs of scientific truth. This was an important development in so far as it helped to prepare the public psychologically to perceive as more and more natural the notion of an objective scientific realm whose truth was set apart from the conditions of immediate perception. The advent of the *optical unconscious* thus played a key role in encouraging the viewing public to accept a 'purer' form of reality lying behind the surface of things. This has implications far beyond the public's growing tendency to believe the objectivity of scientific facts. It also primes a culture for the unproblematic acceptance of the otherwise deeply artificial withdrawal from reality represented by the matrix of media technologies in general and the Matrix of digital matters in particular.

Photography's transparent truth

> ... there is a singular and determining 'way of seeing' within modern Western culture ... the dramatic confluence of an empirical philosophical tradition, a realist aesthetic, a positivist attitude towards knowledge and a technoscientistic ideology through modernity have led to a common-sense cultural attitude of literal depiction in relation to vision ... Visual symbolism, the primary form of symbolism within the culture, is dispossessed of its iconographic, or metaphoric, role and routinely understood as 'correspondence'. Everyday members of the culture are consequently effectively deskilled in their capacities as interpretive beings.
>
> (Jenks 1995: 14)

The notion that 'everyday members of the culture' are divested of the interpretive abilities associated with an earlier symbolic economy means that they are readily enframed by Baudrillard's 'disenchanted universe of the signified'. In this disenchanted universe of technologically mediated withdrawal, the meaning of the technological experience becomes its lack of deeper meaning: 'Photography ... reduces the world to objectively described surfaces with no inherent meaning: to facts. It sees only what is there – not values nor supernatural entities' (Slater 1995: 223). This is the reason for the apparent madness or stupidity of Calvino's photographers or Delillo's barn browsers – the photograph becomes its tautological self-justification. As a result of the combined effect of the qualitatively new way of seeing afforded by the optical unconscious and the quantitative increase in the number of readily available images, the status of the photograph as merely a sign or representation that mediates between the viewer and reality (as would be true of previous representational forms) is no longer as unproblematic as the myth that the camera never lies would have us believe. Its 'merely' representative role is paradoxically complexified by the accuracy and realism with which the photograph depicts reality. The camera introduces a 'super-reality', which as it grows in its dominance comes to supplant what it records: the representative exceeds the represented, the sign the signified or the medium its message. In the case of photography, this happens almost unconsciously, so that we forget the distinction between these two spheres:

> . . . any form of writing is necessarily derivative, a second order representa-
> tion, the sign of a sign. Nevertheless, at its inception the camera largely
> avoided this stigma, and was instead acclaimed as vision without mediation,
> *a medium in which the signifier effaced itself before the force of the signified.* (. . .
> When we look at photographs, we tend not to see them as 'signs', but to see
> only their 'referents'.)
>
> (McQuire 1998: 30 [our emphasis])

This can be taken as particularly powerful instantiation of Heidegger's Danger, that of the forgetting of the withdrawal of Being.

It could be said that the transparency of photography's involvement in the depiction of reality serves to further underline a historical cultural trend within the West that equates visual evidence with a true reality that needs no additional interpretation: the self-evident realism of the content being presented to us precludes self-reflexive, critical consideration of its format. We have argued that a major contribution that photography makes to this process is the way it confuses the sharp distinctions that traditionally existed between the signifier and the signified. Baudrillard's 'disenchanted universe of the signified' takes over from 'the unbreakable reciprocity of social bonds'. This is a crucial moment in the history of the media because it marks the most significant stage in the creation of a realm of images largely freed from their traditional cultural moorings. Benjamin claimed that the freeing of the reproduced object from its previous auratic context constituted a powerful force that undermines tradition. A closer look at his description of the qualities that precipitate this process, however, reveals the disorientating nature of this media-sponsored withdrawal from reality:

> Many of the deformations and stereotypes, the transformations and catas-
> trophes that the world can find in the visual perception in films can also be
> found in psychoses, hallucinations and dreams. And in this way the proce-
> dures and techniques of the camera have claimed for the collective percep-
> tion of the public the individual perceptions of the psychotic or dreamer.
>
> (Benjamin [1935] cited in Caygill 1998: 113)

The universe of the signified may be disenchanted in terms of traditional symbols but, as we see in Part II, we *immerse* ourselves in the manufactured enchantment of commodities that offer themselves as a replacement. We do not have the space in this book to do the theme justice but, in this context Benjamin's exposure of the positive political potential of photography's aura-shattering qualities sits uneasily with the rest of his work's focus – e.g. in his unfinished *Arcades Project* (1999) – upon the phantasmagoric forms assumed by the urban commodity form. It is more consonant, however, with McLuhan's description of the narcotic effects of the media and the Narcissus-like trance they induce and, in particular, with Lash's (2002) identification of McLuhan as important for a full understanding of the new digital order and its unprecedented immanence.

Despite this recognition of the ease with which film readily lends itself to relatively unstructured, impressionistic visual stimuli, Benjamin does not develop the implications of the implicit 'psychosis' of the new collective perception that film inaugurates, preferring to dwell instead on the emancipatory potential of reproductive media. In contrast, Kracauer uses the example of glossy magazines to describe witheringly the cultural consequences of the glut of images that photography brings in its train:

> In the hands of the ruling society, the invention of illustrated magazines is one of the most powerful means of organizing a strike against understanding. Even the colorful arrangement of the images provides a not insignificant means for successfully implementing such a strike. The *contiguity* of these images systematically excludes their contextual framework available to consciousness. The 'image-idea' drives away the idea. The blizzard of photographs betrays an indifference toward what the things mean.
>
> (Kracauer 1995 [1963]: 58 [emphasis in original])

The difference in these interpretations of the decline in aura's implications for the power of the masses is marked. The socialist potential Benjamin hoped for is missing in Kracauer. This is not only because of the quantity, or 'blizzard', of images but also because of the way in which their decontextualized presentation tends to preclude their conceptual interrogation. The resulting 'strike against understanding' takes place as a result of the closely related quantitative and qualitative aspects of the new mechanically reproduced image:

1   the increased quantity of images; and
2   the specific nature of the photographic image.

The increased quantity of images

> This very passivity – and ubiquity – of the photographic record is photography's 'message', its aggression . . . There is an aggression implicit in every use of the camera . . . technology made possible an ever increasing spread of that mentality which looks at the world as a set of potential photographs . . . the subsequent industrialization of camera technology only carried out a promise inherent in photography from its very beginning: to democratize all experiences by translating them into images.
>
> (Sontag 1979: 7)

Sontag's analysis here echoes the pessimism of Kracauer: the democratization she speaks of is an aggressive levelling of particularity, an erosion of difference in favour of the equivalence of the image rather than the socialist potential that Benjamin saw in the medium. The danger she identifies has its origin in the incipient banalization that occurs when every aspect of reality represents a potential photo-opportunity *à la* Calvino. Above and beyond the particular qualities of taking and appreciating photographs, the very possibility of being able to take photographs in the first place has an unacknowledged power and significance, what Sontag's calls the 'aggression' of photography. Benjamin readily praised the way in which cameras undermine the traditional hierarchies of artistic production. But Sontag, writing in the wake of this democratization, notes that 'the modernist revolt against traditional aesthetic norms' (a crucial source of Benjamin's optimistic prognosis) is 'deeply implicated in the promotion of kitsch standards of taste' (ibid.: 81). While Benjamin could find cause for celebration in the nascent conditions of what was to become the 'high' versus 'low' culture debate, Sontag writes with an awareness of the true consequences of the superficial democracy of the photographic image, namely its erosion of aesthetic value. The basis of this harmful nature and its inextricable link with the media is articulated in Rojek's description of the operations of kitsch culture, wherein:

> the conventions of normative order are established by the operations of manufactured novelties and planned sensations orchestrated by the mass-media. In setting the constructed nature of cultural identity and interaction as an *a priori* of normative public encounters, kitsch culture tacitly denies reality.
>
> (Rojek 2001: 23)

From this perspective, not only do the media mediate our perception of direct reality, but they also serve to pervade previously unmediated social interactions with the synthetic, simulated values of media consumption that culminate in the decontextualized (in Feenberg's terms) Matrix where the representation of reality is translated into a self-contained environment premised upon binary impulses.

Where Benjamin tends to pass over the deeper social implications of the public consuming media images in a state of distraction, Sontag attempts to tackle directly an important ambivalence concealed in the apparent democracy of media reproducibility. *A la* McLuhan, she argues that the importance of a medium's form tends to be overlooked in favour of its ultimately less significant but superficially most obvious content, suggesting that photography manages to hide the true import of its democratizing influence by flattering the viewer into believing that he or she has 'a connoisseur's relation *to* the world' whilst all the time encouraging 'a promiscuous acceptance *of* the world' (Sontag 1979: 81 [emphasis in original]). The cultural consequence of this indiscriminate acceptance is illustrated in the apparently unironic comparison drawn by the photographer Edward Weston between ancient Greek marble sculptures and the porcelain of a toilet bowl:

I have been photographing our toilet, that glossy enamelled receptacle of extraordinary beauty . . . Here was every sensuous curve of the 'human figure divine' but minus the imperfections. Never did the Greeks reach a more significant consummation to their culture, and it somehow reminded me, forward movement of finely progressing contours, of the victory of Samothrace.

(cited in Sontag 1979: 193)

Here we see the 'sense of the universal equality of things' that Benjamin spoke of raised to its highest power and, as in his own analysis of photography, there are some seeds of doubt regarding the ultimate cultural effects of a proliferation of images.

The camera's way of seeing – the origins of *Chokerlebnis* (shock effect)

Insofar as photography does peel away the dry wrappers of habitual see-ing, it creates another habit of seeing: both intense and cool, solicitous and detached; charmed by the insignificant detail, addicted to incongruity. But photographic seeing has to be constantly renewed with new shocks, whether of subject matter or technique, so as to produce the impression of violating ordinary vision. For challenged by the revelations of photographers, seeing tends to accommodate to photographs.

(Sontag 1979)

The new perspective that photography brings us irrevocably changes our previous perceptual approaches. One way in which this occurs is through photography's tendency to privilege contingent and superficial details. In *Camera Lucida,* Roland Barthes (1993 [1982]) uses the terms 'studium' and 'punctum' to describe the particular perceptual and emotional effects of individual photographs. The studium refers to the general cultural context with which one approaches a photograph. Thus, in a photograph that is about war, the viewer comes with a stock of previous visual and non-visual knowledge about the concept of war with which the photograph in question will interact to create an 'average' effect. The individual features of the photograph's content, such as gestures, faces and actions, are experienced as part of a wider cultural environment of which the viewer is a member. The punctum, meanwhile, is the quality of a photograph that breaks through the studium:

it is this element which rises from the scene, shoots out of it like an arrow, and pierces me . . . *punctum* is . . . sting, speck, cut, little hole . . . A photo-graph's punctum is that accident which pricks me (but also bruises me, is poignant to me).

(ibid.: 26–7 [emphasis in original])

The relative strength of the punctum over the studium means that, for some commentators: 'photography is a language that speaks only in particularities. Its vocabulary of images is limited to concrete representation' (Postman 1987: 73). The presentation of mechanically reproduced images is, therefore, fundamentally predicated upon a value of fragmentation that promotes the continual consumption of more and more images rather than the development of an understanding of their conceptual significance. This repetitive re-presenting of images, which in their turn are based upon a technology of continuous representation, produces a seemingly endless chain of decontextualized images conducive to the state of distraction that Benjamin noted. This is because a distracted state is most readily achieved if attention has to be focused upon the fresh particularities of each new image rather than the more concentrated and rigorous mental processes required to contemplate the linkages and relationships between the various contexts of the images being presented. Furthermore, in keeping with McLuhan's argument that each particular technology has its own internal grammar or particular task-specific suitability, photography's innate tendency to present the particular means that it is inherently unsuited for the communication of generalizable, abstract concepts. Both the perceptual mode of distraction and the epistemological 'strike against understanding' result from this innate photographic emphasis upon aesthetics over abstract categories of thought – in a similar vein, McLuhan (1995 [1964]) points out that smoke signals are a poor medium for philosophical debates.

This marks an important example of the various forms of the society–technology dialectic (Williams's concept of determination etc.) that we encountered in this book's Introduction. It accounts for the media's role in the creation of a mass body of consumers. We examine in detail in Part II how contemplation is replaced by immersion in flows that appear, first, as the rapidly circulating people and vehicles that overwhelm the *flâneur* and, second, as the closely imbricated flows of images and commodities within those urban settings. Kracauer again uses illustrated magazines to emphasize the profound effect of the camera's way of seeing in a way that illuminates Innis's previously cited use of media bias as a way of approaching the complex issue of 'why we attend to the things which we attend'. Both Kracauer and McQuire highlight the camera's ability to affect society's cultural orientation and values through the redefinition of not only the nature of our experience of reality but our processes of understanding that experience:

> . . . people see the very world that the illustrated magazines prevent them from perceiving. The spatial continuum from the camera's perspective dominates the spatial appearance of the perceived object; the resemblance between the image and the object effaces the contours of the object's 'history'. Never before has a period known so little about itself.
>
> (Kracauer 1995 [1963]: 58)

There is a certain irony in the fact that the original role of the camera as a purveyor of scientific truth has given way to its contemporary role as a key technical element of a cultural alignment with commodity values and their privileging of the emotional over the rational. To this extent, Jenks's previously mentioned claim that the average person is now deskilled as an interpretive being needs reconsidering. The previous close association of media images with scientific truth has been largely replaced by a new correspondence between images and a limited range of predominantly preconfigured meanings. The viewer can interpret, but not in an open-ended way. Meaningful interpretation is in fact paradoxically stymied by the plenitude of visual information, and this is the import of Kracauer's claim that in the illustrated magazines, 'people see the very world that the illustrated magazines prevent them from perceiving'. Whether the viewer is responding to advertisements or the news, images are designed to have close associations with the preferred meanings that result from the conflation of image-based commodity values and the dominant media that replicate those values in their very functioning. We now turn to the claim that these processes create a 'society of spectacle' that is historically significant for the degree to which it is self-contained and self-referential but, as Kracauer argues, ultimately lacking in self-knowledge and fatally prone to withdrawal.

The culture of spectacle

> If the printed book was one of the first serial objects of a nascent capitalism, the photograph corresponds to the maturing logic of commodity production in a world remade by machines. As social life has increasingly been defined by mass production and the rapid circulation of identical objects, photography stands as the very sign of the industrial proliferation of signs.
>
> (McQuire 1998: 49)

Photography played a crucial part in a process of cultural alignment whereby its technical properties were allied with the commodity values of capitalism in a mutually reinforcing relationship to produce the 'industrialization of vision'. The abstracting and decontextualizing qualities of media technologies such as the telegraph and photograph closely matched the social abstractions inherent in the economic realm of commodity production. The case of microphotography provides an interesting early illustration of the way in which the original cultural alignment between mechanically reproduced images and scientific values contained within it the seeds of the eventual dominance and replacement of the latter by the values of commerce. Microphotographs, as the name implies, were photographs that had been reduced to a tiny size so that they could be re-viewed only under a microscope. Maria Benjamin describes how they became an essential part of a Victorian gentleman's study and, although they were frequently marketed under the guise of a useful insight into natural history (microphotographs included such images as pictures of a fly's leg calibrated next to a minute ruler):

> Microphotographs were tailor-made for the 'greedy eyes' that feasted on the culture of spectacle. Like the consumer of stereoscope or lantern slides, an observer could within a matter of minutes, gallop through a succession of images, from a photograph of a Landseer, the moon, the Great Pyramid at Giza, the frontispiece of the *Illustrated London News*, to a portrait of Garibaldi, obtaining *a flow of visual stimulation* more or less on tap.
>
> (M. Benjamin 1996: 117 [our emphasis])

As with more conventional photographs, microphotography as a technology was aligned with the concept of readily accessible consumption, with the single most significant aspect of that consumption being its decontextualized nature. It is the combined effect of this decontextualization allied to the speed and continuity of the supply of images that produces what Maria Benjamin terms 'the culture of spectacle' and which we will soon examine in terms of Debord's phrase 'the society of spectacle'.

Owing to a combination of the increased realism afforded by mechanical reproduction and the ubiquity of the images the process subsequently produces, these images are now freed from their previous dependence upon an original or authentic site. This is a landmark point in the history of media because it represents the beginnings of the hyperreal move away from a specific physical context and the emergence of an independent, self-referential and abstract world of media – thus, 'the microphotographic observer could summon whole worlds into being from nothing' (ibid.: 117). The meaning of images becomes less important than the fact that there is a steady supply of images to be viewed by 'greedy eyes'. The effort of microphotographs was greatly facilitated by the fact that the wider Victorian culture within which it evolved was already becoming accustomed to a large increase in the quantity of images to which it was exposed. In addition to this simple increase in quantity, such images were often presented in a manner that downplayed the significance of their particular context or meaning. Microphotography can be seen as a historical example of Sontag and Jenks's above claims that people become increasingly deskilled as interpretive beings in a visually dominated society. This occurs as a complex mix of technological and ideological factors. The alignment that began to take place between the new quantitative increase in images as a result of their mechanical reproduction and an accompanying cultural atmosphere that encourages the viewing of images and objects divorced from meaningful surroundings reinforced interpretative deskilling in the Victorian practice of microphotography.

The most overt embodiment of this process of cultural alignment was the visual exhibitionism of the Crystal Palace erected in London in 1851. Making use of the new modes of industrial production, the Crystal Palace was a huge glass and steel construction used to display, in the most architecturally transparent manner possible, visual signs of the life gathered under the rubric of Empire.

Exhibits were for the *consumption* of the viewing public and disconnected from any coherent narrative beyond their inclusivity within the overarching concept of the Empire. In microcosm, so to speak, microphotography fulfilled a similar function so that, alongside slides illustrating aspects of natural history, the 'drawing-room scientist' began to obtain access to a large number of slides with no particular meaning. Images of famous landmarks around the Empire competed for attention with technically novel pictures made up of, for example, a large collage of different people's faces all brought together on a minuscule laboratory slide. In their vastly different scales, microphotography and the Crystal Palace both provide early insights into the processes behind media's relativizing impact upon knowledge. In addition, they both illustrate the state of distraction that describes the manner in which their contents were consumed as early precursors of the now largely seamless contemporary link between media and commodity consumption.

The society of the spectacle

> In societies where modern conditions of production prevail, all of life presents itself as an immense accumulation of spectacles. Everything that was directly lived has moved away into a representation.
>
> (Debord 1983: note 1 [emphasis in original])

> A capitalist society requires a culture based on images. It needs to furnish vast amounts of entertainment in order to stimulate buying and anesthetize the injuries of class, race, and sex . . . The production of images also furnishes a ruling ideology. Social change is replaced by a change in images. The freedom to consume a plurality of images and goods is equated with freedom itself. The narrowing of free political choice to free economic consumption requires the unlimited production and consumption of images.
>
> (Sontag 1979: 178–9)

As both Debord and Sontag point out above, the inherently amenable nature of photography to both consumption and production means that it becomes an integral technology to the story of capitalism's development and, as we shall see in more detail in Part II, the privileging of circulation and flows for their own sake. The 'society of the spectacle' is the phrase used by Debord in an attempt to describe this qualitatively new importance to society of images rather than just physical objects. From Debord's perspective, the defining feature of capitalist society's environment has evolved from Marx's strongly materialist emphasis upon the physical production of commodities to the growing centrality of autonomous images. Despite his work's developmental departure from Marx, Debord's intellectual debt remains evident from the opening paragraphs of *The Society of the Spectacle*, in which he reformulates Marx's observation that, with the commodity form, relations between objects become social and, conversely, social relations become objectified:

The spectacle in general, as the concrete inversion of life, is the autonomous movement of the non-living . . . The spectacle is not a collection of images, but a social relation among people, mediated by images.

(Debord 1983: notes 2 and 4)

Marx documented the inherent alienation of the worker's productive efforts, but Debord argues that such alienation has moved on apace:

The first phase of the domination of the economy over social life brought into the definition of all human realization the obvious degradation of being into having. The present phase of total occupation of social life by the accumulated results of the economy leads to a generalized sliding of having into appearing . . .

(ibid.: note 17)

Debord's analysis suggests that the culture of the spectacle signifies a twofold further exacerbation of pre-existing capitalist commodity-induced alienation and abstraction. The advent of commodities introduced a hitherto unknown level of abstraction because they replaced the use-value of objects with an exchange-value derived not from their individual qualities or the haggling motivations of physical buyer and sellers but from a price determined by a deterritorialized market system. The society of the spectacle represents a significant further expansion of an essential paradox of capitalism. Social life is increasingly dominated by largely intangible processes (e.g. exchange-value) that nevertheless have very real, practical effects: 'the abstraction of all specific labor and the general abstraction of the entirety of production are perfectly rendered in the spectacle, whose *mode of being concrete* is precisely abstraction' (ibid.: note 29 [emphasis in original]). The full social implication of spectacular culture is thus that the individual's relationship with commodities and other people is mediated to a qualitatively greater extent than even Marx had previously identified in his, at the time, iconoclastic analysis of exchange-value. The paradox of this new finding is that it continues the circumscribing and inhibiting power of the market, but such power is even more difficult to spot due to its immaterial nature.

Again, within Benjamin – despite his superficially optimistic agenda – lies the beginning of an interesting perspective upon the inextricable cultural alignment between mass society and the media and the origins of the Matrix within the media matrix. Before the term 'mass media' became commonplace, Benjamin drew attention to the way in which the aura-stripping qualities that accompany technologies of mass reproduction create a social sensibility that, in a type of virtuous circle, encourages their further adoption so that 'Every day the need to possess the object in close-up in the form of a picture, or rather a copy, becomes more imperative' (Benjamin 1985: 250 [emphasis in original]). The destruction of aura thus creates new perceptual formats that simultaneously both create and further foster new social attitudes acclimatized to a reduction in the specificity and uniqueness of objects so that:

> . . . the difference between the copy, which illustrated papers and newsreels keep in readiness, and the picture is unmistakable. Uniqueness and duration are as intimately conjoined in the latter as are transience and reproducibility in the former. The stripping bare of the object, the destruction of the aura, is the mark of perception whose sense of the sameness of things has grown to the point where even the singular, the unique is divested of its uniqueness – by means of its reproduction.
>
> (ibid.: 250)

The above 'sense of the sameness of things' initiated by new forms of technological reproduction provides the necessary conditions for the development of a social matrix of homogeneity that complements the abstract market mechanism. Technologies such as photography reinforce such abstract equality by reducing, as Sontag described earlier, disparate objects to the same status as collectible images.

Benjamin identified this trend towards the culturally aligned production of abstraction early in its historical process and, although the main focus of his 'Work of Art' essay is upon the decline in aura brought about by mechanical reproduction and mostly in terms of its perceptual implications for art vis-à-vis photography, beyond this, he saw that it had much more substantive implications for society as a whole. For Benjamin, the advent of photography heralded an important reorientation of our conceptualization of such fundamental concepts as society itself, due to the constitution of a social mass enabled and empowered in new ways by the technologies of mechanical reproduction:

> Thus is manifested in the field of perception what in the theoretical sphere is noticeable in the increasing importance of statistics. The adjustment of reality to the masses and of the masses to reality is a process of unlimited scope, as much for thinking as for perception.
>
> (ibid.: 225)

He proceeds to express himself in terms that leave little doubt as to the paradigmatic nature of these fundamental implications whereby the quantitative increase in perceptual activity ushered in by the camera has produced qualitative social change:

> The mass is a matrix from which all traditional behaviour toward works of art issues today in a new form. Quantity has been transmuted into quality. The greatly increased mass of participants has produced a change in the mode of participation.
>
> (ibid.: 241)

It is in the context of this blurring between quantity and quality that the ideal conditions for both the production and consumption of images and commodity objects (and the increasing conflation of the two) are created. This is the underpinning of the most sophisticatedly intangible mass capitalist commodity form: the brand in its media matrix home.

Sontag concisely summarizes the long-drawn-out but profound contribution photography has made to the cultural alignment of the modern mediascape and late capitalism. She describes how the true epistemological significance of photography resides in the way it laid the groundwork for our contemporary situation in which rationality and concept-driven knowledge has been replaced by image-based, aesthetic values of consumption: 'Photographs document sequences of consumption' (Sontag 1979: 9). She argues that an essential property of photography is its ability to isolate what would otherwise be continuous real-time experience into isolated images for aesthetic appreciation:

> Whatever the moral claims made on behalf of photography, its main effect is to convert the world into a department store or museum-without-walls in which every subject is depreciated into an article of consumption, promoted into an item for aesthetic appreciation.
>
> (ibid.: 110)

The significance of this development is more than merely aesthetic. It is thus no coincidence that Benjamin's *oeuvre* included alongside his analysis of photography an examination of the rise of department stores and their photography-like isolation of commodities for the better viewing of the consumer. The crucial importance of photography in a capitalist context, therefore, is this alignment between the decontextualized visual image for aesthetic appreciation and the similarly decontextualized commodity object shorn of its use-value, which is replaced by its new, inherently abstract and ultimately aesthetic exchange-value. We see this in Benjamin's account of how the movie camera creates conditions directly analogous to the factory floor. Owing to the heavily technological nature of the filming process in which 'The equipment-free aspect of reality . . . has become the height of artifice; the sight of immediate reality has become an orchid in the land of technology' (Benjamin 1973 [1935]: 235), the actor is alienated from the effects of his own performance to such an extent that: 'During the shooting he has as little contact with it as any article made in a factory' (ibid.: 233). Both this commodity quality in production and the previous account of photography's commodity-like consumption result from the inherently fragmentary effect of the representational processes involved in camera technologies, which align neatly with commercial values that tend to promote the presentation of form over content.

Conclusion: the digital or discrete image

The knowledge gained through still photographs will always be some kind of sentimentalism, whether cynical or humanist. It will be knowledge at

bargain prices – a semblance of knowledge, a semblance of wisdom . . .
Needing to have reality confirmed and experience enhanced by photographs
is an aesthetic consumerism to which everyone is now addicted. Industrial
societies turn their citizens into image junkies; it is the most irresistible
form of mental pollution.

(Sontag 1979: 24)

Thus far, we have discussed the nature of photography as a medium and the crucial
role it plays in a process of cultural alignment that brings about a convergence
of the capitalist consumption, subjective perception and technology, in the
service of an overarching matrix. In this capacity, photography has served as the
primary example of the way in which the kind of theories we have addressed
in previous chapters can be seen to operate at the level of specific media. In
other words, it has provided an extended example of the manner in which
withdrawal, *la téchnique*, discourse networks, etc. are realized in the context of
media technologies. Implicit in this account is the way in which earlier networks
or matrices prepare the ground for the current digital matrix – what we have
described, following Kittler, as Network 2000. Although photography is one of
the precursors of Network 1900 and its trinity of ur-media (gramophone, film,
typewriter), it still plays a significant role in the new network: it is an integral
component of digital matters, as the endless recirculation of digital images on
the net demonstrates. But how does the general convergence of media in digital
matters affect the photograph? Do the qualities that led to both its supposed
democratic potential and, conversely, the threat it posed to cultural values
remain when the photographic medium, like all previous media, is absorbed in
the digital über-medium? In order to answer these questions, and to prepare the
ground for the discussion of the digital matrix of flows in Part II, we shall by way
of a conclusion briefly examine the French philosopher of technology Bernard
Stiegler's analysis of the digital image.

The digital image, or what Stiegler terms the analogical–digital image (in
order to distinguish it from the 'pure' digital image or common gateway interface), has its origin in what he terms 'a systematic discretization of movement'
(Stiegler 1996: 153–74). As we have seen, for Barthes, the photographic image
consisted of two moments (punctum and studium) and in itself was marked
by a particular relation to the real, namely that it inherently embodied what he
called the 'this was' (*le ça a été*) – that is to say, the certainty that every photograph
enjoys an unbreakable relation with a particular instance. We have seen that this
dimension of the photographic image was precisely the one that facilitated its
role in the creation of pervasive media network, such that the order of simulation
was bankrolled by the objectivity of the photographic image. The photograph,
understood in these terms, as what Kracauer termed 'a mirror with memory', is
what defines it as 'analogical'. Like Kittler's discussion of the phonographic as an
analogical transposition of the 'real', the photographic is an analogical transposition of a particular moment, a specific constellation of light. This constellation
remains constant despite the photographic image's infinite reproducibility.

Stiegler, drawing on Barthes, calls this its *spectrum*: the photograph is a spectre, a haunting, a ghost of a moment past, and this spectral substance is the spectrum. It is produced by 'touch', a virtual chain – or, in Stiegler's beautiful phrase, 'a *contiguity of luminances*' – that connects the light that touched the subject with the light that touched the film and the light that touches the eye of the viewer. It is this touch from the past that constitutes the photograph as a haunting:

> these people live again . . . as intensely as when their images were captured on the old dry plates of sixty years ago . . . I am standing in their rooms . . . And they in turn seem to be aware of me.
>
> (Ansell Adams cited in Sontag 1979: 202)

The spectre is dependent on the inalterability of the image (this is not to say that analogical photos cannot be altered, but that manipulation is secondary or after the fact). As Barthes says:

> What does the photograph transmit? By definition the scene itself, the literal reality. From the object to its image there is of course a reduction . . . but at no time is this reduction a transformation (in the mathematical sense of the term). In order to move from the reality to its photograph it is in no way necessary to divide up this reality into units: it is a message without a code; from which an important corollary must be immediately be drawn: the photographic message is a continuous message.
>
> (Barthes 1993 [1982]: 196)

It is this continuity that the digital image disrupts, precisely because it inserts digital code where there was contiguity. Instead of an unbroken chain we have a passage through digital matter, 0 and 1, and this introduces a fundamental manipulability into the image. This manipulation differs from that of the analogical image, because it is inseparable from the production of the image itself. This transformation of the image results in a range of new possibilities such as the instantiated in programs like Photoshop; it allows digital images to indexed and searchable, subject to a myriad of algorithmic manipulations, but at the loss of the characteristics that empowered its analogical predecessor. In Part II we shall see how this transformation of the photograph reflects a wider transformation of the m/Matrix, and partakes of the im/materiality we have spoken of. We shall see that this passage from the analogical to the digital is reflection of what Baudrillard defines as the four orders of simulation, in particular the final stage of simulation, which Baudrillard terms the 'fractal'. Moreover, we will see how a range of progressive movements attempt to harness the manipulability of code for aims other than those of the logic of capital.

Part II

Living in the digital matrix: the cultural perspective

5   Urban matrix matters

In this chapter and in Part II as a whole, we build upon Part I's analysis of technological enframement to explore how the abstract perception of technology's apparent autonomy is, in late capitalism, deeply imbricated within the material commodity form. The fantastical properties Marx saw in commodities, Benjamin developed in explorations of both the 'phantasmagoria' of mid-nineteenth-century Paris and the 'lucid dreaming' of the newly emergent cinema. These fantastical properties are now increasingly aligned with the physical world as the commodification of our social environment merges ever more seamlessly with its media representation. In this context, *digital matters* relates to the crucial role digitality plays in promoting a new form of Georg Lukács's (1968 [1922]) concept of *reification*. New commodity forms assume an increasingly informatic appearance that is simultaneously material and immaterial: at once both static elements in our physical environment and in motion or flux (e.g. the spread of franchised stores and logos). We thus build upon Kittler's identification of the city as an information processor to show that a crucial dimension of the digital is its ability to change whole environments into areas ripe for informationalization so that key Marxist notions such as the reversal of relations between people and objects, commodity fetishism, etc. breach ever new thresholds.

Demonstrating how the enframing power of the matrix manifests itself in a seamless web of built environment and media immersion allows us to understand what is indicated by the seemingly oxymoronic term *digital matters*. It provides the reader with a better context with which to approach the matrix that has been dominated by conceptions of the Matrix. Like Ellul, we privilege the Industrial Revolution as the critical threshold in the production of the matrix and its cultural alignment of technology and commodification. We emphasize the manner in which a change in the pace and scale of media technologies is reflected in a commensurate alteration of the urban experience, and add to Ellul's insights by privileging more the role of capitalism and the unifying role it plays in these phenomena. Taking McLuhan and Kittler's identification of the city as an extended informational environment within which human beings operate, we explore the fusion that has taken place between the internal and external worlds of the urban consumer. We develop McLuhan's contention that the city 'translates' people into a more suitable form, and argue that the purpose of this translation is the production of ideal consumers for an environment character-ized by mobility and distraction. The fact that the manufacture of this subjectiv-ity is environmentally determined, rather than the product of individual choice, offers a confirmation of the themes of determinism, *la téchnique* and enframe-ment explored in the earlier chapters. Thus, from a Heideggerian perspective, the city constitutes an environment within which withdrawal from withdrawal is naturalized and urbanity creates a standing reserve of commodities while, from a Kittlerian position, the city represents a macro-processor which lays the groundwork for the naturalization of digital matters.

The city as a medium

> Media can include old-fashioned things such as books, familiar things such as the city and newer inventions such as the computer. It was von Neumann's computer architecture that technically implemented this defi-nition for the first time in history (or as its end). A microprocessor contains a processor, the memory and buses, not just in addition to something else, but exclusively. The processor carries out logical or arithmetical commands, according to the parameters set up in the memory: the buses transmit com-mands, addresses and data based on the parameters of the processor and its most recent command; the memory ultimately makes it possible to read commands or data at precise addresses or to encode them. This network of processing, transmission, and recording, or restating of commands, addresses, and data, can calculate everything (based on Turing's famous proof from 1936) that is calculable. The development of technologic media – from digital transmission media, like the telegraph, to analogue recording media, like gramophone and film, and to the media for their transmission, radio and television – comes logically full circle. Other media can, likewise, be transferred to the discrete universal machine. And this is reason enough to bring together the workings of the city with concepts from general infor-mation science. Reason enough, moreover, to decipher past media and the historical function of what we refer to as 'man' as the play between com-mands, addresses, and data.
>
> (Kittler 1996: 721)

Something of the totalizing nature of Kittler's vision can be appreciated through a marginal text 'The City is a Medium' (Kittler 1996). Here, Kittler's addresses urbanization not as a historical, economic, architectural or social phenomenon, but as an information system. Cities are macroprocessors composed of intersecting networks, and:

> Regardless of whether these networks transmit information (telephone, radio, television) or energy (water supply, electricity, highway) they all rep-

resent forms of information. (If only because every modern energy flow requires a parallel control network.)

(ibid.: 718)

From this perspective the city is to be approached not as a substantive entity, a thing in itself, but as an intersection, a nexus of flows. The city 'exists only as a function of circulation, and of circuits . . . it is defined by entries and exits . . . It is a . . . *network*' (Deleuze and Guattari 1988: 432 [emphasis in original]). It is the site of circulation and exchange, and emerges in relation to these activities; hence the earliest media (money and the alphabet) have their origin in the city (Kittler 1996: 720). Kittler's understanding of what constitutes media – and thus what permits a description of the city as a medium – is unambiguous. Media are means by which data can be stored, transmitted and processed: media consist of commands, addresses and data. Cities, as spaces of flows, as nodes, are sites in which these functions are performed – thus they are computers, the latter for Kittler constituting the final or ultimate medium.

The above passage offers a cogent summary of Kittler's entire project, which (as we have seen) consists of a retroactive reading of societies as information processing systems, as media. The oft-noted analogy between the layout of city grids and that of circuitry is here revealed as more than mere metaphor: cities are digital processors and digital circuits are cities, abstracted and shrunk on to silicon (or any other future substrate). Kittler's project is encapsulated in the final sentence of this extract: past societies and their subjects are revealed as proto-media, as systems of data, addresses and commands. 'Man', or what Kittler dubs 'so-called Man' (*der sogenannte Mensch*), is the product of these systems, these discourse networks, and is at times address, command or data (the last understood as relational). Kittler's media history, which progresses towards the abstract implementation of media in the form of computation, is a history of history as information theory. Such a perspective necessitates viewing people not as objects but as addresses, and goods and communication as data and commands, in other words an abstract dematerialization of communication. This history is marked by a number of crucial junctures. First we observe the *severance of communication and interaction*. This is the birth of the *gramme* (or written mark), a means of perpetuating communication outside of the confines of the embodied voice. This uncoupling of presence and communication in the form of the gramme introduces both McLuhan's principle of redundancy (i.e. each medium has as it content a prior medium), and a coupling of storage and communication. The second break involves the fusion of information and communication, in the form of technical media; the data stored and transmitted no longer have a reference, however tenuous, to a concept of 'sense'. This, then, is the frame in which Kittler's networks are placed, a history of communication retroactively revealed as the autonomization of a postal system.

What is absent in Kittler's identification of the city as a macroprocessor (despite his recognition of money as the first medium born of the city), but explicit in the accounts to which we shall now turn, is the role of capital and commodification in the creation of the urban environment. Benjamin's concern with the cultural and experiential impact of capitalism on the built environment is well documented, and his explorations of major nineteenth-century metropolises provide the first intimation of the kind of totally commodified simulacra that characterize the urban centres, theme parks and malls of the contemporary built environment. Thus, Gilloch (2002) describes how the metropolises of Benjamin's era increasingly became literally concrete embodiments of the perceptual innovation as well as the distraction he believed cinema and other reproductive media to have inaugurated:

> In the contemporary city, human beings are subject not to the daemonic powers of nature, but to the domination and delusions of 'second nature', the human-made environment of commodities, machines and edifices. Nineteenth-century Paris is home to the deceptive allure of fetishized industrial products and consumer goods, to the mystifications promulgated by bourgeois ideology . . . In the 'era of high capitalism' the critical faculties are lulled into stupefied slumber. Benjamin writes, 'Capitalism was a natural phenomenon with which a new dream-filled sleep came over Europe, and through it, a reactivation of mythic forces'.
>
> (ibid.: 124)

Benjamin's analyses of the urban experience (and their points of convergence with the sociology of Simmel), as well as his speculation on the nature and impact of the media technologies of the early twentieth century, allow us to uncover something like an archaeology of the fusion of media, environment and subjectivity that characterizes the matrix. Thus, we can assemble the prehistory of the coalescence of subject, media and space that has been variously described as the 'virtual', 'hyperreality' or the 'postmodern', and which we shall explore in the next chapter. Whether we use the term 'commodity fetishism' or 'mythic forces' to describe this cultural atmosphere, its further proliferation both requires and creates the deterritorialization of existing space. This process of deterritorialization goes to the heart of the paradoxical relationship between immateriality and materiality that underlies our notion of digital matters. Individual physical environments retain their physicality but are denuded of their particularity and replaced with more generic features that stem from a more abstract, underlying system: the matrix.

The dialectic of reification

> [The dialectic of reification] . . . seizes on the properties and the subjectivities, the institutions and the forms, of an older pre-capitalist world, in order to strip them of their hierarchical or religious content . . . what is dialectical about it comes as something like a leap and an overturn from quantity into quality. With the intensification of the forces of reification and their suffusion through ever greater zones of social life (including individual

subjectivity), it is as though the force that generated the first realism now turns against it and devours it in its turn.

(Jameson 1998: 148)

Lukács's (1968 [1922]) famous essay 'Reification and the Consciousness of the Proletariat' may seem an unusual piece with which to address the issue of digitality. Nevertheless, we suggest that his concept of *reification* is still a very useful one with which to make sense of digital matters and the paradox of im/materiality. Reification refers to the way in which otherwise abstract concepts and processes are perceived as *thing-like*. Jameson's above formulation of *the dialectic of reification* neatly illustrates our notion that the colonization of the cultural field by commodity values takes place simultaneously at both material and immaterial levels. His identification of the dialectic in terms of the transformation from quantity into quality mirrors the emphasis placed on this by Benjamin, who, as cited in the previous chapter, explicitly relates the rise of technology and the social matrix: 'The mass is a matrix from which traditional behavior toward works of art issues today in a new form. Quantity has been transmuted into quality' (Benjamin 1973 [1935]: 241). This matches McLuhan's assertion that the social impact of technology is the change in scale and pace it brings to human affairs and Ellul's account of how that same type of change in the Industrial Revolution created a qualitatively different social environment from that of the preindustrial social order. The dialectic of reification reflects a process of *cultural extinction* that lies behind not only modernity's destruction of traditional society but also modernity's own subsequent demise under postmodernity. Society's cultural sphere becomes increasingly pervaded with abstract values inimical not only to the traditional social structures – which Benjamin was happy to see threatened by their decline in aura and which Jameson describes in language reminiscent of Benjamin's dream-world language as: 'spectres of value . . . vying against each other in a vast world-wide disembodied phantasmagoria' (Jameson 1998: 142) – but also to any social structures predicated upon non-commercial values. The quantitative increase in mechanical production is achieved only at the price of the implicit and widespread acceptance of cultural outputs as products. It is at this point of cultural alignment that previous barriers between cultural and economic spheres dissolve ('all that is solid melts into air') as the commodity becomes simultaneously an economic and cultural concept.

The power of the dialectic of reification lies in this recursive interlocking of:

1   *Technologies that encourage perceptual fragmentation.* Visual media like photography, cinema and TV fragment discourse by their very mode of operation in which their tautological images tend to override and displace rational discourse. As we have seen in Chapter 4, Sontag argues that an image speaks for itself in terms of its particular content to the exclusion of expressing more general concepts, and in *Camera Lucida* Barthes (1993 [1982]) uses the terms 'studium' and 'punctum' to describe the way in which the particular-

ity of a photograph's content (punctum) tends to push out the more general conceptual context of the image as a whole (the studium).

2 *The cultural alignment of media technologies and commodity culture.* The tautological element of media technologies' operations helps produce a culture receptive to the image-based emotional appeals of the commodities that dominate its social environment. Just as Lukács states that the commodity can be fully understood only as a concept that dominates an entire society, we have seen how Debord (1983) applies the same definition to the concept of the spectacle in which the commodity and the image are combined to become a socially defining phenomenon.

3 *The proliferation of visual environments.* Such environments, both physical and media based, constantly reflect back to each other commodity values in a *mis en abyme* of self-reflecting images and references.

The dialectic of reification works through all three interlocking processes to produce an ideological matrix for which digital technology is but the im/ material conduit depending upon whether we are talking about it as software or hardware.

Reification and the *Nervenleben*: money, commodity, city

The sociologist Georg Simmel, in his seminal essay of 1903 'Die Grosstadte und das Geistleben' (translated as 'The Metropolis and the Mental Life' in Levine 1971), argued that the event that is the metropolis has at its base the dialectical relationship between what he termed '*Nervenleben*' and '*verstand*' (the life of nerves and of the intellect respectively). In keeping with a Hegelian dialectic, he argued that the relation between these terms constituted the *Vergeistigung* (the process by which *Geist* is realized). This argument is significant because he identifies those very processes of reification we have outlined at the heart of the metropolis; furthermore, in the context of the analyses we have explored so far, the term '*Nervenleben*' is particularly interesting. This life of the nerves appears to recall the psychophysical fragmentation that Kittler argues is integral to the emergence of the new media of Network 1900 (Kittler 1990: 316): this insight, combined with his comments on the city qua macroprocessor, hints at the dialectical interplay between subject, media and space that we are attempting to uncover. Cacciari notes of Simmel's *Vergeistigung* that: 'it is the geist, not the individual, that of necessity inhabits the Metropolis' (Cacciari 1993: 4) and, adopting Kittler's post-dialectical terminology, we may understand this *Geist* in terms of a decentred network. What Simmel apprehends (as does Benjamin) is that the metropolis results in a new form of subject, a Kittlerian subject that is voided of its interiority: 'The psychological base form which arises from the metropolitan personality is the intensification of the life of the nerves, which results from the rapid and uninterrupted transformation of external and internal impressions' (Simmel 1971 [1903]: 220). For Simmel this is the result of commodification, which can be seen as participating in a dialectical relationship with the intellect such that 'the monetary economy and the dominion of intellect are very deeply connected' (ibid.: 221). The intellect abstracts or commodifies its objects through their conversion into signs, which become interchangeable with the economy of language/thought; capitalism carries out an analogous operation by converting objects into their exchange-value.

The metropolis is the site of this process, a space in which intellect, environment and commodity are fused in a process of continual production and exchange. Simmel described the effect of this fusion on subjectivity in terms of the emergence of an endemic metropolitan sensibility, the 'blasé type':

> The essence of the blasé attitude consists of the blunting of discrimination . . . the meaning and differing values of things, and thereby the things themselves, are experienced as insubstantial. They appear to the blasé person in an evenly flat and grey tone; no one object deserves preference over any other. *This mood is the faithful subjective reflection of a completely internalised money economy . . . All things float with equal specific gravity in the constantly moving stream of money.* All things lie on the same level . . .
>
> (Cacciari 1993: 8 [our emphasis])

The blasé attitude is thus the most direct expression of the *Vergeisigung*; here the monetary economy becomes a rule of mind in which availability of all objects as exchange-value negates the object itself, resulting in a 'devaluation of the entire objective world'. The blasé attitude is that of the perpetual consumer, or consciousness commodified, illustrating Adorno's observation that: 'the fetish character of commodities is not a fact of consciousness, but dialectic in the eminent sense that it produces consciousness' (Adorno's letter to Benjamin [1935] in Jameson 1980: 111). We will see how this commodification of the object, subject and space is subject to a complex descent through the twentieth century. Given this, it is important to grasp the paradoxical nature of the blasé attitude, since it represents the first interplay between materiality (object) and immateriality (subject) that, we argue, reaches its fullest expression in the im/material matrix of digital matters. Thus, on the one hand the blasé type as an expression of the *Vergeisigung* represents the negation of individuality, since the subject falls under the spell of economic forces, in that it becomes the 'subjective reflection of a completely internalised monetary economy'. But this is achieved through a process of hyper-individuation; in the welter of the metropolis, the subject assures its integrity only through the cultivation of maximal difference. Thus, as Simmel puts it:

> The deepest conflict of modern man is not any longer in the ancient battle with nature, but one in which the individual must fight to affirm the independence and peculiarity of his existence against the immense power of society, in his resistance to being levelled, swallowed up in the social-technological mechanism.
>
> (Simmel cited in Cacciari 1993: 10)

For Simmel, fashion was the battlefield on which the individual sought to affirm his difference and yet was forever consigned to a pyrrhic victory, since the hyper-individuation that fashion afforded served only to reinscribe the hegemony of the metropolis over all, in that it 'encompasses both the emergence of extreme individuality in the totality of the social and the constant internalisation of this totality in the individual' (Simmel 1971 [1903]: 220).

Benjamin's reading of the figure of the *flâneur* in Baudalaire can be said to delineate the same transformation in subjectivity and space as Simmel's blasé type. Baudelaire described the urban wanderings of the *flâneur*, a mid-nineteenth-century quasi-fictional Parisian figure who can be conceived of as a short-lived personification/imaginative representation of the role soon to be taken over by the camera's lens. The *flâneur* was a man *in* the crowd but not *of* the crowd; he was a dandyish figure with enough time on his hands to observe the constant motion of the vibrant city that passed him by as an impartial spectator. This elegant bystander viewed the cityscape as a mysterious code to be deciphered, and the gaze with which he observed these scenes was immortalized in various Impressionist paintings. In his 'Painter of Modern Life', Baudelaire famously elaborated upon the historical epoch the *flâneur* was witnessing: 'By "modernity" I mean the ephemeral, the fugitive, the contingent' (Baudelaire 2003 [1859]: 12). The experience of the *flâneur* and his perambulations amidst the rapid social change of nineteenth-century Paris serve as a usefully illustrative precursor of the increasingly fragmented and culturally dislocated nature of the social environment within the m/Matrix. Vice and transient sensation become the economy of the *flâneur*'s experience:

> The crowd is not only the newest asylum of outlaws; it is also the latest narcotic for those abandoned. The flâneur is someone abandoned in the crowd. In this he shares the situation of the commodity. He is not aware of this special situation, but this does not diminish its effect on him and it permeates him blissfully like a narcotic that can compensate him for many humiliations. The intoxication to which the flâneur surrenders is the intoxication of the commodity around which surges the stream of customers.
>
> (Benjamin 1973 [1935]: 43)

This constellation of themes in which environment, subjectivity, narcosis and commodification are interwoven is a powerful one and we shall encounter it in various guises as we trace the transmutations of the m/Matrix. In *The Naked Lunch,* Burroughs (1995 [1959]) observes that addiction represents the ultimate triumph of capitalism, and junk the ultimate product – the addictive cycle representing a condition in which all energies are directed to the acquisition of a product that is pure surplus value. Historically, the city has been the site of such economies, and its earliest anatomists in many ways incarnated this convergence. For instance, we might note that De Quincey (whose 1986 [1821] *Confessions of an English Opium Eater* Baudelaire translated) moves with the grace and indifference of the true *flâneur* through the poverty and splendour of Regency London and that in his writing the bliss of the crowd and that of narcosis are intertwined as to be one pleasure. Likewise, Poe, whose *Man in the Crowd* (1840), in Benjamin's words, 'contributed to the early physiognomics of the crowd', shared the same intertwined concerns (and was also translated by Baudelaire). Indeed, we might recall in this context Benjamin's own essay 'Hashish in Marseilles' (1986). This theme is continued in cyberpunk – for instance, Case, the protagonist of Gibson's *Neuromancer*, is introduced as an 'octogan'-swallowing dealer, his nervous system artificially wired to accommodate the flows and hustle of the cityscape, transporting 'a brick of . . . ketamine' (Gibson 1984: 15), and it is in cyberpunk that we arrive at an inseparability of narcotic, informational and urban flows. This world of prosthesis and extension, of the fusion of commodity, flesh and data, attains its headiest expression in the fictions of Noon, in which space, mind and data coalesce, in a post-pharmacological meltdown.

For the *flâneur*, then, the crowd is bliss, as Baudelaire wrote:

> The crowd is his element, as the air is that of birds and water of fishes. His passion and his profession are to become one flesh with the crowd. For the perfect flâneur, for the passionate spectator, it is an immense joy to set up house in the heart of the multitude, amid the ebb and flow of movement, in the midst of the fugitive and the infinite. To be away from home and yet to feel oneself everywhere at home; to see the world, and yet to remain hidden from the world . . . the lover of universal life enters into the crowd as if it were an immense reservoir of electrical energy.
>
> (Baudelaire 2003 [1859]: 9–10)

However, the pleasure of the *flâneur* comes (as will the future pleasures of cyberpunk) at a cost. To participate in the crowd is to undergo a transubstantiation into a commodity; the *flâneur*'s pleasure is that of 'the commodity around which surges the stream of customers' (Benjamin 1986: 57). For Benjamin, Baudelaire's ecstasy is a profane or material spiritual intoxication: 'when Baudelaire speaks of the big cities' "state of religious intoxication" the commodity is . . . the unnamed object of this state' (Benjamin 1983: 75). We should pause here to note the presence of the recurrent trope of liquidity and dissolution, a fluxion that is at once that of the metropolis and that of the commodity. Thus, Caccirari, in describing Simmel, speaks of 'all things floating . . . in the constantly moving stream of money', Baudelaire of the 'ebb and flow' of the crowd and Benjamin of the surging of stream of customers/commodities. As we have indicated, this theme of flows and dissolution finds its echo in contemporary analysis of the matrix, for instance in Lash (2002) and Bauman's (2000) discussions of 'liquidity' and 'flows'. In this manner the newly created urban flux of modernity prefigures the informational flows of the postmodern.

Chokerlebnis: metropolis/media/modernism

We have established that in the nineteenth and early twentieth centuries a quantitative and qualitative transformation took place in the urban landscape, a transformation that affected not only external space but also the interiority of the subject, as embodied in the form of the *flâneur*. We have seen, following Simmel, that these transformations can be viewed in terms of a dialectical interplay between the intellect, commodification and representation. In the following section we hope to establish how these trends were consolidated and accentuated by the technological explosion of the twentieth century, one that built upon the nineteenth-century Industrial Revolution (*à la* Ellul) but massively accelerated its effects. In particular, we will explore the impact of media technologies, those crucial elements of Kittler's network of 1900, and explore how they extended the paradoxical immateriality of the *flâneur*'s experience, and so resulted, at the outset of the twenty-first century, in a urban landscape that has (in certain privileged sectors) fused with its own representation.

In the early decades of the twentieth century the conditions that had given arise to the *flâneur* underwent a qualitative transformation. The urban space became something at once more exhilarating and threatening than the boulevards and streets through which the *flâneur* had strolled, dispassionately reading the physiognomics of the crowd. Now the urban experience became a *Chokerlebnis*: an insult to the sensorium, a shock to life or a life of shocks. This shock was that of the intensified mechanization of the city, and also that of the confrontation, for the first time, with technological media, i.e. those conditions identified by Kittler as the discourse network of 1900. As we have seen, Benjamin registered this assault in the very language he used to herald the arrival of reproductive media – 'the dynamite of a tenth of a second', 'the rubble of the world' etc. This shock was also registered in the practices of an emergent avant-garde, which encompassed the spectrum of the arts (architecture, cinema, visual art, graphics, music and literature) and expressed itself in the form of a proliferation of movements (Dada, Futurism, Vorticism, De Stilj, Imagism – the list is almost endless), each of which marked its debut in the form of the production of febrile manifestos. These manifestos were unified in their denunciation of the aesthetics of the nineteenth century and in their recognition, indeed positive celebration, of the rhythms of the machine and the novel, bewildering sensory assault of the city.

The avant-garde movements of the opening years of the last century rejected the aristocratic passivity of the *flâneur* and blasé type, embracing the reconstituted subjectivity of the metropolitan inhabitant. As Adolf Loos put it, European modernism 'must have American nerves'. In the Introduction, we stressed the diagnostic value of literature, and literature in the form of Musil's (1979 [1930]) *The Man without Qualities* provides us with a synecdoche for this transitional period. Its description of the aftermath of death of a pedestrian (*flâneur*-type figure) in the busy streets of Vienna in the 1920s is a seminal moment, not just in literature but in our understanding of the material forces and vectors that lie behind the media's impact upon our culture. Modernity's flux and vectors of speed kill the *flâneur*. The ephemerally contingent is something that literally runs him down. In his status as pedestrian he is sacrificed to the *Chokerlebnis* – and Musil's description of this accident's aftermath brilliantly captures the emerging, uncontrollable pace of the mechanized metropolis:

> Motorcars came shooting out of deep, narrow streets into the shallows of bright squares. Dark patches of pedestrian bustle formed into cloudy streams. Where stronger lines of speed transected their loose-woven hurrying, they clotted up – only to trickle on all the faster then and after a few ripples regain their regular pulse-beat . . . *the general movement pulsed through the streets . . . Like all big cities, it consisted of irregularity, change, sliding forward, not keeping in step, collision of things and affairs, and fathomless points of silence in between, of paved ways and wilderness, of one great rhythmic throb and the perpetual discord and dislocation of all opposing rhythms, and as a whole resembled a seething, bubbling fluid in a vessel consisting of the solid material of buildings, laws, regulations, and historical traditions.*
>
> (ibid.: 3–4 [our emphasis])

The crowds of Baudelaire and Poe will have to learn to watch out. As Ferguson notes of Balzac's portrayal of the changing relation of the *flâneur* to the city, he [*sic*] now becomes:

> a truly hapless soul, whom the city overwhelms rather than fascinates. Far from empowering the walker in the street, the altered urban context disables the individual. Distance and inactivity no longer connote superiority to the milieu, but suggest quite the opposite – estrangement, alienation, anomie.
>
> (Ferguson 1994: 33)

Musil's 'collision of affairs and things' is reflected in the machine aesthetic of modernist films such as Vertov's hymn to city and technology *Man with the Movie Camera* (1929) and Ferdinand Leger's *Ballet Mechanique* (1924), which through abstract montage offer a literal rendering of the 'perpetual discord and dislocation of all opposing rhythms'. Likewise, it can be seen in the abstract kinesis of the works of Futurists, or in the welter of details and voices in Eliot's *The Waste Land* (2002 [1922]) and Joyce's *Ulysses* (1990 [1922]).

It is cinema that perhaps offers the most direct contact with these disorientating juxtapositions, and Benjamin's analyses of both film and the city are characterized by their emphasis on shock and decomposition. Thus, he notes that, even in the case of Baudelaire's poetry and prose, the 'shock' of the city remains the hidden impulse that drives him to write: 'he placed the shock experience at the very center of his work' (Benjamin 1973 [1935]: 165). The shock that inspired Baudelaire becomes that of the coalescence of city and machine under the solvent power of capital. This assault takes place at the level of the nervous system, inducing Simmel's *Nervenleben*. The city-machine subjects 'the human sensorium to a complex kind of training', from the haptic movements whereby 'one abrupt movement of the hand triggers a process of many steps', not least that of the 'snapping' of the photographer, whereby a 'touch of the finger now sufficed to fix event for an unlimited period of time', to the scopic education:

> . . . supplied by the advertising pages of the newspaper or the traffic of a big city. Moving through this traffic involves the individual in a series of shocks of collisions. At the dangerous intersections, nervous impulses flow through him in rapid succession, like the energy from a battery.
>
> (Benjamin 1973 [1935]: 176–7)

This offers another example of the irreducible interplay between the material and immaterial in the matrix that will attain its fullest expression in the form of digital matters. The mechanical, mediated metropolis does not simply dehumanize, or substitute a life of the mind for that of the body; rather, it involves a retraining of the body, which must be reformatted in order to receive and process its impressions. Baudelaire described the metropolitan subject in terms of 'a *kaleidoscope* equipped with consciousness' (recalling Kittler's thesis that the media of 1900 involved the breakdown and reconstitution of a previous unified sensorium). This kaleidoscope is transmuted into cinema, a medium that, like the cities of the twentieth century, raises the shocks of the nineteenth century to a new level and necessitates new forms of subjectivity. In this light, Benjamin argues that the experimental aesthetics of the avant-garde movements are 'avant' precisely because they prefigure the experience of cinema, commenting upon Dada's 'extravagances and crudities' that 'it is only now that its impulse becomes discernible: Dadaism attempted to create by pictorial – and literary – means the effects which the public today seeks in films' (ibid.: 239).

The theme of the cinema as shock is well established. For instance, Kittler discusses the shock of cinema in terms of a doubling, a disturbing replication of the subject in the form of the image on the screen, which induces a sense of the uncanny or the unnatural. For this reason Kittler argues that the proliferation of narratives involving doubles, sleepwalkers and other figures possessed of a shadowy and threatening autonomy, particularly in films such as *The Student of Prague* (1913), *Der Golem* (1920) and in German Expressionist cinema, arises directly from the confrontation with the (re)animated image. Indeed Edison, the single most important inventor for Network 1900, committed to film in 1910 that most emblematic of doubles: *Frankenstein*. For Kittler, cinema 'undermines the mirror stage' – it introduces the subject to those forces that have been subsumed under the illusion of a self-present self – and it is for this reason that it is disturbing. Similarly, Benjamin notes that 'the feeling that overcomes the actor before the camera . . . is . . . of the same kind as the estrangement felt before one's own image in the mirror. But now the reflected image has become, separable, transportable' (Benjamin 1973 [1935]: 233). The image is abroad like the tenebrous figures that haunt the world of the waking in the cinema of the doppelganger. This condition affects not only the actor but, more importantly, the audience, who move from being a sentient kaleidoscope to take 'the position of the camera'.

Writing of the shock of the city, Tafuri notes that the problem faced by capital was 'how to render active the intensification of the nervous system (*Nervenleben*): how to absorb the shock provoked by the metropolis by transforming it into a principle of dynamic development' (Tafuri 1979: 89). Cinema, as the site of what Deleuze describes as its *nooshock* – that is 'a shock to thought, communicating vibrations to the cortex, touching the nervous and cerebral system directly' (Deleuze 1989: 156) – finds itself in an analogous position. It too must translate its shock and render it productive. As Benjamin observed:

> Man's need to expose himself to shock effects is his adjustment to the dangers threatening him. The film corresponds to profound changes in the apperceptive system-changes that are experienced on an individual scale by the man in the street in big-city traffic.
>
> (Benjamin 1973 [1935]: 252, note 19)

For Benjamin, this takes the form of commodification, in the form of the introduction of confected glamour in lieu of the aura that this reproductive media has extirpated:

> The film responds to the shrivelling of the aura with an artificial build-up of the 'personality' outside the studio. The cult of the movie star, fostered by the money of the film industry, preserves not the unique aura of the person but the 'spell of the personality', the phoney spell of a commodity.
>
> (ibid.: 233)

Despite the threat of this commodification, Benjamin remained convinced of film's revolutionary potential. The mass production and reception of its rapid juxtaposition of fleeting and contingent images gives film its iconoclastic power and induces the state of distraction inimical to traditional forms of communication and expression (thereby making it for Benjamin an intrinsically radical form). In Benjamin's analysis, the increased quantity of media output has a destructive effect upon traditional art forms because of the decline in their auratic quality that it induces. Rather than being subordinate to the canonized art works and the institutions that surround them, this loss of aura liberates the masses, allowing them to directly confront the meaning of their own historical situation.

Our analysis of Heidegger has shown that he shared Benjamin's perspective about the waning power of traditional art and craftsmanship in the face of new media technologies – but to quite different ends. For Heidegger the work of art's voice is that of its poiesis understood in terms of its genesis, its mode of disclosure. The loss and subsequent replacement of that aura with the voice of the media leads Heidegger to a different interpretation of the masses' confrontation with their own historical situation. From this perspective, the transformation of art's reception from the contemplation of art to the state of distraction is an important one – but for reasons directly counter to those offered by Benjamin. He sought within the newly emerging mass media the basis of a social power to counter the rise of Fascism in his time. He saw Fascism to be based upon the appropriation of traditional and mythical art heritage, an appropriation that is fatally undercut by the mechanical reproduction of media content that the masses can lay their hands on directly. However, mechanical reproduction does not so much destroy tradition as ossify it in the constant repetition of the individualized commodity form for essentially individual consumption. Thus, the shift from quantity to quality that Benjamin identified as a source of socialist power has continued beyond Benjamin's analytical framework to such a degree that, as Jameson previously pointed out: 'the force that generated the first realism now turns against it and devours it in its turn'. In later chapters we shall explore in much more detail the increasing manifestation of 'fictive reality' within contemporary culture and the way in which this serves to blur the traditional boundaries between the individual's inner world and the external physical reality. At this point we will suffice by pointing out and re-emphasizing the basis of this process in the speed of the quantity to quality shift that mechanical reproduction heralds. Digital matters both stem from this and represent a new departure in so far as its information flows are of a yet higher order of speed.

Spectacular city

In the passage from Musil cited above, the metropolitan crowd is seen to resemble 'a seething, bubbling fluid in a vessel consisting of the solid material of buildings, laws, regulations, and historical traditions'. In the light of the themes of our analysis we might liken this turbulent fluid to the flows of capital and commodity still regulated by the history and the forms of the built environment. But under capital, all that is solid melts to air: the apparently durable constraints that held this fluid themselves dissolve in the solvent of capital and so these flows recast the city in their own image (a process accelerated in Europe by the destruction of the War). For recognition of this transition we turn to the Situationists, and in particular the theories of Guy Debord (see Chapter 4). From the 1950s to the 1970s, the Situationist Internationale conducted an anatomy of society founded in the concept of the *spectacle*. What is significant in the context of the present discussion is the way in which this critique of the spectacle was at one and the same time a critique of the city, and in this capacity the Situationists elaborated the connection established by the avant-garde artists and theoreticians of the early decades of the twentieth century. However, what distinguished the Situationist critique from these earlier reflections was that, while, for the former, the city was recreated in the image of the industrial machine – 'objectively structured like a machine for the extraction of surplus value, in its own conditioning mechanisms the city reproduce[d] the reality of the ways of industrial production' (Tafuri 1979: 81) – for the latter a new form of machine, or rather machine system, has become central to the image of the city. This system was the spectacle understood as an all-encompassing media network. Marx had discussed the technologies spawned by the industrial revolution in terms of *fixed capital*, i.e. as the concretization of the actions of living labour, abstracted and replicated by machines (see Chapter 8). Debord's analysis suggests that this fixed capital has mutated in accordance with capitalism's rapacious drive for commodification, that the process of reification that we have seen in both Simmel and Benjamin's accounts finds its fullest expression in the spectacle – defined as 'capital accumulated to such a degree that it becomes an image' (Debord 1983: part 1, note 34).

The crucial point here is that, in this form, capital is not simply accumulated as fixed capital, i.e. the hardware of the media; instead it is reality itself that has become commodified. The spectacle is not the 'product of the techniques of mass dissemination of images. It is, rather, a Weltanschauung which has become actual, materially translated' (ibid.: part 1, note 5). We have seen how the shock of the new was a problem both for the media of reproducibility and for the accelerated metropolis, and how the experiences of these terms were dialectically entwined. Here this relationship is raised to a new power: urban space, the technologies of the spectacle, and the subjectivity that participates in them are convergent. But while the shock and fluidity of the early twentieth century was exhilarating, its dissolution of the regulative operation of older forms has allowed it to encompass the entire socius. With this unbinding comes a certain homogeneity: like a cooling liquid, it moves in the direction of dissipation, it cools into a non-space. Particularity is levelled into an amorphous interchangeability: 'capitalism has unified space, this unification is at the same time an extensive and intensive process of banalization' (ibid.: Part I no. 165). The isomorphy of media and city is reflected in the parallel strategies that Debord *et al.* formulated for overturning them in favour of the 'situation': if the spectacle could be defined as 'the autonomous movement of nonlife' (we note here the similarity to the double of cinema, and to Marx's definition of the machine) then *the situation* represents the recovery or liberation of moments of pure 'life' from the stultifying equivalence of the spectacle. In the case of the media this was to be achieved through *détournement* – the reverse or, better still, perverse engineering of media messages through the juxtaposition of inappropriate words and images. This technique can be seen in Debord's 'détourned' film of 1973 *Can Dialectics Break Bricks?,* which overdubs an obscure martial arts B-movie with dialogue concerning the alienated workers' struggle against a spectacular economy. This media *détournement* operated on the principle that the media offered their own immanent critique. They did not need to be exposed via a transcendental perspective; rather, all that was needed was for their elements to be recombined so that the spectacle would utter its own contradictions. The situationist's urban strategy was that of the *dérive* or 'drift' – urban space was to be reclaimed through a form of nomadism attuned to the singularities of the city that lay below the surface of its commodified space. The city was to be remapped according to a new logic, that of chance encounters and juxtapositions, rather than the centrally planned, rationalized space of the urban planner.

These dual strategies were aimed at reclaiming the fusion of space and information that is the spectacle and returning it to an authentic life, in other words an affective insurrection, a revolution of the everyday, as Vanniegan (1972) put it. At the start of the twenty-first century this revolution seems an anachronism, the faded song of a lost time. Debord's own *Comments on the Society of the Spectacle* (1990) suggested the process of 'recuperation' (the tendency of capitalism to neutralize and spectacularize critique and resistance) that the Situationist Internationale warned against had ultimately triumphed. The media-based process of enframement we have outlined is thus abetted by the co-optation of any cultural resistance that may arise to it. Such co-optation can be seen at a broad cultural level by the way in which the abstract modes of expression from such initially rebellious artistic movements as the avant-garde of the 1920s have become the mainstay of contemporary advertising: 'our entire system of commodity production and consumption today is based on those older, once anti-social modernist forms' (Jameson 1998: 149). At the level of the *détournements* of street culture, this stalling of any potentially empowering aspects to the reifying dialectic is illustrated by such examples as the way in which the US ghetto-street fashion of socially alienated blacks quickly became a 'look' to be imitated in the white suburbs. Thus, within the present context, what is more significant than the admittedly noble aims of the Situationist Internationale is the critique on which they drew, in other words the situationists' lucid recognition that space, media and subjectivity had fused within the spectacle, and that this convergence was the logic ripening logic of the dialectic of reification whose history we have outlined.

'Welcome to the Desert of the Real': the ever-enframing matrix

> Malls have achieved their commercial success through a variety of strategies that all depend on 'indirect commodification', a process by which nonsaleable objects, activities, and images are purposely placed in the commodified world of the mall. The basic marketing principle is 'adjacent attraction', where the most dissimilar objects lend each other mutual support when they are placed next to each other ... This logic of association allows noncommodified values to enhance commodities, but it also imposes the reverse process – previously noncommodified entities become part of the marketplace. Once this exchange of attributes is absorbed into the already open-ended and indeterminate exchange between commodities and needs, associations can resonate infinitely.
>
> (Crawford 1996: 14–15)

In this section we consider the millennial extension of this critique, one which, unlike its optimistic precursors, has largely abandoned the possibility of reclaiming or overturning the spectacle. We have seen in our previous discussion of the dialectic of reification how initially disruptive juxtapositions of cinema and photography are tempered by commoditization and thus adapted for consumption. These features of a media-induced process are physically manifested in the form of the shopping mall, the specific purpose of which is to provide a site for the accumulation of commodities for consumption, and this consumption is facilitated by the use of visual displays and imagery. The idiosyncratic bricolage of images thrown up by the reproducible image thus serves, in the shopping mall, a much more functional and culturally aligned purpose. The juxtaposition of disparate subject matter is refashioned into a commercially orientated but ever more inclusive logic of association that Crawford defines above in terms of 'indirect commodification' or 'open-ended and indeterminate exchange'. In other words, more and more aspects of the mall (and by extension the wider society) are either commodities themselves or, alternatively, a standing reserve milieu for the promotion of commodities. There is a growing tendency for urban centres, and in particular malls, to adopt the trappings of theme parks. Theming becomes a means of creating exotic associations that, like the advertising of which they are a subset, and like the essentially tautologous nature of media, are based upon emotional appeal rather than rational discourse.

Commercial appropriations of perception thus depend not just upon the decline in aura described by Benjamin but also on the parodic or simulacral rec-reation of aura in the form of the sign of authenticity. In place of aura's depend-ency upon unsubstitutable physical particularities, the intrinsic circulation of commodities means that aura becomes a much more arbitrary and ultimately manipulable phenomenon. A *non-space* of abstract commodification is created in which the particularity of a space is expunged (see Augé 1995). This paradoxical phrase captures the physical consequences of an exclusively commodified social environment. It encapsulates the im/material ambiguities that have informed the previous chapters and provides the basis to the social matrix that throughout this book we argue is the single most important matrix, and of which digital matters are but an extreme and more explicit representation. In practical terms, this space is typically experienced at first hand in the mundane homogeneity of airports, chain hotels, etc., a homogeneity vividly captured in Jem Cohen's recent film *Chain* (2004), in which footage of the suburbs, malls and business parks of seven different nations are spliced together in a continuous whole to reveal a Ballardian interzone that covers continents. The concept of the city itself has become affected by this banalization of space to the extent that cities themselves risk becoming less particular locations but spectacles that compete with other cities as spectacles, thus:

> their 'imageability' becomes the new selling point . . . in this marketing war, style-of-life and 'liveability', visualized and represented in spaces of conspicuous consumption, become important assets that cities proudly display.
>
> (Boyer 1996: 193)

In other words, cities have become, as a result of the marriage of images and the capitalist market, little more than the circulation of their own signs. This commercial reappropriation of aura also explains why it is common in theme parks and shopping malls to effectively suspend reality by simulating anachronistic and geographically inappropriate mixes of different cultural, technological and fictional themes – the pastiche of styles and aesthetics that went by the name of postmodernism. The dominance of freely juxtaposed images over rationally linked context occurs across a range of social environments that all become subordinate to the subtle influence of 'indirect commodification', which tends towards the conflation of various image-driven activities:

> . . . shopping with an intense spectacle of accumulated images and themes that entertain and stimulate and in turn encourage more shopping. The themes of the spectacle owe much to Disneyland and television, the most familiar and effective commodifiers in American culture. Theme-park attractions are now commonplace in shopping malls; indeed the two forms converge – malls routinely entertain, while theme parks function as disguised marketplaces. Both offer controlled and carefully packaged public spaces and pedestrian experiences to auto-dependent suburban families already primed for passive consumption by television . . .
>
> (Crawford 1996: 16)

It is this fluid way in which commercial values circulate through various levels of society (Jameson's 'suffusion through ever greater zones of social life') that lies behinds Baudrillard's (1983) claim that Disneyland's existence merely distracts us from the fact that the whole of America is essentially Disney. It also makes visiting shopping malls increasingly akin to the disparate effect achieved by 'channel hopping', in terms of both the nature of the visual experience and the content being viewed: 'The system operates much like television programming, with each network presenting slightly different configurations of the same elements. Apparent diversity masks fundamental homogeneity' (Crawford 1996: 9).

To oppose the anonymity and abstractness of commodified non-space, in *The Practices of Every Day Life,* Michel de Certeau (1988) calls, as did the Situationist Internationale, for the reinscription of place as *practised space.* This is to be achieved through the use of playful and exploratory approaches to one's environment. The self-augmentation of the matrix mitigates against such strategies. The shopping mall, for example, is designed for an apparent oxymoron – the distractedly purposive pedestrian consumer – who has replaced the *flâneur.* A positive quality of the *flâneur* in de Certeau's terms was the way in which his apparent purposelessness served to resist the excessive instrumentality of commodity culture and its tendency to colonize social space into a standing-reserve of potential consumption. In the consumerist sites that now dominate, privately run surveillance cameras replace the detached gaze of the *flâneur,* and further fuse the non-space of the commodity with the technologies of representation.

The serendipitous *dérive* is negated by the 'retail grammar' of market planners, who design the sights to be seen, and even the likely pace of the 'air-conditioned nightmare' of the space of consumption. A further isomorphic regimentation of experience occurs in suburbia, where the eclectic mix of the bustling city is replaced by the elective affinities of homogeneous demographic groups.

In so far as the *flâneur* was 'in the crowd' but 'not of the crowd', he arguably contained the early signs of the solipsistic nature of the subsequently commodified and atomized way in which the contemporary city is increasingly experienced. Morse (1998) points out that, for writers such as Canetti and Bakhtin, the city was a site where individuality was subordinated to the amorphous mass of the crowd. In contrast, the mall experience is based upon a similar state of distraction or dream-like solipsism to that of the consumption of movie images identified by Benjamin. Instead of losing individual identity in the crowd, in the mall the individual seeks the completion of his or her character by buying into the spectacle of consumer objects. The use-value of such objects is increasingly much less significant than the image they provide of a lifestyle in which the individual can seek self-expression, momentarily ignoring the mass-produced nature of such commodities that would seem to contradict this aim. In Chapter 7 we will return to this issue of the relationship between the individual and the mass in terms of the cyberpunk's solipsistic relationship to the digital Matrix, but before that we continue to explore the roots of digital flows in the consumerism of the city.

The conflation of the immaterial/material in the matrix

> Metropolitan life suggests the disintegration in space and time of individual's various dwelling places. Often living in 'communities without propinquity', the individual metropolitan must somehow confront the task of reintegrating his or her environment . . . One does not dwell in the metropolis; one passes through it between dwelling places'. This task of reintegrating a social world of separated, dislocated realms is accomplished by means of an internal dualism, of *passage* amid the *segmentation* of glass, screens, and thresholds. Thus, each form of communication becomes a *mis-en-abyme*, a recursive structure in which a nested or embedded representation reproduces or duplicates important aspects of the primary world within which it is enclosed.
>
> (Morse 1998: 107 [emphasis in original])

As Morse points out above, the primacy of circulation within a society in which the physical and the representational are culturally aligned produces a recursive, multilayered, but ultimately self-referential and enclosed environment which, following Luhmann, can be described as an autopoietic system (see Chapter 6). The loss of the living aura of traditional communities produces a need for the recreation of a sense of a unified environment. This is achieved by the seamless reintegration of images and the physical environment to produce the im/material. Explicitly there are commercial logos and advertisements, franchised storefronts, etc. Implicitly, there is an underlying background or frame of reference that exists behind both these images and their environment. The consumer comes to them already inculcated in the notion of social life as circulation within an enframed, standing reserve of commodities/commercial experiences – a commodity matrix. Morse points out that Aristotle identified mobility as an aspect of causality and subjecthood:

> But mobility also suggests the opposite of subjecthood, the freely displace-able and substitutable part, machine or human, which enables mass pro-duction and a consequent standardization brought to the social as well as economic realm.
>
> (ibid.: 112)

The individual in the culture of mechanical reproduction experiences circu-lation in two distinct forms. The first is the paradoxical and uniquely modern experience of travelling through space at high speed in vehicles whilst one's own body remains predominantly static. The second mirrors this effect in the realm of commodities. The shopping mall consumer passively views motionless objects: 'But the shops passed in review are themselves a kind of high-speed transport, the displacement of goods produced in mass quantities in unknown elsewheres into temporal simultaneity and spatial condensation' (ibid.: 112). The 'elsewhere' reaches its most developed form in capitalism's non-space, but its roots are evident in the self-absorbed perambulations of the *flâneur* and his imaginative conceptualization of the metropolitan scene in front of him. The *flâneur* is thus perhaps the earliest example of a 'mobile subjectivity'/'mobile privatization':

> A 'bubble' of subjective here-and-now strolling or speeding about in the midst of elsewhere is one of the features that constitute new, semi-fictitious realms of the everyday.
>
> (ibid.: 112)

a subjectivity whose aggregate effect culminates for writers such as J. G. Ballard and the cyberpunk authors of Chapter 7 in dystopian descriptions of an unreal world of social anomie.

Screens play a fundamental role in the creation of these semifictitious realms. They come in various forms. They can be the literal ones of televisions and computers, but they are also underwritten in our social fabric by the less obvious but supporting screens of car windshields and the branded images that, more metaphorically, *screen* our consciousness. The phrase *mis en abyme* has perhaps been overused in contemporary cultural discourse, but its familiarity should not blind us to its utility in capturing the hall of mirrors that is techno-commodity culture. More and more, people experience social life as a Matryoshka doll set in which physical mediation is progressively reflected within media reproductions: you observe through the screen of the car windshield an outside world of commodified images, brands and other easily recognizable structures whilst a sociability within the car tends to be limited to the solipsistic consumption of mediated forms of commercial radio, compact discs, etc:

> ... the interior of the auto is disconnected and set in the midst of a new kind of theater of derealized space, the experience of what is normally the paramount reality – the experience of self-awareness in a here-and-now – becomes one of unanchored mobility. This mobile subject in the midst of elsewhere is a cultural *novuum* and the model for a new kind of fiction effect, a fiction of presence unbound and uncircumscribed by the fourth wall, without a 180 degree line to separate the world of the imaginary and the subjunctive from the commonplace.
>
> (Morse 1998: 111)

We are, as T. S. Eliot's put it in *Burnt Norton*, 'Distracted from distraction by distraction' (Eliot 1943, Part 3); in other words, we have forgotten our forgetting. The semifictional effect of this distracted experience of life comes to resemble the suspension of disbelief that accompanies our experience of a play or movie: 'Freeways, malls, and television are the locus of virtualization or an attenuated fiction effect, that is, a partial loss of touch with the here-and-now, dubbed here as *distraction*' (Morse 1998: 99). It occurs in a number of activities that range from physical travel to sedentary viewing because of the underlying structural conditions that reside behind seemingly disparate activities. Immaterial media forms have aligned themselves with our wider cultural and physical environments, and Morse borrows Williams's term 'mobile privatization' to describe the loss of this balance. She accounts for the unprecedentedly high level of commodification in contemporary culture by tracing the complex interrelationship between mediated experience, commodity forms and the physical environment.

As we have seen, this interrelationship can be traced from the Marxian analysis of the predominance of exchange-value over use-value, through the dialectic of reification explored by Simmel and Benjamin to that offered by Debord, wherein reality itself has become exchange-value. The rising importance of exchange-value as witnessed by the *flâneur* in turn evolved into the immaterial, but materially informed realm of sign-value. But what has changed is the degree of participation. The man in the crowd was engaged in a commodity dialectic by attempting to distinguish himself within the crowd, but now the whole environment becomes a site for the consumption and differentiation of signs, so that physically distinct environments, such as vehicle interiors, shopping malls and electronic screens, mesh together to create the liquid nature of advanced capitalist society that we have seen discussed by various writers. This liquidity has rendered the recuperative powers of capital all the greater. Resistance, whether it is in the form of Debord's *dérive* and *détournement* or de Certeau's 'curious walking', is increasingly difficult to effect under conditions of a semiotic capitalism that is adroit at recuperating any attempt at resistance.

Conclusion

> A commodity appears, at first sight, a very trivial thing, and easily under-
> stood. Its analysis shows that it is, in reality, a very queer thing abounding in
> metaphysical subtleties and theological niceties.
>
> (Marx 1983 [1887]: 76)

> For distraction both motivates and promotes the 'liquidity' of words and
> images in economic exchange by undermining a sense of different levels of
> reality and of incommensurable difference between them.
>
> (Morse 1998: 122)

The juxtaposition of the above two quotations highlights the link between the
passage from Marx's commodity form to the affective commodification of the
contemporary cityscape. In this chapter we have used Morse's work on *distraction*
and *mobile privatization* to articulate the important role played by the process of
mystification, so vividly described by Marx in terms of fetishism, which results
in the subsumption of more and more aspects of reality under the rubric of the
commodity. Distraction was a concept used by Benjamin in his 'Work of Art'
essay but which remained rather underdeveloped. It described the new way in
which, like architecture, people experience media in a non-contemplative, more
habitual manner. Mobile privatization illustrates Raymond Williams's emphasis
upon the dialectical relationship between technology and society. The media
serve to mediate between the increased personal mobility of individuals in urban
settings and the socially fragmented nature of that mobility. Broadcast media
reintroduce a superficially social element within an ultimately individualized
context and as such serve a social purpose (but of a devalued nature). We have
seen how both processes of distraction and mobile privatization are heightened
by the increased informationalization of social environments facilitated by
digital technologies. Bauman (2000) refers to the subsequent effects in terms
of 'liquidity', and Lash (2002), furthering Williams's work, also defines them in
terms of 'flow'. This analysis is in keeping with our central focus upon digital
matters as a complex, imbricated mix of both the immaterial (in terms of the
growing independence of an abstract coded realm) and material (in terms of
the traces of that coded, formulaic world that plays a bigger and bigger part
in our physical surroundings. Franchise stores provide a good example of this
process: store logos are abstract signs but also interact with standardized shop
interiors to produce the overall franchise effect. They provide a predictable
material environment able to keep up with the privately mobile consumer
and their fluid, informational social realm and, as the next chapter shows, the
development of the im/materiality of digital matters gives rise to the hyperreality
of social matters.

6 Social matters in the matrix

> Today the scene and the mirror have given way to a screen and a network. There is no longer any transcendence or depth, but only the immanent surface of operations unfolding, the smooth and functional surface of communication.
>
> (Baudrillard 1988: 12)

In Part I, the conceptualizations of the abstractness that underlies digital technology culminated in Kittler's approach, which presents the digital as the über-medium we do not, and cannot, fully understand yet. In this regard, Kittler shares the perspective of McLuhan, who, notwithstanding the title of his book *Understanding Media* (1995 [1964]), argues that seeking to understand the social significance of the media is like trying to drive a car by only looking at what is in the rear-view mirror: you only see what you have already left behind.

We disagree somewhat with Kittler and Foucault's concept of discontinuous networks or epistemes. We do find a likely discontinuity due to the different pace at which change is facilitated by the digital, but we also see continuities with the previous Network 1900. For example, in the previous chapter we briefly examined the notion of reification and the alienation from the productive process that reification signifies for the individual. We saw some of the processes through which inhabitants of the city become translated into elements of an urban flux. In this chapter we will attempt to develop the conceptual ramifications of this transformation through an exploration of the continuities (cultural alignment) between urban and digital flows. This process (accelerated by information technology) increases the quantity of flows to produce a qualitative change so that the process of translation, facilitated by digital technology, creates a complex combination of social environment, commodity and subjectivity that results in the seemingly autonomous realm known as cyberspace.

To explore this complex admixture, we trace here the early origins of commodity culture in the nascent urbanization of the Industrial Revolution that Ellul singled out as the Archimedean point in the changed relationship between human society and its technologies, drawing upon the work of various social theorists in order to further explore the notion of the city and metropolitan life as being fundamentally recast by informational flows. We show how the matrix, commonly conceived as an underlying network of computer systems, in fact has its roots in a culturally aligned matrix of commodity culture, and technological reproduction had its inception in the Industrial Revolution from which, contra Kittler, the Information Revolution can be seen to descend directly.

In the above quotation Baudrillard emphasizes the functional and operational nature of networks made for circulation. The fetishization of commodities that Marx identifies in terms of their 'metaphysical subtleties and theological niceties' is aptly complemented by a society in which such metaphysical attributes are relayed in a self-enclosed network of screens devoted to the reproduction of self-referential images. We have already seen how the roots of this process can be approached in terms of traditional Marxist analysis – e.g. with Lukács's concept of *reification* – and we continue this use of historical analyses of capitalism to show better how commodity circulation has reached such a new pitch. Having traced the evolution of the interplay between media and technology, subjectivity and the built environment, in this chapter we examine in more detail the broader social and theoretical implications of this transformation. In addition, it will provide the conceptual ground for the next chapter, in which we will examine cyberpunk in terms of a future projection of the past and present trends we have hitherto explored. With the combined effect of these perspectives we hope to produce at least some hints of the determining features of the socio-technical matrix of Network 2000 and thus gain a more culturally and historically informed sense of why the digital matters.

The previous chapters have provided important background material for considering the extent to which new digital forms represent both an extreme manifestation and/or a significant development of the abstract processes of enframement encountered in Part I. There, we introduced the notion that, beyond a certain threshold, technology can no longer be seen in terms of a instrument deployed by a society but must be approached as a substantive entity in its own right: technological enframement begins to determine the structure of society. This qualitative development is a shift that reflects the quantity/quality pole we have consistently emphasized as a dominant theoretical presence in the work of Benjamin, McLuhan and others. Thus, what we saw begin with the mechanical reproduction of objects and media reaches a markedly new level in the digital matters identified by Baudrillard above. The surface-level operations of computer code replace in-depth communication. We thus explore in this chapter the work of various writers, such as Baudrillard, Lash, and Luhmann, in order to grasp the significance of this process, understood in terms of the increasing priority of information in contemporary society. McLuhan (1995 [1964]) asserted that once you have the assembly line it does not matter substantially whether you produce Cadillacs or cornflakes on it: *la téchnique* is dominant whatever the output. This levelling out of content has an even more powerful effect when, in the realm of digital matters, material objects and immaterial media content are conflated to exacerbate the tension of the im/material. Building upon the previous chapter's concepts of distraction and mobile privatization, we look at the way in which this diminishment of the material has a disorientating effect upon the individual and tends to isolate him/her from a material social context.

Reality becomes a much more complex proposition to relate to when the digital matters.

Phantom objectivity – fluidity and the origins of the inside/outside confusion

> . . . man in capitalist society confronts a reality 'made' by himself (as a class) which appears to him to be a natural phenomenon alien to himself: he is wholly at the mercy of its 'laws', his activity is confined to the exploitation of the inexorable fulfilment of certain individual laws for his own (egotistic) interests. But even while 'acting' he remains, in the nature of the case, the object and the not the subject of events. The field of his activity thus becomes wholly internalised: it consists on the one hand of the awareness of the laws which he uses and, on the other, of his awareness of his inner reactions to the course taken by events.
>
> (Lukács 1968 [1922]: 135)

Early in his essay, 'Reification and the Consciousness of the Proletariat', Lukács identifies as a crucial question: 'how far is commodity exchange together with its structural consequences able to influence the total outer and inner life of society?' (ibid.: 84), a problematic that we have seen is taken and accentuated by the complex interplay between subjectivity and environment that characterizes the development of a metropolitan sensibility. Lukács identifies the dialectic of reification in which the 'individual' (under capitalism) confronts an 'external' reality that increasingly objectifies the nature of his or her thought processes. This has some similarity to Kittler's vision of the determinate nature of discourse networks; nevertheless, there is a difference in the strength of their claims. For Kittler, scriptorial networks are entirely determinant, rather than a dialectic 'that produces consciousness in the eminent sense' (to quote Adorno); the consciousness of 'so-called Man' is solely the product of the ratios between different media. However, rather than subscribing to the extreme anti-humanism of Kittler, we shall develop a more neo-Marxist reading, which we believe gives a great scope for understanding the multiplicity of factors involved in digital matters, as well as holding out the possibility of contesting the terms under which the m/Matrix is formulated.

Both Marx's declaration that the commodity is marked by its 'metaphysical subtleties and theological niceties' and Benjamin's unfinished opus *The Arcades Project* (1999), in which he sought to develop this vision of the commodity through an exploration of the phantasmagorical nature of commodities in nineteenth-century Paris, provide embryonic descriptions of the growing domination of social reality by second-order images and forms. This leads directly to the manner in which this growth in phantasmic commodity forms serves to confuse the boundaries between the internal psychological world of the individual and their external social environment. We will shortly investigate how this accelerated development of urban reality in the past two centuries has been portrayed in the futuristic fictions of cyberpunk in terms of a hyperbolic process. But, before exploring this extrapolation of the coalescence of inner and outer worlds, we will first establish the theoretical framework within which it is articulated.

Chapter 5 demonstrated how the concept of reification goes directly to the heart of the manner in which digital technology reconfigures the abstract and the material in an unprecedentedly complex amalgam. Lukács, however, is interested in the concept of reification not for its own sake but rather as a means of apprehending the social processes that result in a situation whereby the true relation between people is refracted through an accretion of objects and processes. To quote:

> The essence of commodity structure has often been pointed out. Its basis is that a relation between people takes on the character of a thing and thus acquires a *'phantom objectivity'*, an autonomy that seems so strictly rational and all-embracing as to conceal every trace of its fundamental nature: the relation between people.
>
> (Lukács 1968: 83 [our emphasis])

In this light, it is interesting to compare Lukács's perspective with that of Georg Simmel. The latter also explores the interplay between the 'commodity structure' and 'modernity' (as was shown in his discussion of the hyper-individuation of the blasé type explored in the last chapter). These two elements, one apparently internal and the other external, are increasingly imbricated and provide one of the first instances of the apparent paradox of the im/material that lies at the heart of digital matters and which is physically manifested in the city. It is in the city that the phantom objectivity of the commodity form manages to assume both external physical shapes but also an invasive immaterial presence in the mind of the nascent consumer – the phantasmagoria of 'dream objects' (as Benjamin described them). The mobile privatization engendered by the city reflects Simmel's Marx-like observation that increasingly the individual's experience becomes one in which forms are fluid. As he puts it:

> The essence of modernity as such is pyschologism, the experiencing and interpretation of the world in terms of the reactions of our inner life and indeed as an inner world, the dissolution of fixed contents in the fluid element of the soul, from which all that is substantive is filtered and whose forms are merely forms of motion.
>
> (Simmel cited in Frisby 1986: 38)

For Simmel, the internalization of the monetary economy results in a non-local 'psychologism', the world, as a solute dissolved in the flows of commodity, takes on the fluid of the mind and, in turn, the world reflects this fluidity. The urban experience consists of a paradoxical and disorientating situation whereby the repeated experience of reality in fluid form gives such fluidity more apparent substance than the physical the fluid has largely superseded.

Prefiguring Morse and Bauman's emphasis upon the liquidity of the contemporary experience, a major element of Simmel's thinking can thus be seen as an exploration of the previously emphasized notion from Marx and Engels that, as a consequence of the ubiquitous spread of the commodity form, under capital 'all that is solid melts into air'. Like Marx and Lukács, who emphasize *phantom objectivity*, Simmel speaks of the 'spectral' and, as Frisby argues, his work 'is located within the context of a permanent and accelerating opposition between subjective and objective culture' (ibid.: 41): precisely the juncture that we believe to be the locus of the emergence of the im/material. Simmel's *Über sociale Differenzierung* of 1890 argues that 'the increased externalization of life that has come about, with regard to the preponderance that the technical side of life has obtained over its inner side, over its personal values' (cited in Frisby 1986: 42), a sentiment that recalls the positions of Ellul and Heidegger. But, whilst our previous discussion of Heidegger and Ellul was couched in rather philosophical terms, Simmel and his fellow commentators, in addressing modernity's social elements, flesh out what it means to live out the implications of these philosophical changes. Of particular relevance to our examination of digital matters is Frisby's succinct summary of the central effect of a pervasive sense of fluidity (which recalls Ballard's description of the realignment of the external and internal worlds quoted in this book's Introduction). He asserts: 'The external world becomes part of our inner world. In turn, the substantive element of the external world is reduced to a ceaseless flux and its fleeting, fragmentary and contradictory moments are all incorporated into our inner life' (ibid.: 46). In other words, unbeknownst to us, humanity has created an all-pervasive sociotechnical assemblage that redefines our own conditions of subjectivity. *La téchnique* is not simply a matter of an external rationalized system, but redefines the nature of inner life; the training of the sensorium that the city-machine induces operates at the affective level. This blurring of the boundaries between inner and outer environments leads to a situation in which the reproductive process no longer require an initial model, grounded in the real; instead, the objects and commodities of the external world begin more and more to be determined and to reflect the needs and desires of the subject. In this manner the category of the object becomes further divorced from the material process of its own production.

This transformation in the nature of the object is borne out in various ways by many of the thinkers we address. Thus, *The Philosophy of Money*, Simmel's (2001 [1907]) sociological analysis of objects and our relationship to them, like that of Heidegger, grants a privileged position to the artist/craftsperson and prefigures the work of later theorists such as Baudrillard, who in his *The System of Objects* (1997) provides practical examples of the otherwise abstract descriptions of technological change we encountered in Part I's discussion of the 'letting be' of furniture. For both Simmel and Baudrillard, the example of furniture illustrates how these processes make themselves physically apparent in the bland functionalism of objects designed with an a priori sense of their position relative to background systems of style and fashion. This argument can perhaps best be explained by contrasting flat-pack furniture with inherited family furniture. The former is both bought within a functionality-led warehouse system of codes and catalogues and then placed in the home in a modular manner that is highly adaptable to new fashions or later additions from the same or similar furniture ranges. The basic physicality and appearance of such furniture, from its colours to the material it is made from, are subordinate to the systemic qualities it holds in relation to the overarching systems of fashion and the furniture company's total product range. In the case of furniture traditionally handed down between generations, the physical appearance is imbued with the patina, marks and associations of the family's history, and its basic material of wood is more likely to have particular qualities worthy of attention in its own right.

Simmel's analysis emphasizes the way in which these traditional, practical or emotional values of objects are all thrown into the melting pot of exchange-value, which, despite its inherently changeable flux-driven nature, becomes a paradoxically unifying and stabilizing force: despite its immaterial nature it assumes qualities of substance. In Simmel's perspective, which prefigures Baudrillard's later privileging of the symbolic exchange typical of non-technological 'primitive societies' over the exclusively commodified exchange of capitalist society, the blurring of the inside/outside distinction stems from the crucial role the abstract nature of the capitalist exchange system plays in colonizing, in a form of cultural extinction, the traditional life world that preceded capitalism and replacing it with an enframed matrix.

The economic origins of cyberspace

Our examination of the work of Simmel and Benjamin has demonstrated the degree to which the recasting of the subject and object within the context of urban results in a reconfiguration of space, one in which the distinction between the inner and the outer, consciousness and commodity, reaches a new threshold. We have also seen how this process may be treated in terms of a dialectic of reification, in which capital acts as a solvent that puts into suspension previously apparently durable structures. Lukács spoke of this process and of the crucial role that technology played within it when he declared that 'man':

> . . . is a mechanical part incorporated into a mechanical system. He finds it already pre-existing and self-sufficient, it functions independently of him and he has to conform to its laws whether he likes it or not . . . a process mechanically conforming to fixed laws and *enacted independently of man's consciousness and impervious to human intervention, i.e. a perfectly closed system, must likewise transform the basic categories of man's immediate attitude to the world: it reduces space and time to a common denominator and degrades time to the dimension of space.*

> (Lukács 1968 [1922]: 89 [our emphasis])

In this manner, his work prefigures both Heidegger's emphasis upon craft/ enframement and Ellul's notion of *la téchnique*. More relevant still for digital matters is the way in which his focus upon the circumscribing and calculative nature of capitalist laws of production serves to identify a key point in the formation of cyber*space*. Thus, building on Marx, Lukács identifies the same quantity/quality relationship explored by Benjamin and a key element of McLuhan's thought. Lukács describes how:

> Quality no longer matters. Quantity alone decides everything ... Thus time sheds its qualitative, variable, flowing nature; it freezes into an exactly delimited, quantifiable continuum filled with quantifiable 'things' (the reified, mechanically objectified 'performance' of the worker, wholly separated from his total human personality): in short, it becomes space.
>
> (ibid.: 90)

This is very similar to Benjamin's previously cited assertion of the symbiotic relationship that exists between the matrix and the mass: 'The mass is a matrix from which all traditional behavior toward works of art issues today in a new form. Quantity has been transmuted into quality' (Benjamin 1973 [1935]: 241). This is a vital point. It both shows how digital technologies share the same root by which they create qualitative change from quantitative increases and illustrates how the same fundamental creation of qualitative differences from quantitative change serves to separate the mechanical (Network 1900) from the digital (Network 2000). In the digital, despite the dominance of the phrase cyberspace, space is actually less important than the speed and the social flux it causes: 'The principal factors in media impact on existing social forms are acceleration and disruption. Today the acceleration tends to be total, and thus ends space as the main factor in social arrangements' (McLuhan 1995 [1964]: 94). The fact that it is space that is still the nominal focus of the Matrix, despite digitality's undermining of it, is in keeping with McLuhan's concept that we tend to emphasize a feature of our understanding just as it is being made increasingly irrelevant by the newly dominant technology: 'Just before an airplane breaks the sound barrier, sound waves become visible on the wings of the plane. The sudden visibility of sound just as sound ends is an apt instance of that great pattern of being that reveals new and opposite forms just as the earlier forms reach their peak performance' (ibid.: 12). As we have seen Kittler conclude, by converging previous technologies and dramatically increasing their speed of output, the digital represents a radical departure.

In analysing contemporary history, Lukács argues that the essential focus needs to be upon the commodity form and its central role in the structures of the subsequently capitalist society that is built around it: 'The commodity can only be understood in its undistorted essence when it becomes the universal category of society as a whole' (Lukács 1968 [1922]: 86). Lash, however, suggests that the digital information age may have superseded this category. Commodities themselves have become subordinate to their prior status as informational flows: '. . . the spread and ubiquity of the information and com-munication networks cannot be reduced to commodification' (Lash 2002: viii) and 'it may no longer be commodification that is driving informationalization, but instead informationalization that is driving commodification' (ibid.: 3). It is interesting to note in this context that the cyberpunk novelist William Gibson's latest work, *Pattern Recognition* (2003), illustrates how his previous fascination with information flows has evolved *à la* Lash into the informationalization of the commodification process. The culture industry has been described as psy-choanalysis in reverse, to the extent that it is premised upon not uncovering and curing our deepest neuroses and complexes, but rather discovering them in order to massage them and exploit them for commercial gain. For Gibson, this psychoanalysis-in-reverse uses information to effect the process as effectively and subtly as possible. As one of his characters, the head of a cutting-edge adver-tising agency, puts it:

> I want to make the public aware of something they don't quite yet know that they know – or have them feel that way. Because they'll move on that, do you understand? They'll think they thought of it first. It's about trans-ferring information, but at the same time about a certain lack of specificity.
>
> (ibid.: 63)

In the digital, what matters is not an object's essential qualities but its position within a set of relations. This set of relations has evolved from Marx's notion of exchange-value.

For Marx, exchange-value was a distortion of use-value; now, the separation of use-value from a particular object is taken further. The alienation associated with the production of goods for an abstract market beyond the immediate needs of the good's producer (exchange-value) is transformed into the informational processing of those needs themselves. Lash's analysis highlights the central issue repeatedly encountered in McLuhan's work (and later in Baudrillard's in the form of *reversibility*) whereby quantitative increases pushed to their limit produce qualitative change. Likewise, Lukács points out that the basis of the qualitative change from use-value to exchange-value is the quantitative increase in supply, and this is mirrored in the cultural sphere with Benjamin's analysis of the social effects of the mechanical reproduction of photographic images: the quantitative increase in their output leads to a qualitative change in their mode of recep-tion. In Lash's analysis digital technology represents a further qualitative change whereby the old use-value/exchange-value dualism is replaced by a new, 'imma-nentist' logic: 'It explodes and partly marginalizes the exchange-value/use-value couple' (Lash 2002: 9). This new logic is about rapid circulation rather than time for reflection, it is about 'all at onceness' rather than temporal depth.

Lash's analysis is thus similar to the fundamentally new social implications Benjamin saw accompanying the advent of photography. Lash's use of the phrase 'explodes' is resonant of Benjamin's previously cited reference to dynamite to describe the way in which photography destroyed traditional conceptions of art and brought reality closer to the masses. In keeping with Kittler's assertion of the discontinuity of networks, Benjamin describes how photography destroys traditional art forms but fosters exchange-value; writers such as Lash and Baudrillard argue that with digital matters exchange-value has morphed into a yet stranger form. Thus, we appear to arrive at another threshold. Although cyberspace may have its origins in the transformation of space and commodity that we have traced throughout the last chapter, in the digital we arrive at a new scenario in which flows of information appear to take precedence over flows of commodities. Information appears to subsume all of the previous flows outlined and to determine the distribution and direction of these flows. In order to understand what this new informatic status might entail, we will turn in the next chapter to the visions of cyberpunk, which offer fictional extrapolations of current trends; however, before this, we must consider the thought of two theorists whose respective works provide some deeper insight into the increasing informationalization of society, namely Niklas Luhmann and Jean Baudrillard.

Luhmann's autopoietic matrix

> ... the technology of dissemination plays the same kind of role as that played by the medium of money in the differentiation of the economy: it merely constitutes a medium which makes formations of form possible. These formations in turn, unlike the medium itself, constitute the communicative operations which enable the differentiation and operational closure of the system.
>
> (Luhmann 2000: 2)

Like a number of media theorists before him, Luhmann focuses upon mechanical reproduction as a key development in human communication to the extent that it provides the key to the way in which the contemporary media operate: 'it is the mechanical manufacture of a product as the bearer of communication . . . which has led to the differentiation of a particular system of the mass media' (ibid.: 2). Luhmann's theory places the emergence of mechanical reproduction within a unique vision of society and communication, one that is anti-humanist and radically constructivist. Although Luhmann's perspective is marked by a disregard for socio-political questions in favour of a more neutral, structural or quasi-cybernetic model for the evolution of communications media and society, his theory nonetheless offers a number of fruitful points of contact with the body of ideas we have discussed so far. What Luhmann's complex systems theory provides is a crucial insight into how information has emerged as crucial component of the contemporary matrix. The specific relevance of Luhmann's theory for our purposes is its deterministic account of the contribution made by media technologies to the blurring process between representations and reality. This is a major attribute of the media, of which digitality is for Luhmann, like Kittler, but an extended and literal example of the coding that exists in other media forms. And like Kittler, Luhmann approaches society as an information processing system. However, whereas Kittler emphasizes the crucial importance of media technologies, that is to say the nature and evolution of hardware itself, which he views as the *primum mobile* of network transmodulations, Luhmann's approaches is systemic. Society, individuals and the messages that they produce are seen in terms of an evolving system which, through an ongoing process of differentiation and subsequent stabilization, adapts and evolves.

Drawing upon a range of theoretical perspectives (including that of the Frankfurt School, whose influence on our own account is crucial), Luhmann develops an account of society that places communication and increasingly communication technology at its centre. Like Kittler, his basic model is that of information theory, and posits the existence of a sender, message and recipient. The sender's message is not guaranteed to be correctly received by its recipient, since it is subject to the destabilizing presence of noise and the possibility that its recipient will interpret its noise as its signal and vice versa. Thus, communication must evolve in such a way as to exclude the possibility of misinterpretation, and media are a means to ensure this process. However, innovations in media, in turn, introduce further instabilities or occasions for noise and misinterpretation, and so the process is one of constant negotiation or adaptation. In this manner Luhmann places systemic formation via differentiation at the heart of his media theory. Systems (and for Luhmann this term would encompass both society and the individual) are processes of differentiation that establish and maintain dynamic boundaries with their environments; thus, they differentiate themselves from events and operations that cannot be integrated into their internal structures. To describe this process, and the entities that result from it, Luhmann adopts the term 'autopoiesis' (derived from the biological theory of Valera and Mantura). Autopoiesis refers to a system that maintains its boundaries through a process of compensating for the external perturbations to which they are subject. Thus, any stability they possess is entirely dynamic, and their coherence is the result of their continual differentiation. When society and individuals are approached in terms of autopoiesis, media emerge both as agents of destabilization and as elements of coherence. What Luhmann's theory does is to grant priority to this differentiation, such that its apparent terms must always be related back to the differential process through which they are constituted. This position results in a profound reflexivity: through media representation, a system can observe itself via the distinction between the system and its environment through which it has differentially determined itself. In other words, the system's own representations of itself become terms in its ongoing disparation:

> ... the concept of society has to be defined not by an idealized state with compensatory functions but by a boundary, that is, by a boundary-drawing operation. Such an operation produces the difference between the system and its environment and thereby produces the possibility of observing the system, that is, the distinction between the system and its environment. This distinction can re-enter the system, it can be copied in the system and then allows for the stability of the system, for referential oscillation

between observations, respectively indicating external and internal states and events.

(Luhmann 1997: 75)

For Luhmann, then, the environment external to the media system generates McLuhanite frictions with the system itself, but these are still dealt with by the system according to its self-generated values which Luhmann describes as 'condensates of meaning' so that 'topics, and objects emerge as "Eigenvalues" of the system of mass media communication, [which] are generated in the recursive context of the system's operations and do not depend upon the environment's confirmation of them' (Luhmann 2000: 37). This has important implications for our discussion of the complex interplay between internal and external worlds within advanced capitalism and its phantasmagorical commodity forms. According to Luhmann: 'in the system's perception, the distinction between the world as it is and the world as it is observed becomes blurred' (ibid.: 11). Luhmann argues that this is a systemic condition, that is to say that it is not that individuals or collectivities mistake representation for the real, but rather that representation has become an irreducible component of the world, an operator in its ongoing auto-differentiation: '. . . in the operationally current present world as it is and the world as it is being observed cannot be distinguished' (ibid.: 11). Thus, social evolution for Luhmann takes place 'on the basis of very specific evolutionary achievements, such as the invention of coins' (2000: 15). Inventions of this kind create over time a differentiated system so that, with coins for example, a whole economic system is differentially produced. The inherently deterministic element of the process stems from the fact that an artefact has the ability to create 'a productive differentiation . . . which, in favourable conditions, leads to the emergence of systems to which the rest of society can only adapt' (2000: 15). In terms of the other writers we have encountered, this ability to create a differentiated system can be understood as the basis of *la téchnique*, the institutionalization of withdrawal from withdrawal, the synchronicity of a Network etc. Despite the prevalence of such misleading terms as 'interactivity', the mass media function only on the basis of the effective operational exclusion of their audience.

Again, as for Benjamin *et al.,* this starts with the way in which mechanical reproduction creates an increase in quantitative output that leads to a qualitatively new experience of reception. For example, in terms reminiscent of those Baudrillard (1990a) uses to describe the nature of the *fatal masses,* Luhmann describes how the printing press creates a volume of output that by its very nature excludes direct oral participation amongst its consumers, who:

> make their presence felt at most in quantitative terms: through sales figures, through listener or viewer ratings, but not as a counteractive audience. The quantum of their presence can be described and interpreted, but is not fed back via communication.
>
> (Luhmann 2000: 16)

Luhmann accepts that verbal commentary by individuals can of course be made, but the point he emphasizes is that such direct feedback is not essential to the functioning of these operational observations: 'This is how, in the sphere of the mass media, an autopoietic, self-reproducing system is able to emerge which no longer requires the mediation of interaction among those co-present' (ibid.: 16). This is the basis for the important concept of *operational closure*. A definition of *the hyperreal* as the generation of models without origins in reality is here manifested in a system that 'reproduces its own operations out of itself' (ibid.: 16). This is a crucial development because it represents the media's independence from external reality – they are 'instead oriented to the system's own distinction between self-reference and other-reference' (ibid.: 16). The link between such a type of operationally closed system and digital technologies is the way in which the system both defines itself against the external environment and processes its own operations: 'this typically occurs by means of a binary code which fixes a positive and a negative value whilst excluding any third possibility' (ibid.: 16). There is the further irony that, although premised upon a prodigious capability for memory, this system is designed to both remember and forget quickly. It is the flows of information and differentiations made by the system that are privileged, and we now look at depictions of those differentiations and flows in the work of Baudrillard, before turning to cyberpunk fiction and its depiction of the joys and thrills to be found within them.

Baudrillard and the hyperreal

If we were able to take as the finest allegory of simulation the Borges tale where the cartographers of the Empire draw up a map so detailed that it ends up exactly covering the territory (but where the decline of the Empire sees this map become frayed and finally ruined, a few shreds still discernible in the deserts[)] . . . then this fable has come full circle for us . . . Abstraction today is no longer that of the map, the double, the mirror or the concept. Simulation is no longer that of a territory, a referential being or a substance. It is the generation by models of a real without origin or reality: a hyperreal. The territory no longer precedes the map, nor survives it. Henceforth, it is the map that precedes the territory . . . it is the map that engenders the territory and if we were to revive the fable today, it would be the territory whose shreds are slowly rotting across the map. It is the real, and not the map, whose vestiges subsist here and there, in the deserts which are no longer those of the Empire, but our own. *The desert of the real itself.*

(Baudrillard 1983: 2 [emphasis in the original])

Our brief summary of Luhmann's thought outlines the processes by which an informatic capitalism could come into existence. Nevertheless, in adopting a neutral tone and perspective, his account remains curiously 'bloodless' and, since our concern is not only the theory of the matrix but also the cultural and experiential consequences of its institution, we turn to the work of Baudrillard.

Perhaps more than any other theorist, Baudrillard has attempted to articulate the consequences of the fusion of commodity, subject and environment within a generalized space of informatic flows. This blurring is the phenomenon that inspires the plot of the *Matrix* films, and Morpheus (the character who delivers Neo from his enslavement to simulation), when revealing the world that exists outside of the computer-generated simulation in which humanity is enslaved, declares, in homage to Baudrillard, 'welcome to the desert of the real'. Another significant allusion to Baudrillard occurs in the same film, when one of Baudrillard's key theoretical accounts of hyperreality, the book *Simulations* (1983), appears as a literally hollowed out container in which the protagonist's computer disks are stored. We suggest that the pun is deeper than it may appear because Baudrillard's insights are inevitably hollowed out themselves as a result of Hollywood's movie treatment of the simulation phenomenon of which it is a more than willing accomplice. Yet at the same time, these allusions also demonstrate the currency that Baudrillard's account of the modern scene possesses outside the academy, wherein he has often been castigated for the extremity, and the seemingly arbitrary logic, of his claims. Out of the many tropes and figures that Baudrillard has proffered over the years, we will concentrate on one, namely the *hyperreal*, since this term best encapsulates the insidious effect of the logic of enframement and systemic totality that we have hitherto explored. Before we consider the various orders of the hyperreal that Baudrillard has identified, it is necessary to establish some of the conceptual assumptions that underpin his use of this term, and to place these within the context of the ideas we have explored.

Baudrillard is concerned with the gradual occultation of the real by what he terms 'simulation' – a condition we have already touched upon in our discussion of the gradual commodification of space and subjectivity in the transformation of the urban experience throughout the twentieth century. Baudrillard argues that our contemporary condition is that of the *precession of the simulacra*. We might consider in this light his retelling of Borges' tale, quoted above, in which the desire for a perfect cartography results in the production of a map that eclipses the terrain. According to Baudrillard, our current situation is even more surreal. The map does not simply occlude the territory: it has become autonomous. It has been uncoupled from a referent, any necessary relation to a real that precedes it, and this is the order of simulation or the hyperreal. The copy or simulation precedes the real. The terrain formerly known as the real is emptied out, desiccated by the proliferation of representation; it is a desert because it is no longer the site of the life, which is ensnared in simulation, as in the world outside the Matrix that Morpheus reveals to Neo. For Baudrillard, this condition is inseparable from the proliferation of media technologies, what now passes for 'the real is produced from miniaturized units, from matrices, memory banks and command models – and with these it can be reproduced an indefinite number of times' (ibid.: 3). This condition is to be understood in terms of a liberation of signs from their signifieds: simulation begins 'with the liquidation of all referentials'. Relieved from their designatory office and transferred to digital matrices, signs run in an endless loop. Thus, Baudrillard posits a history of the sign and image as representation in terms of successive phases that culminate in this so-called precession of simulacra. First, the image begins as the reflection of a basic reality, then it becomes a mask or perversion of this reality. In time (as that reality withers), it comes to mask the absence of reality and, finally, 'it bears no relation to any reality whatsoever: it is its own pure simulacrum' (ibid.: 11).

The orders of the simulacra

In this manner, Baudrillard identifies four major stages or orders of simulacra in the revolution of our perceptions of social reality as it proceeds to the space of pure simulation. These are:

1   Renaissance perspective and the *trompe-l'oeil*;
2   industrial production and the mechanical reproduction of the image;
3   the advent of the hyperreal; and
4   the fractal.

By way of illustration we might say that, in the first stage, perspectival paintings portray in an abstract, mathematical form a physical reality beyond their canvas, whilst, in the second, photography produces similar, yet even more mathematically accurate, images through a mechanical and chemical process. These first two stages, although aiming at producing independent representations, are still premised to varying degrees upon an external reality that these productions refer or represent. In contrast, the hyperreal and fractal orders are distinguished by the way in which media content increasingly has no external origin: the source of its representations is internally generated. We can see this process with the evolution of the photographic image into the infinitely manipulable digital image. As he is not bound by Kittler's stricture with respect to the impossibility of analysing a contemporary network, for Baudrillard this internal generation of models stems from *la téchnique* reaching a new order of autonomy. The digital translation of external phenomenon into binary 1s and 0s facilitates an enframed order, which, once operational, to a significant degree no longer 'needs' reference to an external reality. Before there are mechanical copies, a representational work of art privileges the notion of an 'original', perspective retains a close link between the observer of scene or object and the representation of that scene (*à la* Benjamin's analysis of aura). With the advent of photography in the second order of simulacra, the strength of the bond between reality and its representations is undermined: the quantitative increase in the number of reproduced images begins to imply a qualitative change in human perception of representations. There emerges a realm of images that is at least partially independent of a prior reality that yielded up those images. The third and fourth orders of simulacra describe the process of this independent realms gradually uncoupling from the real. Let us look at Baudrillard's four orders of simulacra in more detail.

Renaissance perspective, the trompe-l'oeil *and the origins of hyperreality*

As we have seen, the sign and the image are both understood in Baudrillard's theory as originally representational terms that have become increasingly divorced from this function. For Baudrillard their initial function can be grasped through a consideration of the culture of the Renaissance. Here the sign is marked by its constancy; thus, dress as signifying system is not the site of play: 'there is no such thing as fashion in a society of cast and rank . . . one is assigned a place irrevocably . . . An interdiction protects the signs and assures them total clarity; each sign . . . refers unequivocally to a status' (ibid.: 84). As is well known, the Renaissance marked the development of perspective and its essentially illusionary representation of reality that portrays three-dimensional space upon the two-dimensional plane of either paper or canvas, an illusory space that attains its fullest expression in the *trompe-l'oeil* of the Baroque. This portrayal of figures in three-dimensional space provides the initial premise for the subsequent development of autonomous space in its own right, as ultimately embodied in the technologies of virtual reality and computer imaging. The key feature of the representational forms of the Renaissance and Baroque for Baudrillard's schema rests on the fact that, even with the *trompe-l'oeil*'s deception of the eye, there is a clear sense of the difference between the representation and the reality from which it is derived. Simulation is here understood in terms of a counterfeit, analogy or theatre of representation.

Industrial production and mechanical reproduction

Baudrillard focuses upon the difference between the orders of simulation as well as the crucial role of technics in their transformation by juxtaposing the concept of the automaton with the machine. The automaton partakes of the economy of analogy or the counterfeit; it mirrors the functions of the living organism, but in a manner that emphasizes the distance or distinction between them (hence its role in philosophical debate in the seventeenth century). The machine is of another order; it breaks with a play of representation by establishing a functional equivalence. Rather than a mirror of man *in toto*, it extracts and replicates an abstract function, establishing 'an immanent logic of the operational principle' (ibid.: 95). Thus, Marx's analysis of the machine as fixed capital describes it in terms of the exaltation of dead work over living labour. It is work that is reproduced or simulated. The machine is in essence marked by simulation, and it inaugurates an economy of simulation. This is precisely Baudrillard's redefinition of the Industrial Revolution. It is the occasion of mass (re)production of signs and objects, and this resides not in its Promethean liberation of natural and mechanical forces, but in its economy of equivalence. Humans and machines become equivalent, individuals as 'force of work' become equivalent and interchangeable, and 'objects become undefined simulacra one of the other' (ibid.: 97).

Thus, for Baudrillard, the significance of the analyses of Benjamin and later McLuhan is their lucid recognition of the true nature of industrialized capitalism. By making reproduction the locus of industrial culture, Benjamin apprehends the importance 'of what Marx negligently called the nonessential sectors of capital' (ibid.: 99), namely the role of media and later information technologies. Rather than mere superstructural effects, mechanical reproduction reveals technology as media or simulation 'as form and principle of a whole new generation of sense' (ibid.: 99). And, since technology represents the crucial operator in the realization of industrial capitalism, then the latter must be understood as a process of mediatization, of the progressive simulation of the entire social body. Thus, 'Benjamin and McLuhan saw . . . more clearly than Marx . . . the true message: *the true ultimatum was in reproduction itself*' (ibid.: 100 [emphasis in original]). Reproduction, or rather, mediatization – that is the endless productions of copies without an original – was the hidden logic of industrialization and the 'analyses of Benjamin and McLuhan are situated on [the] limit of reproduction and simulation, at the point where referential reason disappears, and where production is no longer sure of itself' (ibid.: 102). In other words, we now inhabit the culmination of the processes first described by Benjamin: the hyperreal.

The hyperreal

The passage from mechanical reproduction to full-blown simulation or the *hyperreal* can again be related to a transformation of the technological matrix. Hyperreality, by which Baudrillard means the absolute triumph of the copy without original, is the result of the replacement of mechanical reproduction by digital or informatic simulation. We have examined Sontag's analysis of the way in which photography tends to transform reality into a tautology, a statement that signals the distance that has been travelled from Benjamin's analysis of reproduction. Reproduction is no longer a death or extirpation of aura, but the impossibility of conceiving of aura; hyperreality is the ruin of the concept of originality. Warhol's serial canvases and prints (of soup cans, Marilyn Monroe, car crashes etc) enact this transition. Here reproducibility does not fall upon an original and replicate it *sans* aura, instead it is implicit in the artwork from its inception. This is at once the fulfilment of the revolutionary potential Benjamin glimpsed in reproducibility (in other words the long-cherished avant-garde dream of the delivering the aesthetic from the canonized work so that it could transform life itself) and its negation: 'art enters into its indefinite *reproduction*: [but] all that reduplicates itself, even if it be the everyday and banal reality, falls by the token under the sign of art, and becomes esthetic' (1983: 151). In world of pure artifice everything becomes art, and so art's specificity or challenge is diffused: 'art and industry can exchange their signs. Art can become a reproducing machine . . . ' (1983: 151).

Hyperreality is marked by the 'oversimulation' of the real; the verisimilitude of the copy is of such exactitude that it negates the original. It refers to the concept of objects and their environments that are *more real than the real itself.* Baudrillard often deploys pornography as a trope for the hyperreal, and in pornography we observe the brutality of overrepresentation, of what Baudrillard calls *the obscene.* His use of the latter term is not moral or pejorative; instead it is an appeal to the etymology of the *ob-scene* – as that which is literally off the scene or stage: that which is not shown. The hyperreal is obscene because it shows everything, nothing is off-stage any more. Again, this is not an appeal for the preservation of modesty, what is sacrificed to the obscene is *seduction,* understood as a play of signifiers that at once reveals and conceals. The erotic is seductive because it both shows and hides. What is shown is charged with that what is concealed or withdrawn (to use Heidegger's terms). What is on display contains within it an implicit dimension; it is this non-present presence that constitutes its seduction. In Baudrillard's work, withdrawal and ambiguity are approached in terms of this concept of *seduction.* A disproportionate amount of the romantic pleasure to be had from human relationships is the ambiguous and indeterminate nature of the likely responses to an amorous advance. Physical desire is kindled and stoked in the stylistic mores of courtship; it is sublimated into a ritualized process of indeterminate/ambiguous advance and retreat/withdrawal of which the eventual physical possession is but the eventual climax point. Such modes of participation are extinguished by technology. The media's technological intrusion into courtship rituals promotes the explicit at the expense of the ambiguous. Pornography is the end product of lenses that provide more physical details to the viewer of the sex act than are immediately available to its direct participants. Pornography exemplifies the obscenity of the hyperreal; its display exceeds ordinary presence and so banishes seduction. In pornography's

> anatomical zoom, the dimension of the real is abolished, the distance implied by the gaze gives way to an instantaneous, exacerbated representation, that of sex in its pure state, stripped not just of all seduction, but of the image's very potentiality. Sex so close that it merges with its own representation.
>
> (Baudrillard 1990b: 29)

This coalescence of act and representation is a direct consequence of technology: pornography is 'a voyeurism of exactitude . . . that can only be revealed by a sophisticated technical apparatus' (ibid.: 45).

This hyperreality can be observed at every level of culture. The Irish theme pub, for instance, instantiates the economy of the hyperreal. An authentic real is transformed into a series of signs including: Guinness, Irish music, the tricolour flag, leprechauns, etc. These signs are then modularized and redeployed as one of a number of possible themed environments. In time, these simulacra infect their progenitor in a semiotic *mis en abyme* as pubs in Ireland begin to take on the appearance of 'Irish pubs'.

The fractal

The ultimate basis of the hyperreal lies in the process of abstraction begun by the act of perspective whereby the physical gives way to increasingly pure forms of representation. Mechanical reproduction thus merely exacerbates a process of abstraction begun with perspective, and hyperreality is a further development of the same process whereby representation is liberated by its dramatic growth to create a new perceptual space no longer closely tied to original sources. The decline in importance of authenticity and originality leads to a rise in a new realm of media and a wholesale recreation of the concept of context. The fractal is the fourth order of simulacra that Baudrillard uses to conceptualize the further qualitative changes that have occurred to perceptual experience as a result of further increases to the mechanical reproduction of images and communication in general, greatly enabled by digital technologies. Thus, the technological foundations of this condition of generalized simulation serve to connect Baudrillard's meditations to the themes we have explored in the preceding chapters.

The hyperreal is inseparable from a transformation of technology and in particular the emergence of information technology. Here, Baudrillard's analysis is particularly incisive, in that it identified in the early 1980s a number of trends that have become fully realized only in the new century. Baudrillard places the question of digitality, code or information at the centre of hyperreality: 'The real is produced . . . from matrices, memory banks . . . and with these it can be reproduced an indefinite number of times' (Baudrillard 1983: 3). When information is digital or digitized, there is no difference between one copy and an infinite number of copies; this, for Baudrillard, is the ultimate state of simulation, an endless proliferation of reproducibility based on information technology. Baudrillard sees this in terms of a fractaline multiverse of code and data: from the information of system of DNA to the structures of the built environment, 'the matrix remains binary' (ibid.: 134), and more and more aspects of the social environment participate in this multiverse and reflect a general economy of informatic replication that with its unchecked spread has taken the previous notion of urban disorientation to a new level. Baudrillard refers to this disorientation in terms of cancerous metastases, viral infections and fractal dispersions. We provide illustrations from cyberpunk fiction of this conceptualization in the next chapter and show how, despite the apparent directionless flux of these processes, they can ultimately be traced as circulations enframed within the matrix.

Conclusion – the Danger of the hyperreal

The notion of the hyperreal helps to clarify Heidegger's ambiguous notion of *the Danger*. The adjective 'ambiguous' is used deliberately because ambiguity is an essential part of Heidegger's notion of Being and the claim that withdrawal from it is actually a crucial part of authentic Being. In Ellul's work we encountered the notion of the overwhelming nature of the simultaneously invasive and pervasive quality of technology to be found in *la téchnique* and its ultimate eclipse of the dialectic. To this foreboding conceptualization we can add Heidegger's application of the *existential analytic* to help grapple with an apparently essential quality of technology that is deeply alienating for human agency. A physical object is always both less and more than a complete self-contained entity. The basis of its existence is its opposition to the greater reality of which it can only ever be but a small and incomplete part. At the same time, it is also more than it appears to be. As part of Being an object partakes of the existential analytic's inherent torsion between past, present and future – its present explicit state also includes implicit qualities derived from its non-explicit past and future. This is what Heidegger refers to as his concept of *withdrawal*.

The concept of the hyperreal and its cultural manifestations put useful flesh on the philosophical bones of Heidegger's notion of the 'withdrawal of withdrawal', by which we have previously seen that he means not simply the withdrawal of Being in presence of technology but the forgetting of Being in this presence. In other words, technology's Danger is the way in which its effects are insidious and/or unacknowledged. Mirroring the essential torsion of Being that is predicated upon disclosure and withdrawal from immediate explicit qualities of physicality, the technological being-in-the-world of the matrix similarly involves both the full disclosure of the physical artefacts we interact with and the much more indeterminate, immaterial mental processes and broader conceptual and technological frameworks that lie behind such overt physicality. The technological object is replete with and presupposes the sedimented meanings of the underlying values of the society that produced it. The crucial difference between Being and being in the matrix is thus that, whilst in the former *ambiguity* and *withdrawal* are an inherent part of the existential analytic, in the matrix they are lacking. The technological object fulfils a predetermined role in the standing-reserve from which it was challenged forth – it plays a precise, unambiguous role in the enframement of Being of which it is one small exactly replicated part. Its most fundamental relationship is not to Being but to the standardizing matrix from which it derives its meaning. The crucial feature of hyperreal phenomena is this way in which they are freed from their dependence upon an original reference point in Being, against which they can be assessed for authenticity. In the next chapter we see how this freedom from dependence upon the Being of reality is embraced as 'withdrawal from withdrawal' and is instantiated in a hypostasized matrix: the Matrix.

In this chapter we began by addressing the concept of reification as it is presented by Lukács *et al.*, and claimed that it was this theory that best accounted for the transformation of identity, space and object in the changing urban landscape of the twentieth century. However, contemporary conditions introduced a new problematic in the form of the flows of information, described by thinkers such as Lash and Bauman. In order to offer some sense of how information and its dissemination could have come to assume such a critical role in an economy that had formerly had as its locus the manufactured object (e.g. the 'dream objects' of Benjamin's Arcades), we turned to bodies of theory, which offer something of a genealogy of information. Thus, in Luhmann's system theory we encounter a model of society as an 'autopoietic' process of differentiation and complexification whose nature is irretrievably altered by the appearance of information technology as at once a product of the ongoing differentiation of society and a term that stimulates further differentiation. In contrast to the evolutionary dynamic of Luhmann's theory, Baudrillard provided us with a 'fatal' or nilhilistic vision of society, in which information became the final term in the triumph of simulation, a concept that owes something to both Debord's spectacle and to Heidegger's notion of the Danger of forgetting the disclosure of Being in conditions of enframement. Despite these differences, both place information and its flows at the heart of contemporary assemblages, and it is to the diagnostic if not prognostic power of cyberpunk's depictions of informational flows that we now turn.

7   Cyberspatial Matrix matters

CYBERSPACE – A consensual hallucination experienced daily by billions of legitimate operators . . . A graphic representation of data abstracted from the bank of every computer in the human system. Unthinkable complexity. Lines of light ranged in the nonspace of the mind, clusters and constellations of data. Like city lights receding.

(Gibson 1984: 67)

He felt a stab of elation, the octagons and adrenaline mixing with something else. You're enjoying this, he thought; you're crazy. Because in some weird and very approximate way it was like a run in the matrix . . . it was possible to see Ninsei as a field of data . . . Then you could throw yourself into a highspeed drift and skid, totally engaged but set apart from it all, and all around you the dance of biz, information interacting, data made flesh in the mazes of the black market.

(ibid.: 26)

We have alluded to the unique sensitivity possessed by creative individuals, their ability to detect and anticipate changes in networks or matrices and, drawing on Deleuze's observations of artists as the 'symptomatologists of society', have spoken of the diagnostic value of literature. Given this perspective, the science fiction subgenre of 'cyberpunk' offers, within the context of the themes of this book, a particularly cogent example of the diagnostic and prognostic powers of fiction. Consider in the first instance the genre's inaugural text, William Gibson's *Neuromancer*, from which the above quotations are taken. Written in the early 1980s, it was here that the term and concept of cyberspace was first articulated; indeed, the text uses 'cyberspace' and the 'matrix' as synonyms for an autonomous, interactive data-space. Other examples could be cited: Neal Stephenson's *Snow Crash* (1992) is often credited as the first instance of the use of the term 'avatar' to describe an individual's virtual representative.

In this chapter we explore the manner in which the world of cyberpunk describes in a deliberately exaggerated form many of our key ideas. In particular, we explore the manner in which it provides a catharsis for the fear and fascination occasioned by the vertiginous change in the pace and nature of modern urban experience. In this respect, cyberpunk is Janus-faced: it both looks back to the conditions hypostatized in the figure of the *flâneur* and its fictional representatives, such as lone male protagonist in crime fiction, while also looking forward, imaging urban landscapes transformed by global diasporas and information technology. From the outset cyberpunk is immersed in the space of flow/flow of spaces that Castells sees as characterizing the network society. The second quotation from *Neuromancer* describes, in terms redolent of Baudelaire (and Kittler's description of the city as a site of information processing), the accelerated sensations felt by the console cowboy (hacker/cyberpunk) protagonist Case as he compares the frenetic urban scene of seething physicality lying in front of him to the experience of jacking into the Matrix. We start this chapter by tracing the links between the fictional figure of the cyberpunk and the less dramatic but ultimately related associations real programmers make with the code they produce. We use the notion of informational intimacy to suggest that, in both reality and fiction, new levels of closeness to informational flows bring both appealing sensations and elements of alienation that need to be viewed in terms of the theories encountered in Part I.

In Chapter 6 we saw the way in which the contemporary consumer learns to circulate within the enframed commodity matrix that the cityscape has become. Individual subjecthood has become largely replaced by circulation as its own *raison d'être* in a manner that mirrors the self-referential qualities of the technological matrix described in depth in Part I. David Harvey (1990), amongst others, has described the postmodern shift from a Fordist economy of durable goods to a post-Fordist one which privileges information-rich commodity forms. As we have seen through Benjamin, Simmel and most recently Baudrillard, this transformation can be located in capitalism's inherent reliance upon the abstract semiological value of products which progressively subordinates their physical use-value: a 'structural law of the code' succeeds a simple materiality. In this theoretical context, cyberpunk's matrix is the imaginative apotheosis of abstract capitalist relations, accelerated and extenuated to such degree that they become a psycho-temporal space. The origins of the matrix reside in the increasing ubiquity and abstraction of code, which results in autonomous realm of self-referential or 'fractal' meaning that subsumes historical notions of the 'real'.

The plots of both Gibson's genre-defining *Neuromancer* trilogy and the Wachowski brothers' *Matrix* trilogy are driven by the notion that artificial intelligences oversee an extreme projection of the matrix we have examined thus far. The complexity of these intelligences is such that they take on an almost demiurgic quality, becoming autonomous operators whose evolution is beyond the comprehension of their putative users. These plots can be seen as visionary extrapolations of our major theme; that is, the way in which changes in quantitative output can create qualitative effects. Thus, throughout the whole of the *Neuromancer* trilogy is the idea that the quantitative build-up of data mystically leads to a qualitative change in the form of a newly found self-awareness of the Matrix. In *Count Zero* (1986), this process is vaguely alluded to – 'Then something happened and it . . . It knew itself' – whilst in *Mona Lisa Overdrive* (1988), this development is simply referred to as 'It changed' (cited in Cavallaro 2000: 60–1). These offhand comments amount to a sense that the Matrix is greater than the sum of its individual parts, that it undergoes bifurcations beyond the awareness or control of its human components.

The concept of autopoietic structures that determine social behaviour can be traced back as far as Adam Smith's infamous 'invisible hand'. What is new, however, is how the simultaneously virtual yet physical nature of digital technology exponentially increases their influence. In the age of digital reproducibility, the process of reification is at once a spiritualization or immaterialization of the external world, since it assumes a form in accordance with our collective conceptualizations of it, yet at the same time this transformation occurs to matter, to objects; the material is not transcended in this process (as the lazy trope of immateriality would have it), rather, it is complexified. The world of the matrix is a material world, where emotional states are mere indexes of the ratio between neurotransmitters, one from which conceptions of a beyond, a soul, indeed the whole range of metaphysical 'fictions' that have sustained humans for millennia, are apparently banished. We say 'apparently' because, as the authors we shall examine demonstrate, we are still haunted by these perhaps necessary fictions. Recognition of this trend, if not sustained political analysis of its significance, is reflected in cyberpunk's numerous occult figures, such as the aforementioned artificial intelligences that recall a polytheistic world where entities must be placated or enrolled. These 'entities' or intelligences can be seen as apotheosis of Lukács's ghostly objectivity: the matrix in a process of increasing autonomy gives birth to semiautonomous 'spirits'.

Let us briefly consider the terms employed by Gibson in his inaugural definition of cyberspace cited above, which can serve to usefully connect the themes of cyberpunk fiction with those of the preceding chapters. Gibson speaks of a 'consensual' hallucination, of an informatic 'nonspace', 'like city lights receding'. The consensual hallucination can be seen as a logical extension of the phantasmagoria of Benjamin's dream objects and the notion presented in Chapter 4 that the camera encourages visual experiences akin to 'psychoses, hallucinations and dreams' (Benjamin [1935] cited in Caygill 1998: 113).

Hallucination, conventionally understood as the extreme of subjectivity, here becomes consensual or collective, in accordance with the recasting of the distinction between inside and outside that we have emphasized. Similarly, 'nonspace' recalls those fusions of commodity and environment that we explored in Chapter 6; indeed, we see the ultimate fictional extension of this tendency in Smith's 'Megamall', in which all society becomes literally enveloped by the model of the mall. Finally, in the third phrase we see how computerized informational flows can be viewed in terms of their origins in the life of the city. The implication from both is that the Matrix has its roots within the matrix we have previously explored: in concepts such as reification and the disorientating realm of the city as a macroprocessor. Gibson's 'Sprawl' is a space that has no 'outside' where even the skies are informatic: 'the colour of television, tuned to a dead channel' (Gibson 1984: 1). Thus,

Gibson condenses . . . the city and the computer . . . the external space of the city is mathematicized, digitized, transformed into a space 'inside' of the computer, while the 'interior' of the computer is given 'graphic representation' in the form of the buildings, thoroughfares, and lights of a virtual city.

(Rutsky 1999: 116)

In this chapter we explore the development of this inceptive conceptualization of the Matrix (as the novel dubs the space its characters traverse) in the fusion of information and urbanism offered by other cyberpunk writers. Thus, in Stephenson's *Snow Crash* (1992) we encounter the 'Metaverse' and in Michael Smith's (1996) *Spares* 'The Gap', while within Jeff Noon's *oeuvre* we find a particularly radical vision in which an abstract map threatens to overwhelm the physical. However, it is to the alienation felt by the individual towards physical reality in these cyberspatial contexts that we will first turn – but before this we will briefly ponder some of Baudrillard's comments on the relation between science fiction and hyperreality.

Baudrillard: theory as science fiction as theory

In an essay on science fiction, Baudrillard (1991) makes a number of observations that can serve to preface the uses for which this chapter employs cyberpunk. Drawing on the history of simulation we outlined in the last chapter, Baudrillard equates traditional science fiction with the order of simulation introduced by the Industrial Revolution and machinery. Science fiction as it was known to most of the twentieth century is dead. It has fallen foul of full-blown simulation, the fourth order that in the previous chapter was referred to as 'fractal'. From this position Baudrillard makes several claims – namely that science fiction is a spent force, that the real in the age of simulacra is itself fictional making science fiction redundant and, finally, that theory and analysis to the extent that it confronts this situation is itself the 'new' science fiction. To quote:

We can no longer imagine other universes; and the gift of transcendence has been taken from us as well. Classic SF [science fiction] was one of expanding universes: it found its calling in narratives of space exploration, coupled with more terrestrial forms of exploration and colonization indigenous to the 19th and 20th centuries. There is no cause–effect relationship to be seen here. Not simply because, today, terrestrial space has been virtually completely encoded, mapped, inventoried, saturated; has in some sense been shrunk by globalization; has become a collective marketplace not only for products but also for values, signs, and models, thereby leaving no room any more for the imaginary. It is not exactly because of all this that the exploratory universe (technical, mental, cosmic) of SF has also stopped functioning. But the two phenomena are closely linked, and they are two aspects of the same general evolutionary process: a period of implosion, after centuries of explosion and expansion. When a system reaches its limits, its own saturation point, a reversal begins to takes place. And something happens also to the imagination.

(Baudrillard 1991: unpaginated)

Phillip K. Dick is often credited with the role of the godfather of cyberpunk, despite the fact that Gibson has discounted Dick as a significant influence. Certainly, it is almost impossible to conceive of the emergence of such an ironic or dystopian brand of science fiction without the influence of Dick's *oeuvre*. Dick broke with a vision of science fiction as a celebration of techno-science's unlimited dominion, with its bloated heroics and one-dimensional heroes. Instead, he practised science fiction as social critique, as a way of satirizing the emergent trends of post-war California. Like the cyberpunk fiction that he would perhaps inspire, Dick's narratives are marked by a confusion of inside and outside: reality is no longer a certainty, identity is multiple and manipulated by corporate and military forces. Given the issue addressed in the last chapter, it worth noting that Baudrillard has, from the 1970s onwards, often referred to Dick, and the condition of hyperreality that Baudrillard's theory convincingly establishes as our own is one found throughout Dick's work. To cite just one famous example, consider the status of animals in his *Do Androids Dream of Electric Sheep?* (1990 [1968]) – which served as the basis for Ridley Scott's equally seminal *Blade Runner*. Animals have become extinct as a result of the effects of some catastrophe, and their rarity has resulted in their transformation into ultimate status symbol, accruing to their owners much distinction but a considerable cost. The android of Dick's story has a fake electronic sheep, and lives in mortal fear that his neighbours will learn of his deception. Here we can see the confusion between model and copy, the exaltation of the sign in direct opposition to its 'reality' that marks the threshold of full-blown simulation. Similarly, in *A Scanner Darkly* (1991 [1977]) one of the characters observes that:

In Southern California it didn't make any difference anyhow where you went; there was always the same McDonaldburger place over and over, like a circular strip that turned past you as you pretended to go somewhere. And when finally you got hungry and went to the McDonaldburger place and bought a McDonald's hamburger, it was the one they sold you last time and the time before that and so forth, back to before you were born . . . Life in Anaheim, California, was a commercial for itself, endlessly replayed. Nothing changed; it just spread out farther and farther in the form of neon ooze.

(Dick 1991 [1977]: 24)

For Baudrillard, Dick's fiction is one of the first recognitions of the fractal order of simulation, noting that 'Dick does not create an alternate cosmos nor a folklore or a cosmic exoticism, nor intergalactic heroic deeds; the reader is, from the outset, in a total simulation without origin, past, or future – in a kind of flux of all coordinates (mental, spatiotemporal, semiotic)' (Baudrillard 1991). Alongside Dick, Baudrillard also cites Ballard as the other author of imaginative fiction whose work registered the conditions of simulacra, and discusses his novel *Crash* ('the first great novel of the universe of simulation') in these terms. While accepting much of Baudrillard's thesis, the material presented below will take a somewhat different approach. It will argue, first, that contra Baudrillard, the prophetic and diagnostic capacity of science fiction remains potent, and cyberpunk illustrates this function and, second, that in contrast to the work of Dick and Ballard, cyberpunk places the flow of information at the heart of the matrix, and in this sense offers a powerful structural analysis of contemporary conditions.

Informational intimacy, objects and alienation

> He closed his eyes . . . It came on again, gradually, a flickering, non-lin-
> ear flood of fact and sensory data, a kind of narrative conveyed in surreal
> jumpcuts and juxtapositions. It was vaguely like riding a rollercoaster that
> phased in and out of existence at random, impossibly rapid intervals, chang-
> ing altitude, attack, and direction with each pulse of nothingness, except
> that the shifts had nothing to do with any physical orientation, but rather
> with lightning alternations in paradigm and symbol system. The data had
> never been intended for human input.
>
> (Gibson 1986: 40)

In the preceding chapters the growth of the im/material has been described in terms of both the acceleration of physical flows and a concomitant delocalization of the physical that leads to the generic, non-spaces of malls, suburbs, etc. The resultant space of flows/flow of spaces finds its logical extension in the delirious speeds, at once physical and informatic, of cyberpunk narratives. A consistent paradox that can be observed in the experiences of both real-world programmers and their cyber-fictional counterparts is that this intimate immersion (in Gibson's world traditional sensory channels are bypassed in favour of cranial jacks), understood as a *collective* abstraction of information, is attended by an isolation or atomization of the participant. As we have seen, this paradox can be traced back to the urban experience of the nineteenth century, as analysed by Simmel and Benjamin. Within the context of fiction, this paradox is perhaps most clearly embodied in the figure of the lone private investigator of hardboiled detective fiction who, like the *flâneur*, is a monadic figure negotiating his way through dirty streets, preserving his integrity in the face of urban flows that threaten to engulf him. The anomie of the private eye as he plies his trade in the anonymous city is reformatted in the figure of console cowboy or lone hacker, who negotiates the lawless immateriality of cyberspace whilst, at the same time, navigating the feral physicality of the post-urban dystopia he struggles to survive within. The cerebral freedom afforded by the former is often enjoyed at a physical price within the latter. Jacking into the matrix is a means to an end of total sensory immersion in environments of pure information not accessible to the average person. The willingness and ability of cyberpunks to enjoy informational intimacy sets them apart as the rhetorical one-eyed man in the kingdom of the blind, but affinity with, and true control of, information may in fact be mutually exclusive owing to the seductively invasive and ultimately alienating qualities of cyberspace.

The profound effect of this decreasing importance of the physical is recognized as an integral aspect of the experience of real-world computer programmers, whose information-dense lives necessitate the embrace of a rather sterile and submissive mindset:

> We give ourselves over to the sheer fun of the technical, to the nearly sexual pleasure of the clicking thought-stream. Some part of me mourns, but I know there is no other way: human needs must cross the line into code. They must pass through this semipermeable membrane where urgency, fear, and hope are filtered out, and only reason travels across ... Actual human confusions cannot live here. Everything we want accomplished, everything the system is to provide, must be denatured in its crossing to the machine, or else the system will die.
>
> (Ullman 1997: 15)

Such experience combines feelings of quasisexual informational intimacy, a profound need to view the world in coded terms, and elements of ontological reversal. The requirements of code begin to supersede refractory reality. Confusion is no longer such a threat, because one either resigns oneself to the certainties of the code or, conversely, revels in its infinite possibilities. Moreover, there is a gendered aspect to this interplay between isolation and intimacy – both the private eye and the console cowboy are marked by a certain hard masculinity, a carapace that ensures their integrity as they enter into the destabilizing fluidity of the city-matrix; indeed, when we recall that the term 'matrix' originally designated the womb, phrases such as 'jacking into the matrix' are cast in a new light.

Noon describes this informational intimacy through vivid and startlingly dystopian portrayals of a world where reality has become subservient to its simulation. In both his novels *Vurt* (1993) and *Pollen* (1995), for example, people are addicted to the thrill of accessing a purely immaterial digital space:

> Into a world of numbers. Falling ... I was still falling down, down towards the snake pit. And all these numbers floating by, pure and naked information, wrapping me up in mathematics.
>
> (Noon 1993: 330)

The profound and disorientating novelty of this reality reversal and the degree of vulnerability is evoked in terms of infantile bewilderment:

Reality following the dream, rather than vice versa. We won't know where we are any more. . . . A map of chaos. The dream will come through this new map. The dream will take us over. We will be like lost children.'

(ibid.: 201)

We have already touched upon the convergence of chemically induced altered states and the vertiginous experience of the *flâneur*, and in cyberpunk this theme is extended so that immersion in the matrix in turn takes on the characteristics of a psychedelic experience, in which the boundaries between individuals, environments and technologies are dissolved. This theme occurs throughout cyberpunk, from works such as Dick's *The Three Stigmata of Palmer Eldritch* (1965) and *Through a Scanner Darkly* (1991 [1977]) to the work of Gibson; however, it is in Noon's fictions that this theme finds its fullest expression. Here accessing information is like: 'falling into bliss and numbers . . . numbers and bliss . . . the numbers overriding the bliss so that the whole world seemed like a mathematical formula . . . full of a slow ecstasy it was, a long, drawn-out parade of tenderness' (Noon 1995: 224), and often when reading Noon we can no longer be sure whether we are dealing with the chemical, the informatic or 'reality' itself. Despite their hyperbole, these portrayals of informational intimacy find their echo in terms used in the non-fictional world of computing, where the pleasures of coding assume the evanescent bliss of the neurochemical:

The world as humans understand it and the world as it must be explained to computers come together in the programmer in a strange state of disjunction. The project begins in the programmer's mind with the beauty of a crystal. I remember the feel of a system at the early stages of programming, when the knowledge I am to represent in code seems lovely in its structuredness. For a time, the world is a calm, mathematical place. Human and machine seem attuned to a cut-diamond-like state of grace. Once in my life I tried methamphetamine: that speed high is the only state that approximates the feel of a project at its inception.

(Ullman 1997: 21)

The association of informational intimacy with sexual gratification implies a degree of hedonic empowerment for the cyberpunk that may in fact disguise an associated cost. Cyberpunk's informational intimacy is portrayed in terms of sexual frisson, but despite the language of physicality such enjoyment contains an essential contradiction since it is premised upon a sense of 'bodiless exultation' – like the pleasure of the drug user it is essential solitary or onanistic. The pleasure of informational intimacy thus implies an attendant loss of contact with the physical. As such, the cyberpunk can be seen as a trope for the wider social trends of commodified nonspace. A character in the 'factional' novel *Microserfs* (Coupland 1996) passionately decries this loss, arguing for Lego as the corrupter of youth, inculcating them into non-space of hypermodernity; Lego, 'Satan's playtoy', brainwashed 'entire generations of youth from the information-dense

industrialized nations into developing mind-sets that view the world as uni-
tized, sterile, inorganic, and interchangeably modular' (ibid.: 258). The excessively manicured lawns at Microsoft headquarters are merely epiphenomena
of an insidious project of social engineering whose goal is the extirpation of all
physicality not accordance with simulation:

> Lego is, like, the perfect device to enculturate a citizenry intolerant of smell,
> intestinal by-products, nonadherence to unified standards, decay, blurred
> edges, germination and death. Try imagining a forest made of Lego. Good
> luck. Do you ever see Legos made from ice? dung? wood? iron? and sphag-
> num moss? No – grotacious, or what?
>
> (ibid.: 258)

Throughout cyberpunk a consistent emphasis is placed upon surfaces in order
to imply a lack of depth to the interactions that occur out of the informational
realm. For example, even areas of houses and apartments most closely identified
with bodily functions partake of a hermetic sterility that forms a pervasive backdrop to a heavily informationalized cultural atmosphere. For example, when
Cayce, the protagonist of Gibson's *Pattern Recognition*, stays at a friend's flat she
finds that:

> ... Damien's new kitchen is as devoid of edible content as its designer's
> display windows in Camden High Street ... Very clean and almost entirely
> empty, save for a carton containing two dry pucks of Weetabix and some
> loose packets of herbal tea. Nothing at all in the German fridge, so new that
> its interior smells only of cold and long-chain monomers.
>
> (Gibson 2003: 1)

And later:

> ... she goes into Damien's newly renovated bathroom. Feels she could
> shower down in it prior to visiting a sterile NASA probe, or step out of
> some Chernobyl scenario to have her lead suit removed by rubber-gowned
> Soviet technicians, who'd then scrub her legs with long-handled brushes.
> The fixtures in the shower can be adjusted with elbows, preserving the
> sterility of scrubbed hands.
>
> (ibid.: 5)

Related to this incipient alienation from organic environments, a central
issue in the process of reification, is the inverted relationship between people
and commodities/objects. Lash's analysis is in keeping with a tradition of media
commentary (such as McLuhan and Baudrillard) that suggests that the quantitative increases in speed have produced qualitatively new scenarios for the
subject–object relationship. The increased informational element of contemporary commodities means that the processes of flux identified earlier are further

exacerbated. Baudelaire identified modernity with the ephemeral, the fleeting and the contingent. In the digital age, this becomes a realm in which the disorientation we witnessed being suffered by the *flâneur* is merely a mild precursor of the fundamental discombobulation that provides such thrills for the cyberpunk. Thus: 'the empirical world of technology and shock experience and speed has leveled Being and Reason into a wasteland, but in which *the transcendental moment is preserved as memory and mourning*' (Lash 2002: ix [our emphasis]). This nostalgia is strikingly expressed in cyberpunk fiction, in which, within a dystopian society, isolated efforts are made to reverse the decline of reality's aura with limited success.

Transience is dominant within cyberpunk so that: 'Memories are nothing more than a book you've read and lost, not a bible for the rest of your life' (Smith 1996: 301) but, amidst the flux and flows, there is a wistful presence of anachronistically simple objects valued for their ability to halt, even if only momentarily, the inexorable flow:

> I passed a couple of children's trikes laid casually on the path, but a nudge with my foot proved what I already knew. They were welded to the path. Show trikes, for atmosphere. Nobody here was letting their kids just ride around the neighbourhood.
>
> (ibid.: 100)

Such nostalgia is dealt with in a more thematically substantial manner in Gibson's *Count Zero* (1986), in which the character Marly discovers a rather old-fashioned robot akin to those presently used in car-assembly work. It is called the 'box-maker' and its purpose is to produce antiquated pieces of art that consist of an odd collection of family objects. The family in question is the Tessier-Ashpool clan, who, if the word is not too material for their mysterious nature, dramatically *embody* Baudrillard's notion of the fourth, fractal, order. Their offspring are genetically cloned to fulfil the needs of the clan rather than those of human desire or love, and this incredibly rich and powerful family seems to hover as a semiautonomous self-replicating entity in the Matrix, giving more than a hint of our previously encountered notion of capital's 'spectral objectivity'.

Gibson neatly summarizes the significance of these apparently anachronistic objects produced by the box-maker in terms of a 'slow-motion hurricane of lost things' (Gibson cited in Cavallaro 2000: 62). The oxymoronic choice of words is instructive. Set against the overwhelming pace of change around them, such objects achieve a compensatory power through their very stillness. In *Pattern Recognition* (2003) this power is something that Cayce clings on to in an attempt to make sense of another form of unreal slow-motion hurricane: September 11th. At the time of the crash, Gibson locates his protagonist in a street nearby, and when the first plane to hit the Twin Towers passes over her very low, with a hint of the internal/external blurring of reality, she assumes that 'They must be making a film'. In a novel whose key focus is the surface level and essential insubstantiality of commodities, it is once again significant that an emphasis is placed upon antiques, so that we read how:

> She had watched a single petal fall, from a dead rose, in the tiny display window of an eccentric Spring Street dealer in antiques . . . The dead roses, arranged in an off-white Fiestaware vase, appeared to have been there for several months. They would have been white, when fresh, but now looked like parchment. This was a mysterious window, with a black-painted plywood backdrop revealing nothing of the establishment behind it. She had never been in to see what else was there, but the objects in the window seemed to change in accordance with some peculiar poetry of their own, and she was in the habit, usually, of pausing to look when she passed this way. The fall of the petal, and somewhere a crash, taken perhaps as some impact of large trucks, one of those unexplained events in the sonic backdrop of lower Manhattan. Leaving her sole witness to this minute fall. Perhaps there is a siren then or sirens, but there are always sirens, in New York.
>
> (Gibson 2003: 135–6)

Later, on her way up to a friend's apartment and before they both witness the impact of the second plane: 'As the elevator doors close behind her, she closes her eyes and sees the dry petal falling. The loneliness of objects. Their secret lives' (ibid.: 136). This instance represents, in the midst of the urban scene of withdrawal, a confrontation with the irreducible particularity of matter. However, such particularity is itself presented as a minute particle of the urban maelstrom with its sonic backdrop and continual wail of sirens. The apparent autonomy of the window objects which 'seemed to change in accordance with some peculiar poetry of their own' seems to appear as a nostalgically manageable counterpoint to the focus of the rest of the novel (and Gibson's extended *oeuvre*) upon Marx's notion of the general independence of the world of objects/technologies that people begin to circulate around rather than vice versa.

Futuristic flu and the dance of biz – im/materiality and the pace of change

> There are too many complaints about society having to move too fast to keep up with the machine. There is great advantage in moving fast if you move completely, if social, educational, and recreational changes keep pace. You must change the whole pattern at once and the whole group together and the people themselves must decide to move.
>
> (Margaret Mead [1954] cited in McLuhan 1995 [1964])

Fully imagined cultural futures were the luxury of another day, one in which 'now' was of some greater duration. For us, things can change so abruptly, so violently, so profoundly, that futures like our grandparents' have insufficient 'now' to stand on. We have no future because our present is too volatile . . . We have only risk management. The spinning of the given moment's scenario's. Pattern recognition.

(Gibson 2003: 57)

In both the above quotations, the pace of social change is taken as an inevitable, enframing, given. Mead advocates 'going with the flow', and the excerpt from Gibson appears as a rather neutral description of the frantic state of play of such a life. However, Gibson's work and the genre in general provide a critical dimension to the optimism of such commentators as Mead. Two related aspects of cyberpunk largely account for its successful resonance with contemporary readers: its inimitably graphic depiction of both the rapid and disorientating technological change and the boundary-blurring and reality-undermining qualities of information technologies. Its basic premise of untrammelled change is recognized in functional non-fictional analyses of cyberculture such as Brown's *Cybertrends*:

Change – the surest sign of life – is now taking on a radically *discontinuous* quality . . . Prevailing relativities change with the blink of an eye.

(Brown 1988: 49 [emphasis in original])

The much-used phrase the 'Information Revolution' is obviously predicated upon a sense of historical development from its industrial predecessor. The Industrial Revolution represented a qualitative shift in human affairs in so far as confusingly rapid social and technological change became the norm rather than the exception.

Futuristic flu is a shortened version of *retro-futuristic chronosemiitis* – both somewhat tongue-in-cheek phrases used by Istvan Csiscery-Ronay (1992) that provide an updated version of *Chokerlebnis* to describe the even greater sense of dislocation and confusion felt at a time of great socio-technical flux that accompanies the advent of cybertechnologies. The 'now' seems almost instantaneously and anachronistically redundant, whilst the future is never quite within reach. Futuristic flu is cyberpunk's distinguishing leitmotif as it takes the accelerated socio-technical change of the industrial revolution to 'warp-speed' levels: 'Night City was like a deranged experiment in social Darwinism, designed by a bored researcher who kept one thumb permanently on the fast-forward button' (Gibson 1984: 14). Elements of the future appear to have collapsed into the present and uncontainable – disorientating change becomes a perverse status. The genre depicts a new experiential order in which the boundaries between the real and virtual worlds are blurred, but it does so with a sophisticated recognition of the ambivalent feelings of exhilaration and fear held towards that order.

In addition to the sheer scale of the new informational capitalist order, whether it be the MegaMall or the Matrix, cyberpunks enjoy the pace of 'the dance of biz'. Thus, the tempo of its dance is such that informational immersion is a sine qua non of survival and requires that you: 'throw yourself into a highspeed drift and skid' (ibid.: 26). Frenetic activity is the background noise of everyday existence: 'Stop hustling and you sank without a trace . . . Biz here was a constant subliminal hum' (ibid.: 14). Life takes on the aspect of a feral fight to survive by means of constant movement so that in Smith's version of the Matrix, The Gap: 'To stand still in The Gap is like stopping swimming for a shark. You sink to the bottom, and can't stop moving again' (Smith 1996: 202). The social environment is downgraded to the husk left over from the cumulative effects of individuals enjoying the flux, so that amidst the hi-tech surroundings in Stephenson's *Snow Crash* (1992) social dystopia reigns to the extent that tramps can be found roasting a dog over an open spit and neighbourhoods have been replaced by private franchised 'communities' and *burbclaves*.

In the same MegaMall where people are reduced to leaving fake children's tricycles out to simulate community, social stratification is literal. Your economic status is reflected by the floor you have reached until you reach the very top, where: 'The people who live that high had so much money they had to be sedated every morning to stop them going berserk with glee' (Smith 1996: 19). Gibson describes the consequences for the communal environment of such societies based upon flux to the exclusion of all else in terms of a near-future part of Tokyo:

> Now it's been Blade Runnered by half a century of use and pollution, edges of concrete worn porous as coral. Dusk comes early, under here, and she spies signs of homeless encampment: plastic-wrapped blankets tucked back into an uncharacteristically littered scrim of struggling municipal shrubs. Vehicles blast past, overhead, a constant drumming of displaced air, particulates sifting invisibly.
>
> (Gibson 2003: 146)

Social alienation from the life world here is matched by alienation from the natural world. Perversely, the organicity of the coral is recovered only by the process of pollution. Frequently, and in keeping with McLuhan's notion of a particular phenomenon being shown in starkest relief just as it is being surpassed by a new form, individual and social alienation is expressed within the immaterial nature of cyberspace in language of exaggerated physicality. Two particularly vivid examples are seen in *Snow Crash* (1992), in which moving against a crowd at a rock concert is compared to walking across a room full of puppies wearing crampons, and the sound of a bullet hitting a bullet-proof vest is described as like that of a wren hitting a patio door. Perhaps most memorably, in *Spares* (1996) we have the following disturbing scene, in which a creature lands in the real world from The Gap:

> It was a bird, of a kind. A bird or a cat, either way. It was featherless but stood a foot tall on spindly jointed legs; its face was avian but – like the body – fat and dotted with patchy, moulting orange fur. Two vestigial wings poked out of its side at right angles looking as if they had been unceremoniously amputated with scissors and then recauterized. Most of the creature's

skin was visible, an unhealthy white mess that appeared to be weeping fluid. The whole body breathed in and out as it sat, as if labouring for breath, and it gave off a smell of recent decay – as if fresh-minted for death. The eyes focused on me, making me instantly, and its beak opened. The hole this revealed looked less like a mouth than a churned wound . . . 'What the fuck is that?' Howie whispered. 'You got me,' I said . . . The bird tried to take a step towards us, but the effort caused one of its legs to break. The top joint teetered in its socket and then popped out. The creature flopped on to its side. The skin over the joint tore like an over-ripe fruit, releasing a gout of matter that resembled nothing so much as a heavy period mixed with sour cream. It was not, all in all, a very beautiful creature.

(Smith 1996: 162)

This creature obviously finds the physical world somewhat difficult to deal with but this merely parallels the traumatizing experience of those humans who enter The Gap, and who we shall see shortly equally provide a particularly dramatized example of the alienation created by the im/material.

Lash (2002) argues that the traditional Marxist model of exploitation based upon the supersession of use-value by exchange-value has made way for a different model based upon exclusion from information flows. This mirrors at a theoretical level the basic theme of much of cyberpunk fiction, which is premised upon the existential desire of its protagonists to be part of the flow of information. In addition, Lash talks in terms of areas within global capitalism that, due to stability of identity, qualify as 'live' or 'dead' zones and 'tame' or 'wild' zones respectively (ibid.: 28–30). In this context, it is therefore interesting to note that language rich with physicality is used to describe the social alienation that accompanies a society disproportionately built upon informational flows. Randal, the lead character of *Spares,* describes the consequences for communities of membership of a live or dead zone:

I saw America itself as one big matrix: bright, dangerous cities crammed with sharp and needy people, interconnected by a spider's web of highways and toll roads and bordered at the edges by the slow coasts peppered with perambulating old people. And in between, in the gaps, a sagging mass of flatline towns which hadn't made it into the twenty second century – alive and technically equal to everyone else, but actually breaking up, losing their cohesion like skin on the face of someone very ill for a long time. The nose might still look sharp, the eyes bright, the cheekbones in place; but the flesh in between falls loosely between the peaks.

(ibid.: 184)

We can thus see how an integral part of cyberpunk's focus upon the abstract and the immaterial is matched by a concern for the material world that is often passed over by uncritical consumers of the genre who Gibson has accused of missing much of the irony of his work.

The rise of the map

> The tie between information and action has been severed . . . we are glutted with information, drowning in information, we have no control over it, don't know what to do with it . . . We suffer from a kind of cultural AIDS.
>
> (Postman 1990: 6)

> It was a time of happenings and flower power. A time of changes. That's why this hayfever wave is exciting me so much, despite the danger. It's got me in two minds, this fever. The flowers are making a come back, and the world is getting messier. The barricades are coming down. This city is so fucking juicy right now.
>
> (Noon 1995: 166)

Cyberpunk deals directly with the blurring we have previously discussed in terms of the inside/outside with its own conflation of the real and the surreal. The sickly bird-like creature falling out of The Gap illustrates the genre's tendency to address ontologically unstable environments that mark a much darker side to Gibson's notion of the Matrix, where nightmarish qualities replace the consensual hallucination: '. . . it was seepage, stuff that should be unconscious becoming conscious. The planet's dreams, seeping through the wall like hallucinations on the edge of sleep' (Smith 1996: 156). For our discussion of the strained relationship between external reality and internal individual psychological autonomy, Kracauer offers the evocative phrase 'herbarium of pure externality' (cited in Frisby 1986) to describe the world so produced. Both Lash's concept of wild zones and Kracauer's phrase are particularly apt concepts with which to approach the 'bio-punk' fiction (i.e. work that emphasizes the conflation of informational environments and biological forms) of Jeff Noon. His dystopian *oeuvre* develops cyberpunk's informationally saturated world by giving imaginative licence to the implications of the increasing convergence between information as an abstract entity and its embodied manipulation in biological DNA. Marx and Engels's vision of sublimation, of the melting of all that was formerly solid, is pursued with fervour in Noon's fiction, which offers repeated references to conventional notions of reality being marginalized and undercut by increasing levels of fluidity. Fear of ontological reversal and this ubiquitous fluidity combine as a major theme: 'These days the doors between the two worlds were slippery, as though the walls were going fluid' (Noon 1995: 92). Gumbo, a Noon character, talks of this process in a manner reminiscent of Chip Tango and Nietzsche as he rhetorically sneers at the traditional forces of law and order: ' "Don't you realise the whole fucking world is ruined now. What you cops gonna do, uh? Arrest a dream?" Gumbo started to laugh. "Reality is fucked." . . . The story took hold of reality's hand, imagine . . .' (ibid.: 248).

In *Pollen* (1995), Noon describes a near-future Manchester struggling to cope with the after-effects of the widespread dispersal of a powerful fertility drug called Fecundity 10. The city is over-run by exponentially proliferating flora and fauna that combine in a frenetic confusion of unlikely hybrid genetic couplings, a situation which provides a grotesque metaphorical representation of Postman's 'cultural aids', and its concomitantly perceived loss of a previously coherent societal frame of reference. An inability to control the growth of information is represented in Noon's work as a blurring of previously distinct genetic categories. His fiction 'fleshes out' the notion of ontological reversal with a sustained depiction of futuristic febrility and fecundity:

> The world in those days was on a constant knife-edge between species.
>
> (ibid.: 63)

> Every combination was there. Not many pure dog or pure human, but hundreds of crazy messed-up mutants in-between. Evil-looking creatures for the most part; bits of dog sprouting from human forms, scraps of humanity glimpsed in a furry face.
>
> (ibid.: 95)

> The Zombies were dancing and blooming around the shit and the dust, flowers sprouting from their tough skins, petals falling from their mouths. It was a fine show of fauna and flora, all mixed into one being. New species.
>
> (ibid.: 117)

Noon's *Nymphomation* (1998) has his usual setting of a near-future Manchester being used as a testing site for a National Lottery based upon a domino-like game. The neologism that provides the novel's title continues his key theme of fecundity but applies it to the abstract world of numbers, which begins to reproduce in pseudosexual terms. 'Nymphomation' is thus used: 'to denote a complex mathematical procedure where numbers, rather than being added together or multiplied or whatever, were actually allowed to *breed* with each other, to produce new numbers, which had something to do with 'breeding ever more pathways towards the goal' (ibid.: 119). Fecundity in this setting does not only apply to the informational and biological environments but is also apparent in the meme-like transmission of a pervasive copulatory zeitgeist: 'The naked populace, making foreplay to the domiviz, bone-eyed and numberfucked . . . Even the air had a hard-on, bulging with mathematics. Turning the burbflies into a nympho-swarm, liquid streets alive with perverts . . .' (ibid.: 65). Such general fecundity is specifically manifested in a glut of commercial activity which the authorities no longer seem able to control:

> The streets of Blurbchester were thick with the mergers, a corporate fog of brand images. People had to battle through them . . . The Government was

at a loss regarding the overwhelming messages; they knew the experiment had gone wrong . . . but how to right it?

(ibid.: 240)

Postman's notion of an informational flood becomes with Noon a reproductive frenzy whereby corporate messages breed literally like flies. Gibson's *biz* becomes an actual *buzz*:

> As the burbflies went out of control, blocking out the streetlights, making a cloud of logos. It was rutting season for the living verts, and all over the city the male blurbs were riding on the backs of females. Biting their necks, hoping for babyverts. The city, the pulsating city, alive with the rain and colours and the stench of nymphomation Mathemedia. Here we go, numberfucked . . .

(ibid.: 159)

Columbus, a character from Noon's novel *Pollen*, succinctly summarizes the situation of ontological blurring in terms akin to Benjamin's notion of ludic dreaming when he asserts that, 'What is presently inside the head will shortly be outside the head. The dream! The dream will live!' (Noon 1995: 193). Baudrillard's use of Borges' map finds dramatic resonance in Noon's work, and Pollen's plot is premised upon the explicit development of the notion that the map is gaining primacy over reality. In this surreal world of excessively fecund fauna and flora, a map of Manchester seeps into the real:

> For too long now, the map has followed reality. Now reality will follow the map . . . If this new map succeeds, there will be no freedom in the city. The city will change to suit the map.

(ibid.: 42)

This close reading of cyberpunk has demonstrated the inimitable 'exaggerated clarity' with which it explores the emotional and social atmosphere of a world whose paradigms are based upon the primacy of simulated or coded structures over direct experience. It has also indicated, however, elements that can be better understood in terms of 'exaggerated anxiety'.

Mind the gap – fear and anxiety in the Matrix

> It was the same in The Gap. I just did my time and tried to stay alive. I guess I managed it, but sometimes my life feels like a piece of demo software, all the key or interesting features disabled, running on a fourteen-day trial period which just repeats over and over again without ever becoming mine.

(Smith 1996: 175)

In the material world, the *process* of technological change causes confusion; within cyberpunk the confusion is instantiated in both the physical and informational environments within which cyberpunks operate. In Gibson's early work, the 'dance of biz' is generally portrayed as an exhilarating manifestation of speed enjoyed at its fullest in simulated informational environments. In the work of subsequent cyberpunk authors the exhilaration of confusion becomes more anxiety-ridden and the blurring of the im/material is more threatening. In Smith's version of cyberspace, 'The Gap', for example: 'Cohesion, order, chronology; The Gap was the place where you learnt those three words meant nothing at all' (ibid.: 208). The Gap reveals the dark, complete flipside of Ullman's calm and mathematical world where, 'human needs must cross the line into code. They must pass through this semi-permeable membrane where urgency, fear and hope are filtered out, and only reason travels across' (Ulllman 1997: 15). It consists of the unbridgeable distance between the material and its immaterial representation in a manner reminiscent of Noon's flowery fecundity: 'they said computer code was at fault, the little lines of syntax we'd thought were perfect and inviolate . . . the chips in the wild inside, flowering up through meaning into function' (Smith 1996: 198). Smith dramatizes the anxiety using a psychoanalytical approach suffused with images redolent of the Vietnam War: soldiers in The Gap are described as mostly eighteen or nineteen years old, drug use amongst them is rampant, villagers in thatched huts resist the troops and children are used to smuggle mines, while the fighting takes place amidst dense (virtual) trees. Distrust and fear are the dominant feelings in this alien environment, echoing Noon's previously quoted use of childhood bewilderment. Thus: 'We were like baffled, terrified children alone in a dark multi-storey car park full of sadists' (ibid.: 204).

The Gap represents not only the imaginative culmination of Lash's previously cited notion that 'speed has leveled Being and Reason into a wasteland', but also that of a 'digital exclusion' from informational flows. The Gap is about: 'Falling between the cracks, being cut out of the loop, consigned to dead code which has lost its place in the program and nobody remembers any more' (ibid.: 200). In addition to being another version of Gibson's cyberspace, however, The Gap – as the introductory quote to this section shows – also usefully represents a negative consequence of the process of withdrawal for the individual. Smith's comparison of life with a piece of demo software echoes the language used in Coupland's *Microserfs* (1996) (see Taylor 1998 for more detail), which mediated on the price the individual pays for identification with a process of coding that is itself co-opted by software giants such as Microsoft. Nearly fifty years ago, McLuhan argued that this blurring of collective and individual was an inevitable consequence of media technologies: 'it is ridiculous to talk of "what the public wants" played over its own nerves. This question would be like asking people what sort of sights and sounds they would prefer around them in an urban metropolis' (McLuhan 1995 [1964]: 68). As we have seen, the equation of mediascape and cityscape is no chance conjunction but registers the historical unfolding of a dialectic between information technologies and urban environments, one that is increasingly sublated into an overarching network of flux.

This emergent network of flux is distinguished by its apparent status as the commons of the corporate sector. Benjamin's examination of Paris in the nineteenth century highlights the phantasmagorical nature of the new commodity form, but arguably the strangeness of this new form tended to outweigh the immediate implications of its commercial nature. In cyberpunk, these implications become much more explicit. Notwithstanding Lash's assertion that commodities have been superseded by informationalized flows, a common thread of both cyberpunk and more 'factional' accounts such as Coupland's *Microserfs* is the stress they place upon the strict inseparability of digital matters and commodification. Again, this analysis is prefigured by McLuhan, who succinctly described the particular suitability of the new electronic sensorium for commercial colonization:

> Archimedes once said, 'Give me a place to stand and I will move the world.' Today he would have pointed to our electric media and said, 'I will stand on your eyes, your ears, your nerves, and your brain, and the world will move in any tempo or pattern I choose.' We have leased these 'places to stand' to private corporations.
>
> (ibid.: 68)

McLuhan's emphasis upon 'pattern' presciently foregrounds the themes of Gibson's *Pattern Recognition* (2003) in which Cayce – in contrast to Case, the buccaneering console cowboy of *Neuromancer* – is so sensitive to the corporate colonization of society's life world that she exhibits a phobic physical reaction from too much exposure to brands and logos: 'she is a "sensitive" of some kind, a dowser in the world of global marketing . . . a morbid and sometimes violent reactivity to the semiotics of the market place' (ibid.: 3). She thus provides a striking illustration of McLuhan's assertion that we feel the full impact of electric technologies with our whole body.

Conclusion: from fiction to fact – futuristic flu in practice

> He has this whole edged-out participation mystique: how we have to allow ourselves so far into the investigation of whatever this is, whatever you're doing, that we become part of it. Hack into the system. Merge with it, deep enough that it, not you, begins to talk to us. He says it's like Coleridge, and De Quincey. He says its shamanic. That we may all seem to just be sitting there, staring at the screen, but really, some of us anyway, we're adventurers. We're out there, seeking, taking risks. In hope, he says, of bringing back wonders. Trouble is, lately, I've been living that.
>
> (Gibson 2003: 255)

The previous analysis illustrates how cyberpunk provides a powerful vehicle for the otherwise unarticulated concerns and tensions that result from society's digitally induced futuristic flu. The genre's various representations of a cyberspace all portray information in dramatic psychospatial terms, the intuitive vividness of which contrasts sharply with the much murkier and confused implications otherwise confronting those who would seek to interpret Network 2000. The plots of cyberpunk novels suggest that console cowboys, like the rest of us, are ultimately subordinate to the whims of the Matrix; however, their direct confrontation with its flows and eddies suggests that they at least avoid the charge of being oblivious to Heidegger's Danger. Unlike the majority of people within the matrix/Matrix, their participation in its informatic flux means that they do not lose sight of the way in which technology implies a withdrawal from the world – in fact, they embrace that withdrawal. They may be susceptible to other dangers such as excessive identification with the mentality of the standing reserve, but that identification is self-conscious and a source of inimitable enjoyment.

On the other hand, it can be argued that, rather than offering a solution to the problems of enframement encountered in Part I, the cyberpunk's accommodation of the social confusion caused by the inside/outside blurring and the pace of social life confusion can be seen as the ultimate consummation of Heidegger's forgetting: in their active delight in synthetic pleasures, in their evacuation of themselves into the matrix, they have entirely forgotten the genuine 'showing forth' that marks authentic production. Here the cyberpunk is merely the 'meat puppet' of the matrix, the biological apparatus of an overarching system, rather than an entity capable of co-participating in the self-disclosure of Being.

A consistent quality of the modernity/postmodernity described by the writers in this and the other earlier chapters of Part II is the way in which the Heideggerian concept of Being is emptied out in an environment in which withdrawal from withdrawal has become an object of fascination. The cyberpunk arguably manifests the individual's surrender to the danger; the social tension of a speeded-up world is ameliorated only through the narcosis of accessing of information flows rather than life-affirming social discourse. The viral spread of unmitigated capitalist values as meme-like behaviour accounts for the dystopian social environments that appear to be the material consequence and corollary of the strength of the Matrix. Throughout the genre, traditional and coherent notions such as law and order and community have been effectively replaced by the false choice proffered by privatized, formerly public services. Cyberpunk's protagonists seem fully cognizant of the negative aspects of this breakdown in social cohesion, but tend to overlook such drawbacks, preferring to revel in the excitement the resultant flux and confusion. Rather than celebrations of technological ingenuity, cyberpunk narratives highlight the dehumanizing ways in which the calculative logic of instrumental reason becomes a brightly lit, enfranchised space where our desires are determined, simulated and met. Most disturbingly, perhaps, the Matrix is a *consensual* hallucination. But are there alternatives? In order to answer this question we now turn to real-world alternatives to the Matrix to see if room can be found for human agency after all. To this end, we will examine practices that attempt to introduce dissensus into this space, to argue for alternatives and differences that are within the matrix.

8   Rewiring the matrix

The network is a matrix, a womb, the mother-matter that spawns us all. But the matrix was always wired. Despite its biological roots, the word itself came to denote a host of technological tools and practices: a metal mould or die; a binding substance, like cement in concrete, or the principal metal in an alloy; a plate used for casting typefaces; a rectangular grid of mathematical quantities treated as a single algebraic entity; and, of course, the dense pattern of connections that link up computer systems. The matrix forms the context for emergence; it is the medium, the motherboard, through which events, objects, and new linkages are grown.

(Davis 1998: 328)

Until now, we have considered the matrix as a sign of enframement. Part I dealt with, first, the general principle of technological development and its implications for the way in which we confront reality through technology (Heidegger's withdrawal from Being), and second, the particular attributes of media technologies which facilitate technology's enframing qualities in a particularly powerful way – as their very name implies media technologies mediate our culture. We have seen in Kittler's work, for example, how cities have come to constitute what are effectively large-scale prototypical computers. In Part II we have traced the im/material tension that is at the heart of digital matters and the paradoxical nature of a withdrawal from reality by means of very real technological artefacts. We have seen how this tension is reflected in various pressures of urban life. Within cities, detectives, *flâneurs* and cyberpunks all represent emblematic figures of the attempt to impose human meaning on the increased pace and scale of the flows that result from the combined effect of the media and urban im/materiality. At its most extreme, the emblematic confrontation with technology's withdrawal was portrayed in Chapter 7 in the dystopian excesses of the Matrix as an ambiguous place residing in the gap (and The Gap) of the im/material. In the blockbuster eponymous film it is the suffocating grid into which we are plugged for nourishment and exploitation, like human fuel cells.

Returning to this book's early theme of optimism and pessimism, in this chapter we offer a positive counterpoint to negative conceptualizations of digital matters, and we consider more positive ways of viewing the matrix. We consider it in the context of dynamic, potentially empowering processes of emergence and linkage. The groups we consider here offer a vision of an empowered mode of intervention within the matrix and hold out the promise of a more equitable relation to our technological systems. Instead of Neo and company's neo-gnostic breakout from the demiurgic simulation of a totally Matrix-enframed world, we consider more immanent modes of intervention in the digital matrix – not a new form of loom-smashing but an attempt to recast technological systems in accordance with a different, more agency-driven logic than that provided by global capital. Elsewhere we have traced this process with our explorations of the new technologically informed social movement of hacktivism (see Jordan and Taylor 2004; Harris and Taylor 2005). Here, in order to explore this potential recasting of the matrix we focus particularly upon the Free or Open Source software movement, which has sought to challenge and renegotiate the terms of digital culture.

The Free software movement has been taken up as a potentially revolutionary praxis by a number of thinkers, who identify within it the possibility of new, non-exploitative modes of production. In order to explore this potential, this chapter will draw on range of post- or neo-Marxist theories that have emerged out of the work of Italian Autonomists – a group of related thinkers including Antonio Negri, Mario Lazzarato and 'Bifo' Beardi – and Deleuze and Guattari. Together these thinkers offer a reformulation of Marxist theory in the context of a shift from a Fordist to post-Fordist mode of production. This transition was commensurate with a constellation of challenges to traditional Marxism, including: the collapse of the Eastern bloc; the exhaustion and or co-optation of the revolutionary movements of the 1960s; the apparent triumph of consumerist capitalism and the globalization of markets; and, last but certainly not least, the Information Revolution. Marx's so-called 'Fragment on Machines' and the concept of the General Intellect found therein is a crucial conceptual resource in this project and it is therefore worth looking at it in more detail.

The General Intellect: Marx's matrix?

The 'Fragment on Machines' is to be found in the *Grundrisse* (Marx 1973 [1841]), the notebooks produced by Marx in his efforts to work through the ideas that found their mature expression in *Das Kapital*. In the 'Fragment', Marx observes that:

> . . . once adopted into the production process of capital, the means of labour passes through different metamorphoses, whose culmination is the *machine,* or rather, an *automatic system of machinery* . . . set in motion by an automaton, a moving power that moves itself; this automaton consisting of numerous mechanical and intellectual organs, so that the workers themselves are cast merely as its conscious linkages.
>
> (ibid.: 690–711)

Here, Marx suggests – in diametrical opposition to Ellul's previously cited assertion that 'capitalism did not create the world: the machine did' (Ellul 1963 [1954]: 5) – that machinery is the product of capitalism and results from the absorption of the means of production into the process of capitalism itself. Machinery is not an 'accidental moment of capital, but is rather the historical reshaping of the traditional, inherited means of labour into a form adequate to capital' (Marx 1973: 691). Technology as an autonomous system is the material concrescence of the autonomous system that is capitalism itself, and just as the workers are merely terms in the reproduction of capital, so they become simply 'conscious linkages' or the 'intellectual organs' of a technological leviathan (this has obvious resonance with McLuhan's Butlerian notion of humans as the bee-like reproductive organs of technology).

In this scenario, the worker no longer exists independently so much as acts as the fleshy appendage of the machine, overseeing its activity: objectified labour (in the form of technology) determines the activity of living labour. In the first instance, this subsumption of living labour is mechanical or energetic; it is the worker's force and gesture that is technically replicated. However, Marx prophetically envisaged a time when 'the accumulation of knowledge . . . the general productive forces of the social brain' would be absorbed 'into capital, as opposed to labour, and hence appear as an attribute of capital, and more specifically of *fixed capital*'. In other words, a time when machinery replicated not only the motive action of the worker, but the activities of the intellect; an era in which 'general social knowledge has become a direct force of production, and . . . the conditions of the process of social life itself have come under the control of the general intellect and been transformed in accordance with it (ibid.: 706). The real significance of the 'Fragment', however, resides not so much in the content of Marx's pronouncements but in the analyses of contemporary conditions it has inspired. Drawing on the 'Fragment', the Italian Autonomists have, in the form of the journals *Futur Antrieur* and *Multitudes* and texts such as *Empire* (Hardt and Negri 2000), developed an armoury of powerful concepts for understanding and challenging technological capitalism. In turn, these concepts have been invoked in an attempt to understand the nature of digital production and consumption, and in particular the Free/Open Source software movement(s), which certain commentators have seen as a hypostatization of Autonomist theory.

Immaterial labour and mass intellectuality: work in the age of the social brain

Contemporary conditions both confirm and refute Marx's General Intellect in the sense that we do now inhabit an environment made of externalizations of many operations formerly confined within the skull, but, whereas Marx argued that in the form of the General Intellect, 'capital thus works towards its own dissolution as the form dominating production', at present, this remains a consummation devoutly to be wished for but hitherto unfulfilled. Globalization, as a fusion of information and transportation technologies, has almost silenced all (formal) opposition – aside from the protest movement that came of age in Seattle and which draws its theories from texts such as *Empire* (Hardt and Negri 2000) and Klein's *No Logo* (2000) – thus, as Virno puts it, what strikes the reader of Marx's 'Fragment' today is 'the full factual realization of the tendencies described in the *Grundrisse*, without, however, any emancipatory – or even merely conflictual – reversal' (Virno 1996: 267). The simultaneous accuracy and inaccuracy of Marx's account has inspired a number of crucial concepts whose purpose is to correct Marx's deficiencies with a fuller understanding of the nature of labour in the context of a digital economy. Amongst these are the two interrelated concepts of *mass intellectuality* and *immaterial labour*. Mass intellectuality constitutes an informed re-evaluation of the General Intellect in terms of the transition from a Fordist economy (based on the factory as the paradigm of production) to a post-Fordist information economy. Within this new context, information and knowledge creation become significant factors in wealth creation. As a consequence labour assumes an informational component (crudely put, we move from the industrial sweatshop to an informatic sweatshop – from the factory to the call centre). Mass intellectuality presupposes a 'a labour of networks and communicative discourse' (Dyer-Witheford 1999: 294) in which the tools of production are not simply technologies but the knowledge and information that is necessary to use them and that flows through them. As Castells has observed, within the network society there is a new relation between:

> . . . the social process of creating and manipulating symbols (the culture of society) and the capacity to produce and distribute goods and services (the productive forces). For the first time in history, the human mind is a direct productive force, not just a decisive element of the production system.
>
> (Castells 2000: 31)

It is the General Intellect that is the source of capital, and it resides in the minds and bodies of labourers; work is no longer the sale of naked labour but the exploitation of subjectivities and individual knowledge. The extremity of this bipolar system is novel in terms of its ubiquity and both its breadth and depth of reach. Its macroscopic extension (literally mondial) is matched only by the intricacy of its microprocesses: digital matters are both pervasive and invasive. It is precisely this paradox that is captured in the phrase 'mass intellect' – the intellect traditionally bound within the confines of individual has become 'massified', generalized.

Within this context, language, or better still 'writing' in the widest sense, comes to play a critical role: mass intellectuality signifies 'the era in which information and communication play an essential role in *each* unfolding production process, *the era in which language itself has been put to work*' (Virno 1996: 271). Writing as that which couples the subject and network is necessarily the locus of a distribution that operates in a 'glocal' manner, the roots of which we have explored in relation to Kittler's discourse networks. Technological media (as

Kittler would describe all the media of 1900 and after) beyond the information technologies that perform the 'real' work of the general intellect are an integral component of what the Autonomists term 'immaterial labour', i.e. 'labour that produces an immaterial good, such as a service, a culture product, knowledge or communication' (Hardt and Negri 2000: 291). Under these conditions work is no longer the expenditure of energy but the exploitation of the intellect and emotions, or what is termed the 'affective'. In this regime of 'affective' labour, everybody works pretty much all of the time, since all of our activities, whether remunerated or not, are recuperated by capital. Since subjectivity and its capabilities are the site of production, this renders the whole field of subjectivity a potential site of production. Our joys and desires are locked into the system of consumption, assuming the status of labour and generating profit. This immateriality affects not only workers or producers but also the corporations that direct them. These too become 'weightless': production and the ownership of the means of production become a necessary but irritating encumbrance outsourced to the developing world. As Klein argues in terms reminiscent of the pseudo-immortal capitalists of Gibson's *Neuromancer* trilogy, the real action is in the brand, the 'intellectual' edifice of the product, and in its creation and dissemination the true nature of an immaterial capitalism shows itself: 'Machines wear out. Cars rust. People die. But what lives on are the brands' (the Chief Executive Officer of United Biscuits, quoted in Klein 2000: 196).

It necessarily follows that media, particularly digital media, are an integral component of this immaterial production, prompting Dyer-Witheford (1999) to describe the internet as the 'quintessential instrument of the general intellect'. More so than other media, the internet demonstrates the collapse between labour and leisure, producer and consumer, that the Autonomists believe define contemporary capitalism. It also highlights the particular nature of the operations performed by capital 'itself' in an effort to recuperate its own revolutionary conditions. The internet offers a vivid example of the kind of immanent contradiction that characterizes the General Intellect. For instance, it offers an unparalleled potential unbinding of previous products and services from those who seek to make profit from them. For instance, all media, as they pass through the digitalization that capital demands (for the purposes of cheaper distribution or even, as in the case of recorded music, films, television programmes, etc., to generate fresh revenue from a product that has already been consumed in another format), are potentially liberated from the control of their distributors. This is demonstrated by the spectacular proliferation of pirated media and its dissemination across various peer-to-peer networks. Here, capital engenders its own countermovement, and struggles (in an increasingly draconian manner – witness the suing of twelve-year-olds in an effort to crack down on online file sharing) to recuperate the very forces it has set in motion. This, however, is not the kind of crisis envisaged by Marx. Rather, within the context of mass intellectuality this kind of 'de/reterritorialization' – as Deleuze and Guattari (1988) call it – becomes business as usual for late capital. Mass intellectuality abounds with this exploitation of limits, with this transgression and resurrection of its boundaries, and the operations of this dynamic can be observed in disparate areas of production and consumption.

This dynamic may be seen as that of *control* as defined by Deleuze in his 'Postscript to the Societies of Control' (1992). Here he argues that the regimes of power identified by Foucault are in their twilight – it is for this reason that we witness everywhere the crisis of those institutions associated with the disciplinary regimes (family, school, the factory and the state). These disciplinary societies are, Deleuze suggests, to be succeeded by the societies of control (in keeping with Beninger's work in *The Control Revolution* [1986]). In contrast to the self-enclosed, regimented spaces of the disciplinary societies that operated through successive 'striations' or discrete enclosures, such that 'one was always starting again (from school to the barracks, from the barracks to the factory)', the societies of control are characterized by a 'variable geometry'. Within this variable geometry, boundaries become permeable. As a consequence, societies of control announce themselves as a general 'crisis' of all 'interiors', such that in the societies of control 'one is never finished with anything'; instead we encounter only 'limitless postponements'.

Deleuze highlights the differing dynamics of these regimes through the distinction between *moulds* (or 'molds') and *modulation*: 'Enclosures are molds, distinct castings, but controls are a modulation, like a self-deforming cast that will continuously change from one moment to the other, or like a sieve whose mesh will transmute from point to point' (Deleuze 1992: 5). Modulation describes a form of power that is no longer exerted through the medium of a given institution and its practices, but which exceeds and escapes the boundaries of institutions, and which thus puts boundaries themselves into question. Modulation is marked by constant variation, and the subjectivity that characterizes control is 'undulatory, in orbit, in a continuous network' (ibid.: 6). In this regard, Hardt and Negri (2000) suggest that Marx's notion of the revolutionary mole with his subterranean tunnels from which he periodically surfaces to protest needs to be replaced in the Information Age with the figure of the undulating snake moving across the communicational surfaces of global capital. Indeed, to the extent that control operates immanently, contra discipline's (apparent) transcendent perspective (as in the panopticon), subjectivity itself is the locus of its modus operandi. Control is, in the words of Hardt and Negri (2000: 330), 'the self disciplining of subjects, the incessant whisperings of disciplinary logics within subjectivities themselves': the unprecedentedly invasive property of digital matters.

It should be stressed that neither moulding and modulation nor discipline and control are to be seen as oppositional categories. Here we are dealing with a difference of degree rather than a difference of kind; thus, 'modulating is molding in a variable and continuous manner' while molding can be understood as 'modulating in a constant and finite manner' (Deleuze 1979: unpaginated). Similarly, control does not spell the end of discipline and the institutions associated with it; rather it consists in raising to the highest power those modulatory operations implicit in the discrete 'castings' of the disciplinary regime. This results in a general 'metastability' of institutions, such that 'carceral discipline, school discipline, factory discipline and so forth interweave in a hybrid production of subjectivity' (Hardt and Negri 2000: 331).

This immanent control at once produces subjectivity and constrains or channels this subjectivity into expressions suitable for recuperation by capital. Thus, Lazzarato (2004) has discussed contemporary management techniques that aim to stimulate subjectivity and the exchange between subjects while firmly subordinating such exchange to the corporation. Similarly, Alex Galloway (2001, 2004) has argued that this logic of control is embodied in the protocols that facilitate the digital environment of the internet, suggesting that, rather than the anarchic, rhizomatic space of the hyperbolic commentary of the mid-1990s, the internet is characterized by a decentralization underwritten by the immanent controls of protocols. The internet is decentred only to the degree that control is distributed throughout the network: it reveals a horizontal rather than vertical logic of control. In this manner, the General Intellect liberates and constrains, often in the same instance. The transgression of boundaries characteristic of the General Intellect is at once an opportunity and a threat for capital, and in many ways the analyses offered by the authors we are drawing upon here aim at identifying this inherent equivocation, since it is within this instability that the possibility of challenging contemporary capital resides (Hardt and Negri 2000: 29). In short, the Autonomists argue (perhaps wish) that capitalism plays a dangerous game in adhering to such a modus, since the possibility of resisting capital that they identify resides precisely in this operation. Thus, it is hoped by the radical left that it is the internet, that 'quintessential instrument' of mass intellectuality, which reveals most clearly the potential for subversion, for a collective resistance to the logic of mass intellectuality.

Free software: late capital's hidden reverse

Before discussing the significance of Free software within the framework of the ideas presented above, we must establish the basic principles of Free or Open Source software, and the following definitions apply to both the free and open 'flavours' of this praxis. Free software is essentially a question of *code*, of the information involved in the development and implementation of software. The latter is understood as informatic systems or structures that allow users to access and utilize the capabilities of their hardware. The code with which software is written is called its source code – this is not the information that a computer uses but rather the information that allows a human programmer to interface with his or her hardware.

In the early days of computing, the status of software was subordinate to hardware. Companies such as IBM provided mainframes with their own software, and this software was freely shared and modified by programmers. But in the 1980s the emergence of the 'personal computer' brought about a fundamental shift in the status of software, since it introduced a large number of relatively unskilled users who required user-friendly software to access the resources of their hardware. Companies such as Microsoft embraced this new market and introduced proprietorial software, which is software sold on an individual basis whose integrity is preserved by legal licences. Since a computer does not require the source code with which a program was written to run that program, it is not included in proprietary software. In this manner, proprietary software separates a program from its genesis, an almost textbook example of commodity fetishism in which the product qua product conceals its own process of production. Moreover, since it prevents access to the codes with which a given program was written, it constrains what can be done with that program: it is prescriptive and precludes modifications and adaptations. Often, if there is sufficient demand for a given modification it will be included in another version of the software, which must be purchased and is similarly constrained. There is no technical necessity for this situation; its *raison d'être* is purely economic.

Free software was essentially a response to this situation after Richard Stallman realized that the working methods that had been commonplace in the 1970s were fundamentally threatened by the proliferation of proprietary software. Free software attempts to legally preserve an expression of what has come to be known as the early hacker ethic (see Levy 1984; Taylor 1999). This is an ideal set of values to which the coders of the 1960s and 1970s adhered to varying degrees, and which we (Harris and Taylor 2005) have summarized thus:

1   an engagement with systems;
2   hands-on curiosity applied to *any* technology; and
3   a desire to reverse the original purposes of an artefact or system.

These values have become increasingly marginalized as computing has moved from the preserve of industry and state-sponsored institutions, in which individual programmers enjoyed a considerable degree of freedom, to become the multibillion-dollar industry it is today, a crucial element of the infrastructure of global capitalism. Steven Levy (1984), the first to identify the so-called hacker ethic, described Stallman as 'the last hacker'. But Stallman's initiation of the Free software movement served as a means of consolidating and transmitting a particular element of the hacker ethic, namely the freedom to share and modify source code, so that programmers can comment on and contribute to the development of projects without constraint, and it is this free distribution of source code that defines Free software. Early on it was recognized that the freedom of sharing source code needed to be preserved otherwise those uncommitted to the development of open projects could simply adopt Free software, make minor modifications and release it in a proprietary form. Thus, Stallman created the GNU ('GNU's not Unix!') General Public License (GPL), which legally enshrined the principles of Free software. The terms of licence can be (following Cramer 2000) summarized thus:

1   Free software may be freely copied.

2   Not only the executable binary code, but also the program source code, is freely available.
3   The source code may be modified and used for other programs by anyone.
4   There are no restrictions on the use of Free software. Even if Free software is used for commercial purposes, no licence fees have to be paid.
5   There are no restrictions on the distribution of Free software. Free software may be sold for money even without paying the programmers.

Free software is not freeware or shareware, that is to say it can be sold. However, even if this is the case, the source code remains available and open to modification by the user or other programmers. This is the concept of 'copyleft', which serves to preserve the freedom of code downstream: all programs derived from free code must in turn transmit this freedom to other users/developers. Such a position leads to an important terminological issue with respect to the use of the term 'free', namely that Free software is, as Stallman tirelessly reiterates, *free as in free speech, not free beer*. There is no injunction against profit generation in the General Public License, merely that this motive should not override the distribution of source code. The drive to profit must begin from the principle that source code is freely available and open to modification.

Free software can thus be seen as the site of a renewed struggle against a capitalism understood as a technological matrix – that is, in terms of the sort of simulated, commodified and total environment that we have explored in previous chapters. In keeping with the conditions summarized in terms such as mass intellectuality and immaterial labour, it does not operate in terms of a total opposition to the existing system, it does not set itself outside the prevailing conditions but rather carries out its struggle within these conditions. As a consequence of this proximity to the matrix, Free software is itself riven with the kinds of contradictions that characterize *societies of control*. This is perhaps most clearly revealed in the movement's own fracture into the Free and Open software factions. This split is largely ethico-political and revolves around the relation of the practices of Free software to wider society.

Free software versus Open Source software

Free software has increasingly become known as Open Source or Open software. This is largely the result of the success of the Linux (more properly referred to as Linux GNU) operating system. Its history has become part of hacker lore, and involves the noble labours of a Finn, Linus Torvalds, to write an operating system from scratch: this young man and his operating system have now become major players in a market largely dominated by Microsoft. Torvalds posted his initial attempts on bulletin boards and within a short while programmers from all over the world were checking bugs and contributing code to this system. Torvalds employed the General Public License developed by Stallman and so Linux has been produced and distributed under the principles of Free software outlined above. The growth of Linux was facilitated by the open architecture of the internet (itself the product of Open software), which allowed thousands of programmers to participate and exchange information. Thus, a pool of part-time, unpaid programmers produced a product that is more reliable and flexible than its competitors. As such, Linux stands as the greatest testimony to the effectiveness of the Free software model. However, it has also brought about the fracture of the Free software movement.

In keeping with the hacker ethic, the Free software movement had as its founding principle the ethical value of freedom in and of itself. Stallman and the Free Software Foundation operate with a vision of the freedom of informa-tion, which recalls the ideal function of the university as space that facilitates the free exchange of ideas. As Kittler has argued, the computer has its origins in a piece of intellectual Free software – the concept of the universal discrete machine, an idea produced without copyright and available to all. For Stallman, Free software extends this conception of knowledge to the digital realm where, as in science and the arts, individuals stand on the shoulders of others, utilizing and developing their ideas within a culture that is driven by the desire to share and develop knowledge for all. Thus, the Free software movement is directed by the notion that Free software is good for society, since it enshrines principles that benefit all of its members. This is the notion of the 'commons' – a collec-tive resource open to all and under the control of none. From this perspective, proprietary software is a black box whose function is to create a divide between user and producer, to introduce a hierarchy of power. In this regard it introduces an artificial impediment to the evolution of a given software function.

It is this concentration on power and ethics that has served to split the source-code-sharing community. The substitution of Open for Free can be seen as an attempt to establish a terminology acceptable to corporate clients, purging the movement of any problematic concepts of freedom, and forestalling the kind of critiques that Microsoft (in a deliberate smear campaign) have levelled against Free/Open software, namely that it is 'un-American' or 'communist'. The Open Source 'faction', which would include Torvalds and whose most vocal representative is Eric S. Raymond, claims to offer Open software without 'ideological tub-thumping' and a 'losing attitude and symbolism' (Raymond 2005). Open Source is not about grand notions of freedom, progress and the communal good. It is simply a question of efficiency and choice, which is to say precisely the qualities that the market holds most dear. Open Source, according to Raymond, will triumph not because it enshrines sacrosanct freedoms, but because of its greater affinity with the market. The Open Source faction argues from a position of straightforward pragmatism, the question of the sharing of source code is one of 'engineering efficiency'. Raymond's position is that what is important is that the Open Source method of development works, that it produces a superior product and that this overrides any of the abstract ethical concerns that burden technological development with the baggage of absolute moral values. In accounts such as his seminal *The Cathedral and Bazaar* Raymond (2001) stresses the methodological advantages of Open Source software: its pat-tern of frequent releases; its parallelism, which allows the rapid identification and correction of bugs; the distributed mindsharing of its pool of motivated programmers; and its 'benevolent dictators', who direct the development of given program and determine which contributions will be incorporated into official releases. For Raymond, the bottom line is that Open Source delivers a superior product in a shorter time at a lower cost than the proprietary model of Microsoft *et al.*

Thus, in contrast to the inalienable freedom of Free software, the Open Source movement advocates a neo-liberal conception of freedom. While Stallman talks of what is good for society, Raymond stresses the self-interest of individuals: Open Source works because individuals interested in their own ends, of necessity, must at times cooperate. Free software prioritizes the collective, and judges the action of the individual in relation to its collective benefit; Open Source prioritizes the individual and places collective collaboration against the backdrop of the individual. On one level, it can be argued that Raymond's stance is contradictory: while Stallman is openly ideological, Raymond claims that Open Source is solely pragmatic while at the same time eliding this pragmatism with a range of ideological positions, for instance on gun laws, and a deep-seated American distrust of centralized government. However, Stallman's stance has also been seen as contradictory because it enforces freedom through the use of legally binding licences – to quote De Landa (2001): 'The very fact that the [GNU] license acts as an "enforcement mechanism" for openness shows how far its function is from one of just promoting "freedom" (that is, Stallman's original intention)'. However, most programmers involved in Free software appear to fall somewhere between these two extremes and, like most hackers, enjoy a mixture of financial rewards and intellectual stimulation. Neither faction is opposed to financial gain from their labour; rather, both believe that remuneration can be derived from support rather than from the sale of licensed software. In economic terms, Raymond's model has proved the most successful, both economically and ideologically, since 'Open' rather than 'Free' has become the preferred term for source code sharing. De Landa suggests that ultimately both poles of the debate are equally compromised and that what is important about Free/Open software is its consequences, such as the 'viral' impact of 'copyleft', and that these consequences would encompass elements of both visions.

Free software in the context of the General Intellect and immaterial labour

Commentators such as Barbrook (2002) and Terranova (2000) have offered a number of valuable insights into the relation between Free/Open software and digital capital. Both argue that it is mistaken to see this praxis as inherently anti-capitalist, arguing instead that it confirms the dynamics of global capitalism, while offering an opportunity to understand how this system may be challenged. Throughout this book we have argued that the logic of the matrix is that of commodification and enframement, such that our contemporary condition is one in which commodification has been *concretized* (to use Feenberg's phrase) in a technological environment. However, what analyses such as the neo-Marxist theory outlined above and praxes such as Free software suggest is that this matrix is unstable and sets in motion processes that it struggles to contain. Technology may well be a second nature, a womb in which we are nurtured or trapped, but it is also in flux. The flows of the metropolis in which the *flâneur* immersed himself and which the cyberpunk celebrates are the essence of digital matters, but they are difficult to second guess or corral. This militates against a vision of the matrix as total enframement or hardwired totalitarianism.

Barbrook has argued that the digital realm represents a fulfilment of the anar-cho-communists ideals of the social revolutions of the 1960s articulated in tracts such as Raoul Vaneigem's (1972) *Revolution of Everyday Life*, wherein:

> We must rediscover the pleasure of giving: giving because you have so much. What beautiful and priceless potlatches the affluent society will see – whether it likes it or not! – when the exuberance of the younger genera-tion discovers the pure gift.
>
> (ibid.: 70)

Digital matters thus inaugurate a new gift economy: McLuhan's global village realized in the ultimate medium of the net results in the re-emergence of anachronistic modes of exchange. For Barbrook the internet confounds an earlier form of capitalism because it refuses to play by its rules and thus constitutes a return of the repressed. While the internet's martial origins are well known, Barbrook maintains that what is often forgotten is that its midwife was the university, in which the free exchange of ideas is (at least traditionally) a common practice. The extension of this gift culture emerges in the context of a superabundance of information; when information can be copied and exchanged at little cost, it no longer makes sense to charge for it, and a culture of potlatch (or sharing) emerges, in which largesse becomes symbolic power. The internet's original purpose is as a medium for the exchange and replication of information such that, as Tim Berners-Lee (the inventor of hypertext mark-up language) has put it:

> Concepts of intellectual property, central to our culture, are not expressed in a way which maps onto the abstract information space. In an information space, we can consider the authorship of materials, and their perception; but . . . there is a need for the underlying infrastructure to be able to make copies simply for reasons of [technical] efficiency and reliability. The con-cept of 'copyright' as expressed in terms of copies made makes little sense.
>
> (Berners-Lee in Barbrook 1998: unpaginated)

Thus, Barbrook argues that the design of the internet forgoes concepts of intellectual copyright and assumes that its users should be able to access and manipulate information without impediment. Free or Open software is a natu-ral extension of this situation, and thus it is not coincidence that the internet has played an absolutely critical role in its evolution – for instance the coordination of the development of Linux online. However, Barbrook stresses that this gift economy is a qualified or compromised realization of an anarcho-communist utopia. The net is the site of an irreducible heterogeneity, a mixed economy. Thus, the average web user may in a single session pass from participating in a potlatch (sharing files or posting information on newsgroups or blogs) to participating in economic exchanges as either consumer or producer (for instance trading on sites such as eBay). This miscegenation or paradoxical assemblage of economic forms is reflected on multiple levels and is easily overlooked by commentators from either side of the political spectrum. For instance, Berry (2004: 81) notes that Raymond, in celebrating the 'invisible hand' of the market, fails to acknowledge the degree to which the tools with which this market bootstraps itself are the product of considerable centralized funding, in the form of both the military and the universities. By the same token, the very surplus that presents conditions propitious to the emergence of gift economy is the product of business-as-usual – thus, a not insignificant proportion of the hackers who have contributed to the development of Linux GNU have earned their daily bread in the proprietary software industry.

In fact, the entire debate currently raging regarding intellectual property (of which Free/Open software is a privileged example) can be seen in the context of this irreducible heterogeneity; thus, the apparent difficulties that capital confronts in the form of Open Source, peer-to-peer networks and pirated media and software prove problematic only for certain sectors. And the internet could be said to set sector against sector. For example, bandwidth and hardware are commodities like any other, and the proliferation of the internet's apparent gift culture provides considerable revenue for those that supply them, revenues that only increase as more and more people across the developed world rush to get online to participate in the global potlatch. As Barbrook has observed, this situation is troubling for those who deal in content, and who attempt to maintain an 'enforced information scarcity in an age of information plenty'. Since 'copyright emerged in a world with only limited media' (Barbrook 2002: unpaginated), this represents an attempt (in Kittler's terms) to maintain the conditions of earlier discourse network (based on disparate media that precluded easy replication) in the context of a new network.

Terranova (2000) has argued that this situation of irreducible mixture can perhaps be best understood through the concepts offered by the Italian Autonomists, not least that of immaterial or what she terms 'free' labour. Immaterial labour, as we have seen, operates on two levels: first, that of addition of an increasingly informatic dimension to traditional labour and, second, that of an extension of what constitutes labour so that it begins to embrace activities that traditionally were elements of leisure, escape or simply outside of the market. What immaterial labour suggests is that the boundaries between traditional labour and entertainment or 'play' are dissolved in digital capitalism. In the issues surrounding Open/Free software and in its theoretical erosion of the distinction between users and producers, we observe a conflation of these two vectors. This situation has a certain historical logic. Himanen (2001), in his analysis of the hacker ethic, for example, suggests that the culture that developed around hacking in the 1960s and 1970s was one in which the boundaries between work and play, creativity and labour, altruism and self-interest were eroded. Hackers, although by no means adverse to work, labour in a non-alienated fashion; their hours are irregular and determined by the waxing and waning of their own interest rather than by external dictates. Hackers value not labour in itself, but rather their specific labour: their enthusiasm is less for the material rewards of work, but for the task itself. In this light, hacking at its most basic level is a joyous, playful or creative activity, and the work ethic of the hacker is close to that of the creative artist or the academic, both of whom (ideally) work for the sake of *the* work (Moody 2002: 154). However, in the case of the latter there is a tendency towards individualism, an autonomous even solipsistic aspect that is absent in hacking.

Such a formulation may appear paradoxical given the popular image of the hacker as a socially maladroit loner, happier with code than with people – an image that corresponds, as we have seen, with other analyses of the matrix, for instance Ellul's notion of *la téchnique* as a source of anomie and alienation, or cyberpunk's world of self-serving/surviving protagonists struggling to preserving their individual identity and integrity within conditions of extreme social flux. Such images are brought into question by the deeply socially nature of hacking. Thus, to quote Marvin Minsky: 'contrary to popular belief, hackers are more social than other people' (Minsky cited in Himanen 2001: 52). Hackers, while perhaps solitary as individuals, are as a group or collective highly social. Peer recognition, and a desire to produce tools that are socially useful, is a crucial aspect of their endeavour. Hackers, Himanen suggests, harness the traits of creativity and enthusiasm associated with highly individualized forms of production towards communal or collaborative projects. Indeed, when we consider that the hacking ethic has produced the open architecture of the internet, a medium that in itself has allowed the proliferation of ranges of communities, it becomes necessary to approach the impact of technology on society in terms other than atomization and alienation.

Thus, hacking culture could be said to have anticipated, by virtue of its proximity to the technologies that would transform the working world, the crucial trends of digital matters. Nevertheless, this must be placed within the context of the concepts outlined above: thus, Terranova argues that the gift-economy celebrated by Barbrook and others 'does not exist as a free floating postindustrial utopia but in full, mutually constituting interaction with late capitalism' (Barbrook 2000: unpaginated). From this perspective the fracture of the movement into rival factions, as well as the lack of a doctrinal opposition in either faction to capital itself, cannot be seen as a betrayal of the anarcho-communist principles that Barbrook sees the net as realizing. To quote Terranova:

> Rather than representing a moment of incorporation of a previously authentic moment, the open source question is exemplar . . . of larger mechanisms

of capitalist valorization which are totally immanent to late capitalism as whole. That is they are not created outside capital and then reappropriated by capital, but are the results of a complex history where the relation between labour and capital is mutually constitutive. Free [or immaterial] labour is a desire of labour immanent to late capitalism, and late capitalism is the field that both sustains and exhausts it.

(ibid.)

From this position, Free software as a mode of production is not a challenge to capital but rather something entirely immanent to its current form: it represents a hypostatization of a more general logic, i.e. a logic articulated in concepts such as the social brain or immaterial labour. This is an analysis that is borne out by the success of the Open Source vision of code sharing and the increasingly marginal position of Stallman's Free software model in the marketplace. This might seem a dispiriting position when placed against the vision of free labour as the realization of the revolutionary ideals of the anarcho-communism born of the 1960s. However, what it also suggests is a fundamental instability, which is embraced by capital but at the same time threatens capital, rendering digital matter a complex or chaotic matter subject to sudden reversals and bifurcations. As such, while it perhaps diffuses the possibility of the total transformation of the social field in the sense of the emergence of an fully 'Open Source society', it also holds out the possibility of the continual emergence of new sites of contestation; neither capital nor anti-capital will ever triumph.

Open futures?

The possibility of new areas of political contestation is demonstrated by the spread of Open Source software and more generally the Open Source model. In both Europe and, more importantly, the developing nations, Free software is increasingly being embraced by states, business and individuals. Indeed, in the context of globalized economy, that speaks of the benefits for all while preserving the wealth of the few and actively exploiting the rest of the world's population as its immiserized proletariat, Free software represents one of the few easily accessed infrastructural resources that might offer some hope of equity. As Weerwarana and Weertunga (2004: 51) conclude in their study of the consequences of Open Source software for developing nations, through 'exploiting OSS [Open Source software], it is possible for a developing country to establish a global position in the IT [information technology] driven knowledge of the future'.

An even more radical vision of the future of this freedom has been proposed by Eben Moglen, a member of Stallman's Free Software Foundation, in a series of polemical articles and in a rousing speech delivered at the Wizards of Open Source conference in 2004 (Moglen 2004). He argues for the extension of the freedoms embodied in the GNU General Public License to the entire digital realm. His contention is that, in contrast to earlier revolutionary movements, the Free software movement is concerned not with the realization of a future utopia but with the preservation and dissemination of current liberties. As he puts it, the Free software movement derives its strength from two principles: *running code*, i.e. extant software; and *proof of concept*, that is to say the demonstrable success of the Open Source model. Moglen maintains that the solution to the problems and contradictions of capitalism that we have addressed reside in the institution of a fourfold freedom, namely:

1   Free software;
2   Free hardware;
3   Free spectrum; and
4   Free culture.

Since we have already established what Free software means, we shall briefly outline these other freedoms. By 'Free hardware', Moglen indicates the refusal by the Free software movement of initiatives such as *trusted computing*. This refers to attempts by a consortium of content providers and computer manufacturers to forestall the sort of paradoxical vectors outlined above. Under trusted computing, hardware and software would be ascribed a unique digital fingerprint. This fingerprint would be checked when a given user accessed a particular form of content on the internet, and would tell the content provider the capabilities of the components a user possessed. For instance, if a content provider wanted to preserve the integrity of a given media file, it could choose to prevent the distribution of said file to all users whose software fingerprint indicated that they allowed modification or replication. The basic aim of trusted computing (or, following Stallman, 'treacherous' computing since it abrogates control of hardware to the manufacturer and content provider) is thus to preserve copyright by policing at the level of hardware and software the manipulation of data, in other words to turn the internet (as Barbrook above has described it) against itself. This would result in a situation in which the digital realm would come under the control of a cabal of content providers and hardware and software manufacturers. Certainly, this would represent a major impediment for Free software since trusted computing could effectively ostracize the results of Open Source programming (or limit it to a small number of 'trusted' applications), by refusing to permit computers running it to access a range of online content. Moglen suggests that the most effective way to challenge initiatives such as these is to liberate unfree hardware, to engage in the kind of reverse engineering that has been seen a crucial component of the hacker ethic (see Harris and Taylor 2005).

'Free spectrum' designates the ownership of the electromagnetic spectrum and the issues surrounding the installation of wireless networks. This, it is argued, should be treated as a 'commons' outside of the ownership of corporations or states. The fact that Free spectrum can provide the foundation for self-organizing, non-hierarchical access to wireless telecommunication is already demonstrated by a range of 'wi-fi' initiatives in both the developed and developing worlds. These projects have demonstrated that it is possible at a community level to set up networks that provide high-speed access to the net at nothing more than the cost of installation and maintenance. If these networks were extended, they could result in the creation of digital network, capable of high-speed data transfer outside the control of states and capital. In keeping with the paradox of mass intellectuality and, like the wired internet, wi-fi networks dissolve the distinction between user and provider since the same equipment performs both functions. By 'Free culture', Moglen refers to the issues surrounding intellectual property and asserts a fundamental freedom for all to access knowledge and culture. Since when they are digitized these cultural elements can be provided to all at almost no cost, he argues that they should be accessible to all. Content providers and creators must redefine their activities in the context of Free culture that has substantially revised notions of ownership and copyright. The proliferation of file sharing can be seen as a controversial expression of this freedom. More constructive are projects such as the Creative Commons License, a licence based on the principles of the GNU General Public License, which serves to install the principle of 'copyleft' in the sphere of cultural production.

Conclusion: a 'metastable' matrix?

Together the above freedoms amount to a new vision of a digital commons. What is interesting in the context of the body of theory on which we have drawn is the way in which they creatively engage with the logic of control. Through the use of licences that preserve freedom within the context of a mass intellect, they negotiate the treacherous waters of late capital. Galloway, in his discussion of the way in which the principles of the society of control are embodied in the protocols that organize the net, states that 'Deleuze had the foresight to situate resistive action within the protological field . . . It is through protocol that we must guide our efforts, not against it' (Galloway 2001: 88). In seeking to perpetuate existing freedoms through the use of licences, in consolidating existing conditions rather than engaging in a struggle to realize a future utopia, Moglen's fourfold freedom does exactly this. What we have then is not a challenge to capital by something outside or beyond, but a situation in which capital is riven from within – a 'schizophrenic' capital that engenders its own immanent countermeasures; and a movement that strives to accelerate this process. It may be that this tendency is not simply a result of capitalism and the way that it controls the evolution of technology, nor simply the result of engaging in liberated modes of production, but more radically a vector in technogenesis itself. That is to say that technology intrinsically possesses a tendency toward deterritorialization and as we, individually and collectively, enter into increasingly complex colligation with our technologies we, individually and collectively, become subjects of this tendency.

Something of this tendency may be grasped through the comments of Bernard Stiegler, who, drawing on the work of the French philosopher of technology Gilbert Simondon, has argued that: 'The industrial technical system whose beginnings took root in England at the end of the 18th Century has today been globalised. It has entered an epoch of permanent innovation and can be said to be fundamentally unstable. Technological stability . . . is no longer possible' (Stiegler 2002: unpaginated). Simondon's thesis was that technology constituted a system that evolved over time through its relations with other systems (such as the natural world and human society), and in this evolution ran into periods of contradiction or conflict with these other systems. This situation necessitated the evolution of technology so that it was brought into relation with its ambient systems. According to Simondon, technology displayed its own autonomous dynamic, but he, unlike Ellul, considers this dynamic to be systemic, but rather genetically so – that is to say a quasi-organic evolutionary dynamic that involved the resolution and incorporation of contradictions in its functioning. For this reason, Simondon argued for the existence of a margin of indetermination in the technological itself, such that it does not attain closure but remains open to the future: it is always in becoming, a process of individuation that does not attain closure. This, Simondon described as 'metastability' (a term Deleuze draws upon in his description of the logic of a society of control). Thus, while the individual technical artefact is stable, the technological system is metastable, open to evolution or modification. Since we have arrived at a situation in which technology has become our matrix, in which technology has become the driving force of our society, our society itself begins to partake of this metastability, in particular those sections in greatest proximity to the technological.

The consequences of this metastability are profound for all the parties involved. This metastability means that technology can never be subordinated to the interests of capitalism and, should Microsoft or the various content-providing industries attempt to lock down information networks, this will occur only at great loss to technological innovation itself, and even then is unlikely to succeed. Similarly, efforts at state control, bar the most totalitarian, cannot constrain this inherent instability. This indetermination reveals itself in the practices of Free software as well as in the more disruptive activities of 'cracking', the release of worms and viruses, etc., and in the general problematization of categories revealed by the immaterial labour. The Italian Autonomist Paolo Virno has drawn on Simondon in the context of the general intellect, noting that:

> . . . *individuation is never concluded* . . . the pre-individual is never fully translated into singularity. Consequently, according to Simondon, the *subject* consists of the permanent interweaving of pre-individual elements and individuated characteristics; moreover, the subject *is* this interweaving . . . By participating in a collective, the subject, far from surrendering the most unique individual traits, has the opportunity to individuate, at least in part, the share of pre-individual reality which all individuals carry within themselves. According to Simondon, within the collective we endeavor to refine our singularity, to bring it to its climax. Only within the collective, certainly

not within the isolated subject, can perception, language, and productive forces take on the shape of an individuated experience.

(Virno 2004: 78–9 [emphasis in original])

What the impossibility of technological stability suggests is that we will never be free of these phenomena, that they are an irreducible component of a global information society: the individual, the collective and the technological are all mestastable, involved in a process of mutual accelerated individuation. Success here resides in an ability to embrace and negotiate this indeterminacy or metastability, and capitalism as a whole has done this, by becoming a mode of control by exploiting immaterial labour. But likewise, as the Free/Open software movement demonstrates, so have those who would oppose capital. Technical metastability suggests that these struggles may never cease; the multitude will always escape the striations of capitalism, even as capitalism continues to decode and unbind. Rather than the straightjacket of technical determinacy – an Ellulian enframement in which we are subjects of monstrous rationality – we inhabit a space of flows, of instability. This instability abounds with opportunity, and, as the Free software movement and those who extend its freedoms demonstrate, it offers an opportunity to establish a groundwork for the construction of better world, to overturn the old distribution of power. But this can occur only if these opportunities are embraced and consolidated; otherwise we risk losing them before even recognizing that we possess them. Put a different way: there is everything to fight for.

Bibliography

Adorno, T. (1973) *Negative Dialectics,* trans. E.B. Ashton, London: Routledge.

Augé, M. (1995) *Non-Places: introduction to an anthropology of supermodernity*, London: Verso.

Ballard, J.G. (1995) *Crash*, London: Vintage.

Barbrook, R. (1998) 'The high tech gift economy', available at http://www.firstmonday.dk/issues/issue3_12/barbrook/ (accessed 14 February 2005).

—— (2002) 'Giving is receiving', available at http://info.interactivist.net/article.pl?sid=02/10/12/2031231&mode=nested&tid=12 (accessed 14 February 2005).

Barlow, J.P. (1990) 'Crime and puzzlement', *Whole Earth Review*, Fall: 44–57.

Barthes, R. (1993 [1982]) *Camera Lucida: reflections on photography*, London: Vintage Books.

Baudelaire, C. (2003 [1859]) *The Painter of Modern Life and Other Essays,* London: Phaidon Press.

Baudrillard, J. (1983) *Simulations*, trans. P. Foss, P. Batton and P. Beitchman, New York: Semiotext(e).

—— (1988) *The Ecstasy of Communication*, trans. B. and C. Schutze, New York, NY: Semiotext(e).

—— (1990a) *Revenge of the Crystal: selected writings on the modern object and its destiny, 1968–1983*, London: Pluto Press.

—— (1990b) *Fatal Strategies,* trans. P. Beitchman and W.G.J. Niesluchowski, New York/London: Semiotext(e)/Pluto.

—— (1991) 'Two essays: simulacra and science fiction and Ballard's 'Crash', *Science Fiction Studies*, 18(3), available at: http://www.depauw.edu/sfs/backissues/55/baudrillard55art.htm (accessed 15 February 2005).

—— (1997) *The System of Objects,* trans. J. Benedict, London: Verso.

Bauman, Z. (2000) *Liquid Modernity*, Cambridge: Polity.

Beninger, J. R. (1986) *The Control Revolution: technological and economic origins of the information society.* Cambridge, MA: Harvard University Press.

Benjamin, M. (1996) 'Sliding scales: microphotography and the Victorian obsession with the miniscule', in F. Spufford and J. Uglow (eds) *Cultural Babbage: technology, time and invention*, London: Faber & Faber.

Benjamin, W. (1973 [1935]) 'The work of art in the age of mechanical reproduction', in H. Arendt (ed.) *Illuminations*, trans. H. Zohn, London: Fontana, pp. 219–45.

—— (1983) *Charles Baudelaire: a lyric poet in the era of high capitalism*, London: Verso.

—— (1985) *One-Way Street and Other Writings*, London: Verso.

—— (1986) 'Hashish in Marseilles', in P. Demetz (ed.) *Reflections: essays, aphorisms, autobiographical writings*, trans. E. Jephcott, New York: Schoken, pp. 137–45.

—— (1999) *The Arcades Project,* trans. H. Eiland and K. McLaughlin, Cambridge, MA: Belknap Press/Harvard University Press.

Berman, M. (1983) *All that is Solid Melts into Air: the experience of modernity*, London: Verso.

Berry, D.M. (2004) 'The contestation of code', *Critical Discourse Studies*, 1(1): 65–89.

Boli-Bennett, J. (1980) 'The absolutist dialectics of Jacques Ellul', *Research in Philosophy and Technology*, 3: 171–201.

Boyer, C.M. (1996) 'Cities for sale: merchandising history at South Street Seaport', in M. Sorkin (ed.) *Variations on a Theme Park: the new American City and the end of public space,* New York: Hill & Wang, pp. 181–204.

Brown, D. (1988) *Cybertrends: chaos, power and accountability in the information age*, London: Penguin.

Burroughs, W.S. (1995 [1959]) *The Naked Lunch,* London: Flamingo.

Burrows, R. (1997) 'Cyberpunk as social theory', in S. Westwood and J. Williams (eds) *Imagining Cities*, London: Routledge, pp. 235–48.

Cacciari, M. (1993) *Architecture and Nihilism: on the philosophy of modern architecture*, New Haven, CT: Yale University Press.

Calvino, I. (1985) *Difficult Loves*, London: Picador.

Castells, M. (2000) *The Rise of the Network Society*, 2nd edn, Oxford: Blackwell.

Cavallaro, D. (2000) *Cyberpunk and Cyberculture: science fiction and the work of William Gibson*, London: Athlone Press.

Caygill, H. (1998) *Walter Benjamin: the colour of experience*, London: Routledge.

Cerezuelle, D. (1979) 'Fear and insight in French philosophy of technology', *Research in Philosophy and Technology,* 2: 53–75.

Comor, E. (2003) 'Harold Innis', in C. May (ed.) *Key Thinkers for the Information Society*, London: Routledge, pp. 87–108.

Coupland, D. (1996) *Microserfs*, New York: Flamingo.

Coyle, D. (1998) *The Weightless World: strategies for managing the digital economy,* Cambridge, MA: MIT Press.

Cramer, F. (2000) 'Free software as collaborative text', presented at Interface 5, Hamburg, 15 September, available at http://www.netzliteratur.net/cramer/free_software_as_text.html (accessed 15 February 2005).

Crawford, M. (1996) 'The world in a shopping Mall', in M. Sorkin (ed.) *Variations on a Theme Park: the new American city and the end of public space,* New York: Hill & Wang, pp. 3–30.

Crowley, A. (1929) *Magic in Theory and Practice*, Paris: Lecram Press.

Csiscery-Ronay, I. (1992) 'Futuristic flu, or, the revenge of the future', in G. Slusser and T. Shippey (eds) *Fiction 2000: cyberpunk and the future of narrative,* Athens, GA: University of Georgia Press, pp. 26–45.

Cubitt, S. (1998) *Digital Aesthetics*, London: Sage.

Davis, E. (1998) *TechGnosis: myth, magic + mysticism in the age of information*, London: Serpent's Tail.

de Certeau, M. (1988) *The Practice of Everyday Life*, Berkeley: University of California Press.

De Landa, M. (1991) *War in the Age of Intelligent Machines*, New York: Zone Books.

—— (2001) 'Open-Source: a movement in search of a philosophy', presented at the Institute for Advanced Study, Princeton, NJ, available at http://www.cddc.vt.edu/host/delanda/pages/opensource.htm (accessed 15 February 2005).

De Quincey, T. (1986 [1821]) *Confessions of an Opium Eater*, Harmondsworth: Penguin.

Debord, G. (1983) *The Society of the Spectacle*, Detroit: Black & Red.

—— (1990) *Comments on the Society of Spectacle*, trans. M. Imrie, London: Verso.

Deleuze, G. (1979) 'Metal, metallurgy, music, Husserl, Simondon', trans. T.S. Murphy, unpublished seminar, 24 August 1979, available at: http://www.webdeleuze.com (accessed 15 February 2005).

—— (1989) *Cinema 2: the time-image*, trans. H. Tomlinson and R. Galeta, London: Athlone Press.

—— (1990) *The Logic of Sense*, trans. M. Lester and C. Stivale, London: Athlone Press.

—— (1992) 'Postscript on the societies of control', *October* 59 (Winter): 3–7.

—— (1998) 'An unrecognized precursor to Heidegger: Alfred Jarry', in *Essays Critical and Clinical*, trans. D.W. Smith and M.A. Greco, London: Verso, pp. 91–8.

Deleuze, G. and Guattari, F. (1988) *A Thousand Plateaus: capitalism and schizophrenia*, trans. B. Massumi, London: Athlone Press.

Delillo, D. (1985) *White Noise*, London: Picador.

Derrida, J. (1976) *Of Grammatology*, trans. G.C. Spivak, Baltimore: Johns Hopkins Press.

—— (2001) *Writing and Difference*, trans. A. Bass, London: Routledge.

Dick, P.D. (1966) *The Three Stigmata of Palmer Eldritch*, London: Jonathan Cape.

—— (1990 [1968]) *Do Androids Dream of Electric Sheep?* New York: Ballentine.

—— (1991 [1977]) *A Scanner Darkly*, New York: Vintage Books.

Dyer-Witheford, N. (1999) *Cyber-Marx: cycles and circuits of struggle in high technology capitalism*, Champaign, IL: University of Illinois Press.

Eliot, T.S. (1943) *Burnt Norton*, London: Faber & Faber.

—— (2002) *The Waste Land* [1922], in *Selected Poems*, London: Faber & Faber.

Ellul, J. (1963 [1954]) *The Technological Society*, trans. J. Wilkinson, London: Vintage.

Feenberg, A. (1991) *Critical Theory of Technology*, New York: Oxford University Press.

—— (1999) *Questioning Technology*, London: Routledge.

—— (2000) 'The ontic and the ontological in Heidegger's philosophy of technology: response to Thomson', *Inquiry*, 445–50,

Ferguson, P.P. (1994) 'The flâneur on and off the streets of Paris', in K. Tester (ed.) *The Flâneur*, London: Routledge, pp. 22–42.

Foucault, M. (1972) *The Archaeology of Knowledge*, London: Routledge.

—— (1994 [1970]) *The Order of Things: an archaeology of human sciences*, New York: Vintage.

Frank, T. (2001) *One Market under God: extreme capitalism, market populism and the end of economic democracy*, London: Secker & Warburg.

Freedman, D. (2003) 'Raymond Williams', in C. May (ed.) *Key Thinkers for the Key Information Age*, London: Routledge, pp. 173–90.

Freud, S. (2002 [1901]) *The Psychopathology of Everyday Life*, London: Penguin.

Frisby, D. (1986) *Fragments of Modernity: theories of modernity in the work of Simmel, Kracauer and Benjamin*, Cambridge, MA: MIT Press.

Galloway, A. (2001) 'Protocol, or, how control exists after decentralization', *Rethinking Marxism,* 13: 81–8.

—— (2004) *Protocol: how control exists after decentralization*, Cambridge, MA: MIT Press.

Geidion, S. (1969 [1948]) *Mechanisation Takes Command: a contribution to anonymous history*, New York: Norton.

Gibson, W. (1984) *Neuromancer*, London: Grafton.

—— (1986) *Count Zero*, London: Grafton.

—— (1988) *Mona Lisa Overdrive*, London: Grafton.

—— (2003) *Pattern Recognition*, London: Penguin.

Gilloch, G. (2002) *Walter Benjamin: critical constellations*, Cambridge: Polity.

Griffin, M. (1996) 'Literary studies +/– literature: Friedrich A. Kittler's media histories', *New Literary History*, 27: 709–16.

Gumbrecht, H.U. and Pfeiffer, K.L. (eds) (1994) *Materialities of Communication*, Stanford, CA: Stanford University Press.

Handy, C. (1995) *The Empty Raincoat: making sense of the future*, London: Random House.

Hardt, M. and Negri, A. (2000) *Empire*, Harvard: Harvard University Press.

Harris, J. and Taylor, P.A. (2005) 'Hacktivism', in H. Bidgoli (ed.) *The Handbook of Information Security*, Hoboken, NJ: John Wiley.

Harvey, D. (1990) *The Condition of Postmodernity*, Oxford: Blackwell.

Heidegger, M. (1962) *Being and Time*, trans. J. Macquarrie and E. Robinson, Oxford: Blackwell.

—— (1976 [1966]) '"Only a God can Save Us": the Spiegel interview', trans. M.P. Alter and J.D. Caputo, *Philosophy Today* 20(4): 267–85.

—— (1977 [1954]) *The Question Concerning Technology*, New York: Harper & Row.

—— (1992) *Parmenides*, trans. A. Schuwer and R. Rojcewicz, Bloomington: Indiana University Press.

—— (1993 [1947]) 'Letter on humanism', in D. Farrell Krell (ed.) *Basic Writings*, San Francisco: Harper Collins.

Heyer, P. and Crowley, D. (2003) Introduction to H. Innis, *The Bias of Communication* [1951], Toronto: University of Toronto Press, ix–xxvi.

Himanen, P. (2001) *The Hacker Ethic: and the spirit of the information age*, London: Secker & Warburg.

Hobsbawm, E. (1975 [1962]) *The Age of Revolution: Europe, 1789–1848*, London: Abacus.

Inglis, F. (1990) *Media Theory: an introduction*, Oxford: Blackwell.

Innis, H. (2003 [1951]) *The Bias of Communication*, Toronto: University of Toronto Press.

Jameson, F. (1980) *Aesthetics and Politics*, London: Verso.

—— (1998) *The Cultural Turn: selected writings on the postmodern 1983–1998*, London: Verso.

Jaspers, K. (1978 [1932]) *Man in the Modern Age*, Brooklyn: AMS Press.

Jenks, C. (1995) 'The centrality of the eye in Western culture: an introduction', in C. Jenks (ed.) *Visual Culture*, London: Routledge, pp. 1–25.

Jordan, T. and Taylor, P.A. (2004) *Hacktivists: rebels with a cause?* London: Routledge.

Joyce, J. (1990 [1922]) *Ulysses*, New York: Vintage.

Kellner, D. (1995) *Media Culture*, London: Routledge.

Kern, S. (1983) *The Culture of Time and Space 1880–1918*, Cambridge, MA: Harvard University Press.

Kittler, F.A. (1990) *Discourse Networks 1800/1900*, Stanford: Stanford University Press.

—— (1996) 'The city is a medium', *New Literary History*, 27: 717–29.

—— (1997) *Literature Media, Information Systems*, edited by J. Johnston, Amsterdam: Overseas Publishers Association.

—— (1999) *Gramophone, Film, Typewriter*, trans. G. Winthrop-Young and M. Wutz, Stanford: Stanford University Press.

Klein, M. (2000) *No Logo*, New York: Flamingo.

Kracauer, S. (1965) *Theory of Film: the redemption of physical reality*, New York: Galaxy.

—— (1995 [1963]) *Mass Ornament: Weimar essays*, trans. T.Y. Levin, Cambridge, MA: Harvard University Press.

Kruh, L. and Deavours, T. (2002) 'The commerical Enigma: beginnings of machine cryptography', *Cryptologia*, 26(1): 1–6.

Lash, S. (2002) *Critique of Information*, London: Sage.

Latour, B. (1993) *We Have Never Been Modern,* trans. C. Porter, Cambridge, MA: Harvard University Press.

Lazzarato, M. (2004) 'From capital-labour to capital-life', *Emphemera*, 4(3): 187–208.

Leadbetter, C. (2000) *Living on Thin Air: the new economy,* London: Penguin.

Levine, D.N. (ed.) (2001) *On Individuality and Social Forms: selected writings of Georg Simmel*, Chicago: University of Chicago Press.

Levy, S. (1984) *Hackers: heroes of the computer revolution*, New York: Bantam Doubleday Dell.

Luhmann, N. (1997) 'Globalization or world society: how to conceive of modern society', *International Review of Sociology*, 7(1): 67–79.

—— (2000) *The Reality of the Mass Media*, trans. K. Cross, Cambridge: Polity Press.

Lukács, G. (1968 [1922]) 'Reification and the consciousness of the proletariat', in *History and Class Consciousness*, London: Merlin Press.

MacKenzie, D. and Wajcman, J. (eds) (1985) *The Social Shaping of Technology*, Milton Keynes: Open University Press.

McLuhan, M. (1995) [1964] *Understanding Media*, London: Routledge.

—— (1997) 'Notes on Burroughs', in M. Moos (ed.) *Media Research: technology, art, communication*, Amsterdam: Overseas Publishers Association, pp. 86–91.

McLuhan, M. and Fiore, Q. (1967) *The Medium is the Massage: an inventory of effects*, New York: Bantam.

McQuire, S. (1998) *Visions of Modernity: representation, memory, time and space in the age of the camera*, London: Sage.

Marcuse, H. (1968) *One Dimensional Man,* Boston: Beacon Books.

Marx, K. (1973) *Grundrisse*, trans. M. Nicolaus, Harmondsworth: Penguin.

—— (1983 [1887]) *Capital: a critique of political economy,* vol. 1, London: Lawrence & Wishart.

Marx, K. and Engels, F. (1977 [1848]) *Manifesto of the Communist Party*, Moscow: Progress Publishers.

May, C. (ed.) (2003) *Key Thinkers for the Information Society*, London: Routledge.

Mazlish, B. (1993) *The Fourth Discontinuity: the co-evolution of humans and machines*, New Haven, CT: Yale University Press.

Moglen, E. (2004) ' "Die Gedanken sind Frei": Free software and the struggle for free thought', Keynote Address, Wizards of OS 3, Berlin, June 2004, available at http:// wizards-of-os.org/index.php?id=791 (accessed 15 February 2005).

Moody, G. (2002) *Rebel Code: Linux and the Open Source revolution*, London: Penguin.

Moos, M. (ed.) (1997) *Media Research: technology, art, communication*, Amsterdam: Overseas Publishers Association.

Morse, M. (1998) *Virtualities: television, media art, and cyberculture*, Indianapolis: Indiana University Press.

Mumford, L. (1934) *Technics and Civilization,* London: Routledge.

—— (1966) *Technics and Human Development (Myth of Machine*, vol. 1), New York: Harcourt Brace Jovanovich.

Musil, R. (1979 [1930]) *The Man without Qualities*, vol. 1, London: Picador.

Negroponte, N. (1995) *Being Digital,* New York: Knopf.

Noon, J. (1993) *Vurt,* Manchester: Ringpull.

—— (1995) *Pollen,* Manchester: Ringpull.

—— (1998) *Nymphomation*, London: Corgi.

Postman, N. (1987) *Amusing Ourselves to Death*, London: Methuen.

—— (1990) 'Informing Ourselves to Death', speech given to the German Informatics Society (Gesellschaft für Informatik), 11 October, Stuttgart, available at http://world. std.com/~jimf/informing.html (accessed 9 February 2005).

—— (1993) *Technopoly: the surrender of culture to technology*, New York: Vintage.

Raymond, E.S. (2001) *The Cathedral and the Bazaar: musings of Linux and Open Source by an accidental revolutionary*, Cambridge, MA: O'Reilly.

—— (2005) 'Open Source FAQ', available at http://www.opensource.org/advocacy/faq. html (accessed 15 February 2005).

Rojek, C. (2001) *Celebrity,* London: Reaktion books.

Rutsky, R.L. (1999) *High Techne: art and technology from the machine aesthetic to the posthuman*, Minneapolis: University of Minnesota Press.

Simmel, G. (1971) [1903] 'The metropolis and the mental life', in D.N. Levine (ed.) *On Individuality and Social Forms: selected writings of Georg Simmel*. Chicago: University of Chicago Press, pp. 324–39.

—— (2001 [1907]) *The Philosophy of Money,* trans. T. Bottomore and D. Frisby, London: Routledge.

Slater, D. (1995) 'Photography and modern vision: the spectacle of "natural magic"', in C. Jenks (ed.) *Visual Culture*, London: Routledge, pp. 218–37.

Smith, M.M. (1996) *Spares,* London: HarperCollins.

Sontag, S. (1979) *On Photography,* London: Penguin.

Spengler, O. (1940) *Man and Technics: a contribution to a philosophy of life,* New York: Knopf.

Stephenson, N. (1992) *Snow Crash,* New York: RoC.

Stiegler, B. (1996) 'The discrete image', in Derrida, J. and Stiegler, B., *Echographies of Television*, trans. J. Bajorek, London: Polity, pp. 148–74.

—— (1998) *Technics and Time, 1: the fault of Epimetheus*, trans. R. Beardsworth and G. Collins, Stanford: Stanford University Press.

—— (2002) 'Our ailing educational systems', *Culture Machine,* 5, available at http:// culturemachine.tees.ac.uk/Cmach/Backissues/j005/Articles/Stiegler.htm (accessed 15 February 2005).

Tafuri, M. (1979) *Architecture and Utopia: design and capitalist development*, Cambridge, MA: MIT Press.

Taylor, P.A. (1998) 'Hackers: cyberpunks or microserfs?', *Information, Communication and Society,* 1(4): 401–19.

—— (1999) *Hackers: crime in the digital sublime*, London: Routledge.

Taylor, P.A. (2005) 'From Hackers to hacktivists: speed bumps on the global superhighway?', *New Media & Society*, 7: 625–46.

Temple, K. (1980) 'The sociology of Jacques Ellul', *Research in Philosophy and Technology*, 3: 223–61.

Terranova, T. (2000) 'Free labor: producing for the digital economy', *Social Text*, 18(2): 33–57, available at: http://www.muse.jhu.edu/journalssocial_text/v018/18.2terranova. html (accessed 13 February 2005).

Thompson, J.B. (1994) 'Social theory and the media', in D. Crowley and D. Mitchell (eds) *Communication Theory Today*, Cambridge: Polity, pp. 27–49.

—— (1995) *The Media and Modernity: a social theory of the media*, Cambridge: Polity.

Ullman, E. (1997) *Close to the Machine: technophilia and its discontents*. San Francisco: City Lights.

Vaneigem, R. (1972) *The Revolution of Everyday Life*, London: Practical Paradise Publications.

Veblen, T. (1963 [1921]) *The Engineers and the Price System*, New York: Harcourt Brace.

Virilio, P. (2002) *Desert Screen: war at the speed of light*, trans. M. Degener, London: Athlone Press.

Virno, P. (1996) 'Notes on the "General Intellect"', in S. Makdisi, C. Casarino and R. Karl (eds), *Marxism beyond Marxism*, London: Routledge, pp. 265–72.

—— (2004) *The Grammar of the Multitude,* trans. I. Bertoletti, J. Cascaito and A. Casson, New York: Semiotext(e).

Waks, L.J. (1989) 'The oil in the machine', *Research in Philosophy & Technology*, 9: 155–71.

Weerwarana, S. and Weertunga, J. (2004) *Open Source in Developing Countries*, available at: http://www.seeda.se/publications (accessed 14 February 2005).

Williams, R. (1967) *Communications*, revised edn, New York: Barnes & Noble.

—— (2003 [1974]) *Television: technology and cultural form*, London: Routledge.

Winner, L. (1977) *Autonomous Technology: technics-out-of-control as a theme in political thought*, Cambridge, MA: MIT Press.

Winthrop-Young, G. (2000) 'Silicon sociology, or, two kings on Hegel's throne? Kittler, Luhmann and the posthuman merger of German media theory', *Yale Journal of Criticism* 13(2): 391–420, available at http://www.rudolf-maresch.de/texte/63.pdf (accessed 14 February 2005).

Zimmerman, M.E. (1990) *Heidegger's Confrontation with Modernity: technology, politics, and art*, Minneapolis: Indiana University Press.

Index